Helpful Hints
for Better Living

How to Live Better for Less

Helpful Hints for Better Living

How to Live Better for Less

Hap Hatton
Laura Torbet

Facts On File Publications
New York, New York • Bicester, England

Helpful Hints for Better Living

Library of Congress Cataloging in Publication Data

Torbet, Laura.

Helpful hints for better living.

Includes bibliographies and index.
1. Consumer education.   1. Hatton, Hap.   II. Torbet, Laura.
   III. Title.
TX335.T62   1984   640.73   83-14037
ISBN 0-87196-860-6
ISBN 0-87196-272-1 (pbk.)

Printed in the United States of America
10 9 8 7 6 5 4 3 2 1

For Alison Pearl and Clay Jones,
our inspirations for better living

CONTENTS

ACKNOWLEDGMENTS

Our special thanks go to the following individuals,
some more instrumental than others, in
putting this book together:

Diane Cleaver
Alix Elias
Pat Ethridge

Rod Hardesty
Christine and Earl Hatton
Bob Hutchins

Mike Kennedy
Milly Klingman
Heide Lange

Michael McNeil

Wallace Orr

Allison Pearl
Phil Saltz
Eleanora Schoenebaum
Craig Steadman

Kath Twohill
Jamie Warren
Craig Widmar

Our indebtedness to the hundreds of sources
we called upon also warrants mention. It's
reassuring to see so many dedicated to the
pursuit of better living with less.

Hap Hatton
Laura Torbet

New York City

1

SHOPPING FOR FOOD

1

SHOPPING FOR FOOD

Today's food bill for the average family is staggering. In the past six years we've seen a 35 percent increase in food spending, almost twice the inflation rate; only the costs of medical care and energy have increased as much. Food accounts for a big chunk of your income, but you can cut a big chunk out of your food expenses—at least 20 percent—while improving your nutritional intake merely by changing your shopping habits in the supermarket and by becoming aware of what the American food business is all about.

The United States is unique in that while nearly half of its population is malnourished and/or overweight, poverty or lack of food are *not* contributing factors. Americans have simply lost comprehension of basic food forms and have forgotten that these basic foods can be prepared at home with delicious, nutritious, money-saving results. Instead, we consume food that is factory-canned, instant-mixed, freeze-dried, dehydrated, synthetic, chemically processed, and additive-treated. In doing so, we play right into the hands of the food conglomerates, who often charge us more for the advertising and packaging than for the food itself.

So the first step is to shop more selectively. Even simple substitutions like juices instead of soft drinks, fruit instead of junk food, and cooked cereal instead of sugared flakes will set you on your way to feeling better while saving. And the more you learn about nutrition and food preparation, the more enthusiastic and comfortable you'll become with preparing your own foods simply and quickly.

SUPERMARKET STRATEGY

MARKETING TECHNIQUES TO BE AWARE OF

Most supermarket shoppers don't realize that from the moment they set foot inside today's supermarket they are being barraged by the most sophisticated marketing strategies in existence. Everything's orchestrated—from the Mu-

3

zak to the placement of products on the shelves. One can beat this psychological warfare by being aware of some tricks that supermarkets pull:

- *Basic and popular items are placed far from the store entrance, so when shoppers run in for one thing, they have to walk clear across the store to get it.* The supermarket is banking on a few impulse purchases along the way.
- *High-profit goods are placed near the entrance and exit of the store.*
- *End-of-aisle and other high-visibility displays increase sales up to 600 percent because most shoppers wrongly assume the product is on sale.*
- *Although supermarket specials can save you money, there is an ulterior motive at work here.* You are lured into the store, where additional shopping and especially impulse buying will cancel out the special savings.
- *Markets have been known to mix sale foods and regular-priced goods.* Make sure you're getting the special.
- *Supermarkets place higher-priced items on shelves between neck and waist level.* Higher-priced items also tend to be spread more abreast than lower-priced ones. The wise shoppers stoops, stretches, and saves by buying the lower-profile products.

ORGANIZING YOUR SHOPPING TRIPS

When to Shop

- *Try to set up a specific weekly market time so you can better gauge your weekly food needs, and try to shop only once a week.* Most foods will keep that long, and one big shopping trip saves time and trouble.
- *Most supermarket specials are run Tuesday and Wednesday, and the stores are less crowded then.* Monday is the worst day; stocks are depleted and picked over from the weekend.
- *Some supermarkets up their prices at the beginning of the month because that's when Social Security and welfare checks are received.*

Where to Shop

Prices may vary from store to store, even among those owned by the same chain. You can expect higher prices in higher-income urban areas and lower ones in lower-income, outlying, or rural areas. Naturally you can save by shopping the latter, but take into consideration the gas you use to get there.

Proper Planning

The foundation of saving money in the supermarket is planning your meals in advance, making a shopping list, and sticking to it. Planning your meals while you're shopping can only result in higher grocery bills.

If you need some flexibility, be a little vague in your meal plan. Include such items as "two meat meals, one fish, one poultry dish" on your shopping list. This allows you to take advantage of any specials that fall into your categories.

DO NOT IMPULSE SHOP. Each time you purchase an item you didn't intend to buy you lose another battle in the war against high food prices. If you cannot live without an item you run across in the supermarket, make a note of it on the back of your shopping list. If you still must have it the next time you're shopping, buy it. But in most cases you'll realize you didn't need it as much as you thought you did.

Ways to avoid impulse buying:
- *Don't shop hungry.* (Those who do spend 17 percent more.)
- *Shop alone.* Kids can be a general distraction. Also, they are pushovers for TV commercials and want you to buy everything they've seen advertised.
- *Don't send anyone shopping for you.*

OTHER WAYS TO SAVE

Unit Pricing
Although proper planning is the primary key to saving food dollars, unit prices can be a helpful tool. Comparing prices on a 12-oz. can of tuna to a 14 1/2-oz. can, for example, can get confusing. The unit price label gives you the per pound price per brand, so you know which label is actually costing you less. You'll find the unit price marker on the shelf under the product.

Specials
The one sure sign of a true "special" is a limit on what the customer can purchase. In any case, purchase a product only if you really need it; don't fall into the "giant economy" trap. Bulk-buying can save you money (as with 50-lb. bags of potatoes), but not on an item that's hardly ever used. Buy strictly according to how quickly you will consume.

Seeing the Manager
- *When you buy a faulty product, always return it and get your money back.*
- *Supermarkets will often meet their competitors' prices,* so show the manager any ad listing a lower competitive price. (Some department stores will also do this.)
- *If the supermarket is out of a special, get a "rain check" or "out of stock" slip so you can get the discount price when the product is available.*
- *When scales are available, reweigh marked packages of produce and meats.* If there's any discrepancy, point it out to the manager.

- *If there is a store item that you use with frequency, ask the manager for a special price on a case of it.* You'll often get it.

- *Make sure the food you buy is fresh. Food dating is frequently coded so you can't tell how old the commodity is.* Manufacturers claim that comprehensible food dating would result in older food going unsold while consumers continually bought the freshest. The store manager can explain the code to you.

THE GIMMICKS: COUPONS, REFUNDS, AND TRADING STAMPS

You might say this is the golden age of the coupon and the rebate. A refund is offered on virtually every household product and packaged food by at least one manufacturer. Some 77 percent of American households use coupons. Earnest refunders can save as much as 50 percent of their shopping bill, and even a modest effort can save 10 percent.

Coupon and refund offers are paid out of the general advertising budget of the company and thus represent a truer saving to the consumer than trading stamps. The supermarket pays for trading stamps and passes their cost on to the consumer.

A Hard Look at Coupons and Refunds

- *The majority of the foods that offer coupons are highly processed, expensively packaged, and low in nutrition.* You almost always pay higher prices for them. With a coupon you're getting savings on a product that doesn't contribute to a well-balanced diet.

- *Coupon clipping and sending in refund offers, not to mention organizing labels and coupons, is a lot of trouble and costs a certain amount of money for postage and envelopes.*

Coupon Strategies

There are three ways to save coupons:

- *Save the covering or wrapping of virtually every foodstuff or non-food item you purchase.* (Anything with writing on it.) The average American family discards about $3.00 worth of these daily. Clean them if necessary and file them away. You will then have a backlog of proofs of purchase to match to coupons as you get them. Obviously this system requires a lot of work, but coupon enthusiasts invariably recommend it, swearing that "it pays off."

- *Let the available coupon selection dictate what you buy.* Pick out the best bargains and plan your meals around those items, even if you don't ordinarily eat those foods. You'll save more money, and eat more adventurously, but the trap here is that you'll buy a lot of prepared convenience foods that are relatively expensive even when purchased at a discount. And your payoff is a savings on the full price of an item you might never have bought unless it was on sale. Is this a real saving?

- *Pick up only coupons that correspond to products you need or ordinarily buy, then use those coupons to buy that product or take advantage of the refund offer attached to it.*

More Coupon Hints

- *Watch unit price in relation to your coupon.* The coupon may give you a better deal per pound on a smaller size. If so, and if you have more than one coupon, buy more than one of the smaller packages rather than purchasing the large size.

- *Organization is the key to efficient use of coupons.* Make sure you don't let coupons expire. Arrive at the store well organized. And try to use coupons at the same time that supermarket specials are covering specific products; that way you get double savings.

- *Always shop by comparing, even when using coupons.* Many equivalent store brands cost less than the name brand, even *with* the coupon reduction. Most important, avoid junk foods at inflated prices even if they are covered by coupons.

- *There are various kinds of coupons:* mail in for cash refund; cents off the purchase price; buy a box, second box free or for less; mail in for free or drastically reduced merchandise other than the purchase product; and so on. The mail in for cash refund offers the most substantial savings.

If You're Serious

- *Obtain coupons from stores (be sure to ask if they have any coupons that haven't been put out), from magazines (especially the "family" magazines, which are loaded with them), from newspapers, and from junk mail.* To put your name on a direct-mail coupon list, write to Donnelly Marketing, 1235 North Avenue, Nevada, IA 50201.

- *Trade coupons with friends, neighbors, or relatives or through family organizations such as the PTA, churches, lodges, etc.* Also, the library sometimes has a bin for coupon swapping.

- *These two companies will mail you refund forms upon request:*
  Libby, McNeill & Libby   Proctor & Gamble
  200 S. Michigan Ave.   P.O. Box 432
  Chicago, IL 60804   Cincinnati, OH 45229

Write "Refund Forms" on the envelopes and enclose a stamped, self-addressed envelope.

Trading Stamps

As inflation has climbed, the use of trading stamps has tapered off. In the 1960s there were 2,000 trading stamp companies. Less than a tenth of these are still around. At one time 80 percent of all American households saved them.

Trading stamps are engineered to addict you to the specific stores that give the types of stamps you're saving. The cost of trading stamps is built into the prices you pay at those stores; it's like a direct tax. And if you always shop the same store just to collect the stamps, you lose out on specials at other stores. So buy the specials wherever they may be and collect the stamps if they're available. Be on the lookout for double-stamp days; gas stations and occasionally supermarkets may give twice the number of stamps on certain days (usually during mid-week to get you to shop at that time).

Redemption centers often have specials on items that are last year's models, demonstrators, out of season, etc. Take advantage of these offers. Also, you get the best value on higher-priced items at these centers.

THE FOOD YOU CHOOSE

KNOW WHAT YOU'RE GETTING

- *A valid food philosophy: Healthful food is cheaper.* Food that keeps longer is less nutritious and more expensive because you're paying for all those additives and preservatives.

- *You should always read labels because they tell you what you're getting.* And don't believe claims of "pure" and "natural" on the label; go on to read the ingredients and see for yourself.

- However, *there are certain foods that do not require a USDA listing of ingredients.* You can very well be buying unlisted additives and preservatives in the following:

  — Non-alcoholic beverages
  — Bread and rolls: enriched, raisin, white, whole wheat
  — Fruit butters
  — Natural cheeses
  — Processed cheeses
  — Cocoa products
  — Frozen desserts

— Flour

— Food flavorings

— Canned fruit and fruit juices

— Jellies and preserves

— Macaroni and noodle products

— Milk

— Fruit pies

— Salad dressing

— Canned vegetables.

- *Additives that are label-exempt include fumigants, defoaming agents, and anti-caking agents.*

- *On precooked foods, which you should avoid anyway because of low-quality ingredients and a high portion of chemicals, the ingredients are listed in descending order.* "Noodles and Turkey" means more noodles than turkey; "Turkey and Noodles" requires a fixed amount of turkey, and more turkey than noodles.

BRAND NAMES AND THE ALTERNATIVES

Studies have proven that buying the cheapest label of all products in the supermarket can save you in excess of 40 percent. This could mean a paid vacation by the year's end. When you buy a brand name because you've seen it nationally advertised on television, in a full page color ad in a magazine, or elsewhere, just remember: *It's you, the consumer, who pays for all that hype,* much of which stretches the truth. Think twice when you buy Charmin or Perdue. It's the "no frill" and store brands that can afford to be cheaper because they don't have huge advertising tabs to pass on to you.

Store Brands

Here are some additional facts about store brands:

- *If the product goes by the store name* (for instance, A&P succotash), *it's as good as a brand name product;* if it's under another name (A&P Ann Page succotash) it's of a slightly lower quality.

- *A reputable manufacturer usually produces them.* For instance, Dole and Del Monte supply A&P with canned pineapple and fruit salad; Heinz makes soup for A&P, Grand Union, Pantry Pride, and Giant, among others; Morton, Diamond, and International supply salt; and Borden and Sealtest make ice cream for the chains.

No-Brand or Generic Products

Food, cleaning, and paper products in plain white boxes can save you up to one-third the cost of the equivalent brand-name products and are often just as good.

The following items have the same chemical composition *no matter what the label*, so there's no sacrifice of quality in buying a generic or store brand.

- Baking powder
- Baking soda
- Bread crumbs (unflavored)
- Cooking oils (except olive)
- Corn starch
- Dried fruits (raisins, dates)
- Extracts and flavorings
- Honey
- Lemon juice
- Lime juice
- Molasses
- Nuts (except mixed)
- Powdered milk
- Salt
- Spices and herbs
- Sugar (all forms)
- Vinegar.

Experiment with other generic products to see which ones you like.

SUPERMARKET BAD BUYS

As will be discussed in the Food Preparation section, a key to cutting food expenditures is to buy ingredients separately and put them together at home. The ingredients will be real, so chances are you'll benefit nutritionally as well. Whenever possible, avoid precooked and frozen "convenience foods," such as boil-in-a-bag meals, TV dinners, ready-to-eat desserts, and frozen pizzas.

In addition to this general food category, there are a host of other items to be avoided in the supermarket:

- *Bologna. Consumer Reports* says, "It isn't always fresh, or even clean, and most of it doesn't taste especially good. . . . Bologna is no bargain." *CR* goes on to report that bologna is high in calories, fat, salt, hidden sugar, sodium nitrite, and foreign matter (animal hairs, insect particles, mold, etc.). One-quarter of the samples tested by CR showed evidence of filth and a third contained excessive amounts of bacteria.

- *Franks.* These are 10 percent water and 85 percent meat—the cheapest, most undesirable meat (muscle tissues and throw-away flesh) that is unusable elsewhere. All-meat, all-turkey, and all-chicken franks have as much protein as the more expensive all-beef and all-pork versions. But bear in mind that all sausages—including franks, cold cuts, and bacon—are cured with chemical additives (sodium nitrite in particular) and spices that account for the remaining 5 percent. In addition, these foods are quite high in fat and cholesterol.

- *Cold cereals.* These are generally low in nutrition and high in price (packaging costs). Most contain from 35 to 50 percent sugar, while shredded wheat and many others are nothing more than expensive filler. However, cooked cereals like Cream of Wheat, Wheatina, and oatmeal are a tasty and nutritious bargain.

- *Baby food.* Commercial baby food is the ultimate in trashy convenience products. Here's what you get:

  — Lots of water

  — Canned or frozen vegetables, meat, etc.

  — Salt and sugar (so *you'll* think it's good if you taste it)

  — Artificial flavor and color

  — Thickeners

  — Modified food starches (treated with acid)

  — Dextrines

  — Nitrates

  — Preservatives

  — A jar that costs a third of the total price.

  The high salt content can increase a child's predisposition to high blood pressure later in life. You can feed your child much better, and at a great savings, by mixing batches yourself. See page 44 for simple ways to make your own baby food. Also, those convenient juice bottles that baby nipples screw onto contain a watered-down product that sells for over a dollar a quart. You can do better by squeezing your own or using ordinary bottled juice.

- *Refined carbohydrates (white flour and brown or white sugar).* These cost more than their natural counterparts and are being directly linked with mental and physical problems such as obesity, heart attacks, and ulcers. Buy whole grain flours and honey.

- *Gelatin desserts and puddings.* Save 300 percent and more by avoiding prepackaged gelatin desserts such as Jell-O. Those dessert powder mixes are about 85% sugar, 10% gelatin, and the rest chemical flavor and color. Buy pure unflavored gelatin (such as Knox) and flavor it with fresh fruit, fruit juices, or coffee. The time consumed in making them is essentially the same.

- *Snacks.* These can add 10 percent to the weekly food bill, and most have no nutritionally redeeming qualities. Substitute cheaper fresh fruit or whole-grain crackers.

- *Prepared stuffings.* With a few extra minutes you can make your own from fresh ingredients or left-overs. (See page 68.)

- *Pancake syrups.* From *Consumer Reports:* "Nutritive value of all pancake syrups is practically nil. They consist primarily of water and sugars— empty calories." See page 69 for a recipe for nutritious homemade syrup, or stick to pure maple syrups.

- *Jams and jellies.* If you purchase commercial jams and jellies, you'll be getting a product that's 55 percent sweetener and 45 percent fruit or fruit juice (the legal minimum). Commercial brands have to list their ingredients, which usually include pectin (to get jelly to gel), citric acid, chemical antifoaming agents (to prevent foaming during man-ufacture), benzoic acid/sodium benzoate (to fake freshness), and spices. Jams that say "no artificial coloring, flavoring, or preservatives" still have the 55 percent sugar content. No major brands use honey instead of sugar, because it's more expensive. Mint-flavored and green-colored jellies are almost always totally artificial.

- *Margarine.* Although the cheaper price of margarine is a selling point, most people buy it for its unsaturated (vegetable) fats that are supposed to be cholesterol free. But this is a myth. When solidified into mar-garine form, the unsaturated fats have to be hydrogenated, which converts them into saturated fats, just like those found in real butter. (The softer the margarine, the lower the saturated fat content.) The difference is that butter contains dozens of nutrients, while vitamins A and D are the only nutrients added to margarine.

  Federal regulations insist margarine must be at least 80 percent fat; the remaining 20 percent is made up of artificial color and flavor, synthetic vitamins, preservatives, and so on. Check the label. Diet margarines may be anywhere from 38 to 57 percent water, and cost about the same as regular margarine.

By far the cheapest butter substitute, which *Consumer Reports* rates as "acceptable," is a product called Butter Buds. It is sold in the form of a dry powder which, when mixed with hot tap water, makes a yellow liquid resembling butter. It has only 6 calories per tablespoon (this is 94 percent fewer calories than butter or margarine) and, thus, may be a boon to the dieter. It has the added advantage of being lower in sodium than either butter or margarine. Although the manufacturers don't recommend it for frying, this product might be worth a try on toast or on popcorn.

For cooking, use vegetable oil. It is often cheaper than any kind of margarine, certainly cheaper than butter, and can generally be used in any kind of cooking that calls for shortening. Vegetable oil is usually higher in polyunsaturated fats than margarine—but check labels to be sure.

- *Vacuum-packed or instant coffee.* Whole beans usually cost less, last longer, and taste better than vacuum-packed or instant coffees. They're cheapest in bags like those the A&P stocks. Many stores will grind the beans at the checkout counter for you.

  Ideally, you'll give up coffee altogether and save substantially. Even moderate coffee drinkers can consume 15 to 20 pounds a year. Coffee has no nutritional benefits and can cause problems like insomnia, irritability, stomach upset, high blood pressure and rapid pulse. Coffee can also exacerbate conditions like hypoglycemia and ulcers.

- *Canned soft drinks.* A can of the type used for soft drinks consumes a half cup of oil in its manufacture, so you pay exorbitantly for packaging. And considering the contents, in many cases sugar water that causes bad health and cavities, the 40 cents or more you spend is more or less wasted.

- *Fruit drinks and reconstituted fruit juices.* Fruit "drinks," "ades," and "punches" are bad buys because they may contain as little as 1 percent or less natural fruit; the rest is water, sugar, and flavoring. "Fruit juice" must be 100 percent fruit juice, so buy that and dilute it yourself, if you like.

  Imitation or "substitute" fruit drinks are often as expensive as the real things, so why buy them? Frozen orange juice concentrate, for example, costs about the same as frozen orange juice substitute which is only 30 percent orange juice and includes sugar and added chemicals.

  Save money by not buying juices that are reconstituted from concentrate. Buy frozen concentrate and make it yourself. Frozen concentrate is also a better buy than the juices in cans, which have little nutritional value and are lacking in vitamin C; the intense boiling needed for the canning and pasteurization processes destroys the vitamin C. However, the concentrating process also destroys much of the nutritional value. Fresh, as usual, is best.

- *Bottled and mineral waters.* You're being manipulated by advertising here. To prove the point, try a taste test with the members of your family who insist on bottled water and watch them flunk. Many cities provide water that is every bit as good as imported and costly Perrier or Vichy. Schweppes Sparkling Mineral Water (with its "Schweppervescence") is Los Angeles tap water with artificial carbonation and salt added, and New York City tap water has won many a "blind" tasting test.

- *Expensive beers.* Here again, try the taste test. Chances are you won't be able to distinguish among various beers of different prices. In fact, most people cannot distinguish beer from ale.

- *"Water added."* Manufacturers add water to their products to attain a desired consistency or to dilute liquids. The consumer often pays dearly for that water; for instance, canned pet foods can contain up to 74 percent water.

- *Garlic or seasoned salts.* Buy garlic powder or other pure spices and you'll avoid paying up to $1.35 a pound for salt.

- *Elaborately packaged staples.* Buy food in bags instead of boxes. And pick plain rather than fancy containers. A pretty package has nothing to do with what's inside, but it definitely affects the price. The biggest packaging cost is paid by consumers who buy *individually packaged and wrapped items.* The cost of packaging can account for 15 to 20 percent of your grocery bill.

- *Non-foods.* These items—toothpaste, aspirin, toiletries, cleaning supplies, razor blades, garbage bags, etc.—always sustain the highest markups in the supermarket to make up for the lower markup on food. Buy them at a discount house and save.

SHOPPING FOR PROTEIN

Protein is essential for energy, growth, and repair of tissues, so a high-protein diet is generally the most desirable. Despite the sharp increase in meat prices of late, prices can be a pleasant surprise when you really shop for protein. The chart on the following page will help.

The five foods that give you the most protein for your money—soybeans,

Food	Grams of Protein per dollar	Grams of Protein per pound	Price per pound	Calories per pound
Soybeans	224.2	154.7	.69	1,828
Swiss cheese	34.4	119.8	3.49	1,610
Lentils	162.3	112.0	.69	1,542
Tuna, canned	42.9	111.1	2.59	760
Split peas	159.1	109.8	.69	1,579
Kidney beans	118.7	102.1	.86	1,556
Halibut	29.2	94.8	3.25	454
Chick peas (garbanzos)	104.5	93.0	.89	1,633
Lima beans	77.7	92.5	1.19	1,565
Hamburger	34.0	81.2	2.39	1,216
Veal, loin chop	18.0	72.3	3.99	681
Sirloin, bone in	23.8	71.1	2.99	1,316
Cottage cheese	47.8	61.7	1.29	481
Pork, loin chop	20.4	61.1	2.99	1,065
Frankfurters, all meat	27.1	59.4	2.19	1,343
Lamb, shoulder chop	19.7	58.9	2.99	1,082
Chicken, whole	64.5	57.4	.89	382
Eggs, extra large/dozen	43.8	52.1	1.19	658
Bacon	17.3	38.1	2.19	3,016

lentils, split peas, kidney beans, and chick peas—are all from the legume family. Legumes are rich in protein, vitamins, and minerals, and can be used in hearty casserole dishes, served cold with a salad, roasted for a tasty and nutritious snack, and so on. Dried beans are absolutely the best supermarket bargain. Buy them in bulk; they'll last a year if stored in airtight containers such as large mayonnaise jars and set in a cool dry place. By buying them dry and cooking them yourself you can save 50 percent on their cost and avoid the antitoxins that are generally added to preserve color. You'll find a much greater variety of legumes in an uncooked form anyway.

Soybeans are a fine natural source of lecithin, which absorbs fats in the body, making it a valiant cholesterol fighter. Also, soy oil can be used for frying and soy flour for baking. But perhaps most important, soy beans are used to make tofu, also known as bean curd, a white, cheesy-looking food which is low in cost and calories and high in protein. Tofu is very bland. Its texture is smooth, like a very firm pudding. By itself, it's dull, but it takes on the flavor of whatever it's cooked with. If your food budget is failing under inflation's pressures, tofu is a good way to extend the meat dishes you can afford, and to replace the protein that's gotten too expensive. You can slice it into broth, scramble it into eggs, blend it into salad dressing, stir-fry it with vegetables, add it to oatmeal, crumble it and use it like hamburger, or add it to tuna fish salad.

One caution: Legumes are not a complete protein in themselves. In order for your body to use any of the proteins in legumes, the complete family of proteins must be provided in the meal. Therefore, you must supplement a serving of legumes with a serving of nuts or seeds, grains (including wheat and rice), or milk (including cheese or yogurt). Conversely, small amounts of grain protein from bread, pasta, and rice, are magnified when consumed with the complete protein in meat, poultry, fish, eggs, and cheese.

TIPS IN VARIOUS FOOD CATEGORIES

Bread

Always buy bread (and cereals) by weight. There's no bargain in paying for air in bread.

Cheese

Although domestic cheeses cost less than imported, many American cheeses, especially pasteurized and otherwise processed varieties, are higher in additives and lower in nutrition. Check the ingredients; if preservatives are used, by law they have to be listed.

Your best buy in the northeastern United States is usually Muenster; in the southwestern United States it's usually Monterey Jack.

Also, avoid factory-ground Parmesan or Romano cheese. Buy it in blocks and grate it yourself. It will taste better and cost less.

Eggs

Grade for non-meats is determined by factors such as texture, shape, and uniformity of style, not by nutritional value or flavor. For instance, the difference between Grade B eggs and Grade A or AA eggs is that the yokes of the B eggs don't stand as high in the pan. Considering the difference in price, you can certainly do without that. And don't pay extra for brown eggs. They are no different from white eggs.

Fruits and Vegetables

Fresh fruits and vegetables respond quickly to the pressures of the marketplace because of their perishability. When supplies are abundant, the prices decrease immediately to rid the marketplace of the excess. When the item is out of season, or when unusual weather conditions like a drought or unseasonal cold cause supplies to be low, the price is naturally higher. Because the prices fluctuate so dramatically (50 percent and more), the key to saving is to buy in large quantities when the item is most abundant. So when the first early fruits and vegetables appear on the produce shelves, hold off. As the rest of the stock comes in, the prices will drop. When the time is right, buy the produce at various stages of ripeness so you won't have to eat it all at once. Also consider canning and preserving your bounty. (See the appropriate sections in the next chapter.)

Buy fresh fruits and vegetables at site of harvest outlets whenever you can to avoid the middlemen and cut the price. The best bargains are the "pick your own" places; you do your own picking and pay less for the freshest produce. If you find such a place, pick early in the day, before the temperature goes up. Cool your produce as soon as possible, and be sure to bring enough containers.

Your state department of agriculture or county agent of the Department of Agriculture Extension Service will gladly furnish locations of roadside stands, farmers' markets, and pick-your-own fields.

Other tips on fruits and vegetables:

- *The reduced produce section is a bargain bin.* Don't overlook it.
- *Packaged produce isn't the best buy.* The packages may vary in weight but be priced the same. A piece or two inside may be spoiled. And the extra cost of filling those packages will be passed on to you.
- *Frozen vegetables can be a good buy.* Some, such as corn, peas, and cauliflower in large bags, are cheaper than their fresh counterparts. And the vegetables are usually frozen right after harvest, so their nutritional value is intact. When buying frozen vegetables, select chunked rather than cubed. The less the vegetable is tampered with, the cheaper.
- *The price of frozen food goes down in June when fresh is available, and canned food prices are reduced in the fall as new shipments arrive.*
- *Try unusual and unpopular vegetables*—spaghetti squash, celery root, Jerusalem artichokes, cardoons, etc. These are often introduced at supermarkets at a low introductory price.
- *Yellow and white onions are interchangeable, so buy whichever are cheaper.* Store them in a dry place.
- *If you buy unripened tomatoes, which are cheap, choose firm, unblemished ones and place them in paper bags to ripen away from the sun.* The temperature should be 60° to 70°. Once ripe, store them in a refrigerator to preserve vitamin C.

- *Invest during sales of any canned tomato products* (paste, puree, sauce, or stewed). These are endlessly useful.

- *When buying iceberg lettuce avoid the heaviest heads in a given size.* The lighter weight, looser-leaved head of lettuce is of better quality and has a sweeter taste. More of its leaves will be edible. The heavier, more tightly wrapped lettuce has been left longer in the field, has a larger core (which means fewer edible leaves), and also tends to have a bitter taste.

- *Canned fruits, unlike canned vegetables, retain most of their vitamins and minerals* and so are an acceptable substitute when fresh fruit is expensive, unavailable, or out of season.

- *When you buy canned or frozen fruit, remember that pieces are less expensive than wholes,* because whole fruit must be in better condition and requires more handling on the production line.

- *Fruit canned in light syrup or water is cheaper than fruit canned in heavy syrup* (and better for you anyway).

- *Undersized fruit is often inexpensive, although its food value is normal.* And smaller is often more convenient, especially for children who may throw away a half-eaten larger piece. Less attractive fruit can also be chopped for fruit salad or used in cooking.

- *Small apples last better than large ones.*

- *Larger citrus fruits may have thicker skins, in which case they're not the bargain they appear to be.*

- *Oranges with paler color or tinges of green may be cheaper, and they're usually better because they haven't been dyed.*

- *Dark and light (golden) raisins are the same*—both made from Thompson seedless grapes—so buy whichever type is cheaper and use them interchangeably. Dark raisins are dried outside where the sun's rays caramelize them.

Whole Grains, Beans, and Nuts: Some Facts and Tips

- *Staple foods for most of the world have always been whole grains, whole grain flours, seeds, legumes (beans), and nuts.* These foods are easily available, very economical, and totally nutritious.

- *Grains may be purchased as whole stone-ground flours.* The bran and germ—the healthiest parts—are not processed out of these flours, so they have as much nutrition as whole grains.

- *Whole grains, especially bran, provide fiber, which is necessary for normal functioning of the intestinal tract* and has recently been touted as a preventative for intestinal cancer.

- *Consider a hand-operated grain mill to make your own flour.* Many mail-order firms stock them; those with steel and stone grinding burrs work best on harder seeds and nuts.

- *By combining grains and legumes (for example, rice and beans) or adding a dairy product (macaroni and cheese) or a little meat (pork and beans), one creates dishes complete in protein and with all the essential amino acids.* Peas and beans alone are lacking two of the amino acids, so they should be eaten in combination with grains.

- *White rice has been bleached, cleaned, polished, and oiled; it therefore lacks fiber and many nutrients.* Brown rice has only had the tough hull removed (the germ and most of the bran layer remain), thus retaining a much higher nutritional value. Use brown rice *anywhere* you'd use white.

- *The larger the purchase, the lower the cost is per pound.* So buy large amounts and split the excess with a friend. Purchase in health food stores or from suppliers, as supermarkets charge more and don't have complete selections.

- *Here's a listing of bulk food mail-order firms that supply grain (flour, bran, etc.) (G), rice (R), and nuts (N):*

Deer Valley Farms   G,R,N
Guilford, NY 13780
    Catalog $.50, refundable with
    first order

Garden Way   G
133 Ethan Allen Ave.
Winooski, VT 05404

Great Valley Mills   G
Quakertown, PA 18951

Jaffe Brothers   G,R,N
P.O. Box 636
Valley Center, CA 92082

Kenyon's Corn Meal Co.   G
Usepaugh, RI 02892
    12 lbs. minimum order

Koinonia Partners   N
Rt. 2
Americus, GA 31709

Northwestern Coffee
    Mills   N
217 North Broadway
Milwaukee, WI 53202

Vermont Country Store   G
Weston, VT 05161

Walnut Acres   G,R,N
Penns Creek, PA 17862

Meat

Beef is a good place to trim your budget. It's an uneconomical source of protein, and nutritionists say we Americans eat too much anyway. Two dollars in prime ribs gives you no more protein than 70 cents worth of red beans or 50 cents in eggs. All over the world meat is considered a luxury. We've mistakenly grown to consider it a necessity. Even a recent USDA study stated that raising animals for consumption is a wasteful process: "If we ever chose to have a 'no-meat' diet, our current production capacity would feed four or five times as many people as it does. Feeding animals to furnish us with meat is less efficient than direct use of crops for food."

In 1970 the average per capita consumption of beef was 120 pounds of beef and 70 pounds of pork. A decade earlier it was half that. Meat is high in saturated fats and cholesterol, and cholesterol-related diseases have risen proportionally with our meat consumption. Meat is one of the first foods doctors suggest potential cardiac victims cut down on. Meat-providing animals are given a diet of chemically-treated foods, antibiotics, and hormones so they'll grow fatter and faster. Once the animal is slaughtered, additives, dyes, and extenders are added. All this is also being associated with many human disorders.

Shopping for Meat

- *First and foremost, shop the specials.* Buy only meat that is marked down and you'll cut your meat bill up to 22 percent while enjoying plenty of variety in your diet.

- *Buy meat by the number of servings it will yield, not by the number of pounds each package offers.* The yield of edible meat per pound varies according to the amount of bone, excess fat, gristle, and drippings. For instance:

  — Spareribs or chops yield one or two servings per pound.

  — Hamburger or flank steak yields four servings per pound.

  — Stew meat yields as many as six servings per pound (when stretched with vegetables and potatoes).

    A more expensive cut with less bone may be more economical. Boneless beef chuck, steak, and roast, and rump and round roasts have little or no waste, can be tenderized, marinated, grilled, stewed, cut thin, and stir-fried.

- *Think big on most meats, since larger hams, roasts, etc., have more meat in relation to bone and are usually cheaper per pound.*

  — Buy big and cut up your own steaks, stew meat, and lunch meats at home. Up to a third of your meat bill reflects the cost of the meat cutter; you pay more with each whack of the blade. Freeze what is not used immediately.

  — Plan for two or three meals from one cut of meat, for example: a leg of lamb can become a lamb roast for one meal, broiled lamb steaks for another, and shish kebab or curry for a third; a large chuck roast can make beef stew, pot roast, and Swiss steaks.

— Family packages of four or five pounds of ground beef or a dozen pork chops are usually good buys. If your family is small, you can divide it into meal-sized packages and freeze.

• *Shop at the correct times.* Meat prices generally fluctuate as follows:

— Beef is lower in winter, higher in late summer.

— Steak is highest in summer ("cookout" time).

— Roasts are highest in late fall ("oven cooking" time).

— Veal is lower in spring and summer, higher in winter.

Ask at your local market what day of the week the bulk of the fresh meat is put out. You'll get the best selection that day, or you can take advantage of specials the day before.

• *Avoid "meat-in-bulk" plans.*

— *Many are unreliable.* You're not assured of getting the weight you order, nor the quality you could choose yourself from the supermarket. You also pay for the meat before it's trimmed, further cancelling any savings.

— *Using less meat is more healthful.* "Meat-in-bulk" plans place too much emphasis on meat as part of the diet. If you have a freezer full of meat, you'll tend to want to eat it up.

— *Shopping the specials at the supermarket can save you a comparable amount and give you variety to boot.*

Grading

Beef, veal, pork and lamb are graded prime, choice, and good. Meat grading has to do only with tenderness, and for the most part it's choice and good grades that are available in supermarkets. There are two good reasons to buy cheaper grades:

• *The less-expensive cuts are as nutritious and wholesome as more costly cuts.* They just take more preparation. With a little effort these cheaper cuts can be made as tender and tasty as the higher-priced cuts, and they usually have a lower fat content. (See tenderizing meat, page 61.)

• *The good grades have more than likely eaten grass, while the prime and choice grades have most likely been subject to a chemical diet and hormone treatments.*

Some supermarkets buy ungraded meat and do their own grading. The stickers or stamps look like the USDA stamp but lack the USDA lettering. Don't buy this meat unless a low price is attached.

Occasionally, cheaper cuts are mislabeled as fancier cuts. There's very little you can do about it, except to avoid buying cuts you are not familiar with.

Other Tips

- *Restructured beef is made from tougher cut-up parts formed into steaks and can cost you 40 percent less but taste 90 percent as good as steak.*
- *With imagination, less expensive organ meats (liver, heart, kidney, tongue, pigs' feet, brains, tail), especially those from younger animals, can be turned into gourmet meals, as they are in the finest restaurants in Europe.*
- *As for pork, the loin end is less fatty than the rib end, and country ribs are meatier than spareribs. Also, fresh unsmoked ham can be economical, and bacon ends can save you a third to a half the price of regular bacon.*
- *Don't overlook rabbit.* It's often available frozen.
- *Veal is never a budget item.* When on special, shoulder chops and breast of veal are decent buys. Turkey or pork scallops can be substituted for more expensive veal scallops; pork roast can stand in for a veal roast.

Poultry

Consumer Reports determined that brand name chickens (Perdue, Paramount, Foster Farms, etc.) are no better than supermarket brands and can cost 9 to 14 percent more per pound.

- *The larger the fowl (chicken, turkey, etc.) the greater the ratio of meat to bone.* Thus roasters are usually better buys than fryers.
- *Turkey has a higher proportion of meat to bone than chicken does, so if chicken and turkey are the same price, turkey is a better buy.* Larger turkeys can be sectioned for cooking in a variety of ways—cutlet, turkey-burgers, tetrazzini, etc.—besides the classic roasts.
- *Buy chicken whole rather than in pieces and cut it up yourself.* Purchasing chicken by sections costs from 33 to 300 percent more. Your chicken will taste better if bought whole, too.
- *Buy poultry, like meat, by cost per serving, not cost per pound.* The following will furnish a rough idea of yield per pound.
  - Whole fowl yields two servings per pound.
  - Boneless turkey breast (high yield, high cost) yields four servings per pound.
  - Chicken breasts (low yield, high cost, especially if boneless) yield one or two servings per pound.

— Chicken legs and wings (more reasonable) yield two servings per pound.

Seafood

- *Seafood is usually less expensive when purchased frozen.* The labor to bring fish back and deliver it fresh costs much more than to freeze it right on board. Fresh fish tastes better, though.

- *Fillets are the most expensive form of fish, but you can eat up to 100 percent if they are boneless or skinless—*as opposed to 60 percent of the whole (uncleaned) fish.

- *Canned fish—both water and oil-packed—can be relatively inexpensive sources of high-quality protein,* although tuna is no longer cheap.

Sugar

Cutting down on sugar and sweets can cut your grocery bill substantially; it can also cut your dentist's and doctor's bills substantially. All of the nutrients are processed out of refined sugar so all you get are empty calories, which account for 15 to 20 percent of the caloric intake of Americans.

Read the labels on the products you buy. Variations of sugar are sucrose, dextrose, corn syrup, maltose, and fructose. Of the 129 pounds of sugar each of us averages annually, we get 75 percent from prepared foods. Here are some examples and the percentage of their composition that is sugar.

Vick's Throat Lozenges	66% sugar
Hostess Twinkie	32%
Chewable Vitamins	44%
Coffeemate	65%
Quaker Natural Cereal	24%
Heinz Catsup	29%
Shake 'n' Bake	50%
Hershey Bar	51%
Jello	82%

Honey

Since bees have predigested nectar, the sugars in honey are in a form that is readily digested by the human body, whereas refined sugar involves a complicated and debilitating digestive process. Honey is absorbed directly into the bloodstream for a quick and healthy energy boost.

It's also a natural healer. Germs need water in which to multiply, and honey is hygroscopic, meaning it absorbs water. (This is also a reason that it must be stored in an airtight container.) And bees also manufacture several kinds of antibiotics that are passed on to us.

Suppliers feel that a clean, brilliant product will sell better than a darker cloudy one, so they heat honey to retard future granulization, then filter out the pollen and colloids to make for a clear product. The result of this tampering is, as usual, a less nutritious product. So buy darker, 100 percent pure, unfiltered, and uncooked honey.

Tea

Tea is one-fifth to one-third the cost of coffee and has only half the caffeine. Bulk tea is much more economical than tea bags. Brew loose tea in a tea ball or tea strainer, or throw a handful in the pot and pour through a strainer from pot to cup. Herb teas have no caffeine, and most are cheaper than regular tea.

Always avoid instant tea. Isn't fresh tea instant enough? And fresh is free of artificial flavoring and coloring.

Wine

You can usually save around 10 percent of the cost of a bottle of wine if you buy by the case. Store bottles on their sides in a cool, dark place. The ideal storing temperature is 55°.

Countries like Rumania, Spain, Chile, and Yugoslavia produce good wines that are reasonably priced. And don't overlook California wines: they can be excellent.

MAIL-ORDER SHOPPING

If you're having trouble finding good sources for the organic and natural products you want, write directly to the wholesalers. See page 19 for mail-order firms that supply grain, rice, and nuts. Some other, more diversified, suppliers are:

- Shiloh Farms, P.O. Box 97, Sulphur Springs, AZ 72768. Frozen organic meat, nitrate-free sausage. Catalog $.50.
- Starflower, 885 McKinley St., Eugene, OR 97402. A feminist group run and owned by the workers. Catalog $.75.
- Manna Foods, 112 Crockford Rd., Scarborough, Ontario, Canada MIR3C3. Small, high-quality wholesaler. Catalog free.
- Stow Mills, Box 1030, Greenfield, MA 01302. Vitamins and cosmetics as well as foods. Catalog free.

For wholesale cheese:

- Cheese Discount Center, 1 West Ridgewood Ave., Ridgewood, NJ 07450.

- Walnut Acres, Penns Creek, PA 17862.
- Deer Valley Farms, Inc., Guilford, NY 13780. Catalog $.50, refundable with your first order.

There are many more regional sources for good food. Try the yellow pages or check out the listings in the *Whole Earth Catalog* (see page 223) for those near you. Remember that these places mostly deal wholesale. You'll get better service and value if you think through your needs, join with some friends and send in a clear, precise, prepaid order based on the quantities and varieties in the catalog.

Mail-order houses also abound for such speciality gift items as coffee and tea, cheese, fruit, and baked goods. The prices are outrageously high compared even to specialty store tags. Unless you're really in the boondocks, you can probably do better at the gourmet section of your local department store.

EATING AWAY FROM HOME

CUTTING THE HIGH COST OF EATING OUT

- *Always check the menu posted in the window.* If you find nothing but credit card stickers, enter at your own risk: these restaurants are usually more expensive.
- *Restaurants with shorter menus do not have the food wastage other eateries do.* You can save money and get a better meal when the chef is concentrating on a few special menu items.
- *Have your drinks at home before you go out, and avoid the high cost of mixed drinks in restaurants.* This can save you up to a third of the bill. But drive safely.
- *Search out restaurants without liquor licenses.* They often let you bring your own wine, which can mean huge savings because the usual restaurant markup on wine is 100 percent.
- *Stay away from restaurants where you have to tip everyone from the maître d'hôtel to the doorman and checkroom attendant, not to mention both the head waiter and your own waiter.*
- *The neighborhood in which a restaurant is located can make a big difference.* Where rents and overheads are lower, a restaurant owner is able to price food more reasonably.
- *Traveling to ethnic neighborhoods provides authentic and reasonably priced meals.* Look in the window to see if the clientele is ethnic or tourist.

- *Eat lunch out, instead of dinner, and order the day's special.* You can often save half of what dinner would cost. This works every day except Sunday.

- *Organize a gourmet dinner group.* Get together with other people and plan to meet on a regular basis. Each host can prepare the whole meal or the dinners can be team efforts. This is another example of the cooperative effort.

ON THE ROAD

- *While traveling, plan to picnic at rest stops, especially with children, so you can avoid the terrible and expensive roadside food chains and impulse buying.* Pack an iced travel kit with crackers, cheese, fruit, cookies, cold meats, sandwiches, etc. Bring a thermos of fruit juice, coffee, or cool water. You'll need a mug and silverware.

- *Breakfasts are restaurants' most overpriced meals, so buy fruit the day before to have on hand for breakfasts.* An electric skillet can also be very handy for preparing breakfast or supper in your room. Use the hot water tap to make cocoa and coffee (or buy a small submersible electric water heater—the kind that heats a cup or two of water at a time). Or eat dinner leftovers you have asked the restaurant to wrap up for you in foil.

SOURCES

GOOD FOOD FOR LESS

Beat the Supermarkets by Linda Nanfria gives you the lowdown on how to slash your food costs in the grocery store, exposing the marketing techniques that cost us more than we should be paying. Available from Impact Publishing Company, 1601 Oak Park Blvd., Pleasant Hill, CA 94523. $3.95.

A Consumer's Dictionary of Food Additives by Ruth Winter. How to buy food for economy and quality. Available from Crown Publishers, 1 Park Ave., New York, NY 10016. $4.95.

Eating Better for Less: A Guide to Managing Your Personal Food Supply by Ray Wolf is a good guide from the people who publish *Organic Gardening* and *Prevention* magazines, experts in nutrition and holistic health. Rodale Press, Emmaus, PA 18049. $8.95.

The Food Inflation Fighter's Handbook by Judith L. Klinger is *the* food reference book to have. It's comprehensive and covers everything from obtaining food to preparing it, from appliances to eating out. Fawcett Columbine, 1515 Broadway, New York, NY 10036. $5.95.

How to Buy Food for Economy and Quality: Recommendations of the USDA. Informative and understandable. Dover Publications, 180 Varick Street, New York, NY 10014. $1.75.

The Supermarket Handbook by Nikki and David Goldbeck is a fine, informative guide to understanding labels and knowing what you're really buying. A paperback available from New American Library, 1633 Broadway, New York, NY 10019. $1.95.

FRUITS AND VEGETABLES

The United Fruit and Vegetable Association distributes a guide entitled "Publications and Materials" on its approximately 100 publications and kits relating to the growing, harvesting, marketing, consumption, and food value of fresh fruits and vegetables. Write to them at North Washington and Madison Streets, Alexandria, VA 22314. It's free.

WINE

The Wine Buying Guide will provide a free sample of its bimonthly newsletter rating low- and medium-priced wines, which will give you an idea of the market and going prices. Send a stamped, self-addressed $8^1/_2 \times 11''$ manila envelope. Write to P.O. Box 1067, Long Island City, NY 11101. Subscription rate is $7.50.

COUPONS AND REFUNDS

Bunch O' Editors distributes some fifty refunding bulletins. For a list of them, send a large, stamped, self-addressed envelope to Bunch O' Editors, 7626 22nd St., Sacramento, CA 95832.

Cashing in at the Checkout by Susan Samtur (one of the pioneers of the coupon movement) and Thaddeus Tuleja. Published in 1979 by Stonesong Press and available from Grossett & Dunlap, 51 Madison Ave., New York, NY 10010. $6.95.

Coupon Magic by Susan Samtur and Thaddeus Tuleja. Published in 1980 by Grossett and Dunlap, 51 Madison Ave., New York, NY 10010. $4.95.

Coupons, Refunds, Rebates: How to Make Those Money-Saving Offers Work for You by Carol Kratz and Albert Lee. Workman Publishing, 1 West 39th St., New York, NY 10018. $2.95.

The National Supermarket Shopper can, the American Coupon Club claims, put $50.00 to $100.00 in your pocket. A full year membership is $15.00, and a sample copy is $1.50 postpaid. As a bonus for joining you get a free copy of Martin Sloan's *Guide to Coupons and Refunds*, a $2.95 value. The A.C.C. also publishes a book entitled *How to Start a Local Coupon Club for Fun and Profit*. For a copy, send a large, stamped, self-addressed envelope. American Coupon Club, P.O. Box 1149, Great Neck, NY 11023.

Refundle Bundle is a monthly coupon bulletin edited by Susan Samtur. Available from Refundle Bundle, Inc., P.O. Box 141, Centuck Station, Yonkers, NY 10710. A year's subscription is $11.87.

FOOD COOPS

Food Coops for Small Groups: How to Buy Better Food for Less by Tony Villela. How to bypass middlemen and buy from farmers and wholesalers. Workman Publishing, 1 West 39th St., New York, NY 10018. $2.95.

FOOD STAMPS

How to Apply for and Use Food Stamps. If you're having problems making ends meet, maybe you'll be able to clear the federal budget cutbacks and qualify. Free from Consumer Information Center, Pueblo, CO 81009.

GROWING, STORING, AND PREPARING FOOD

GROWING, STORING, AND PREPARING FOOD

GROWING YOUR OWN FOOD

APPROACHING GARDENING

There are two ways of approaching gardening. If you see gardening as a pleasant experience—a form of recreation and exercise—then the initial investment (for seeds and equipment at the very least) will be well worth your while. The hours you spend gardening are healthful hours spent away from more expensive forms of recreation, and the results of your activity can be several hundred dollars' worth of the freshest vegetables available.

On the other hand, if your approach to gardening is purely pragmatic—if you want to be reimbursed proportionately to your hours of labor—be sure to get all the facts before breaking the ground for a new garden. Judith Nelson, in *Money-Saving Garden Magic* (Prentice-Hall, 1978—now out of print), calculates 300 square feet as the break-even size for a vegetable plot, while allotting only one-third the minimum wage for labor. She points out that the initial investment can extend from seeds and equipment to include soil improvement (often necessary), fences, and the services of professional soil-tillers. She goes on to say that "when the crop comes in for you, the crop is at the local farms, too: that's when the prices are at their lowest." And if you don't really enjoy gardening, you're less likely to do the proper research and more likely to neglect your garden for harmful amounts of time.

In general, best results are achieved after several years of growing when the high initial expenses for tools and other supplies have averaged out, and when you've had a chance to learn from your mistakes. But there's really no limit to what you can do with a garden. In recent years, smaller and smaller parcels of land have been made to yield more and more. Duane Newcomb, in *The Postage Stamp Garden Book* (Houghton Mifflin, 1975), shows how a family of four can grow all the vegetables they need in a patch of ground only 15 square feet in size. Even in the city and in crowded suburbs, many people have roof and balcony gardens, windowbox "greenhouselets," garage plots (using artificial light), hydroponic gardens (in which plants are grown without soil and fed water and fertilizer regularly), or small yards where food is grown either in the ground or in planter boxes. And city dwellers have the advantage of a longer growing season since cities tend to be warmer than surrounding areas.

Over half of America's households grow something, if only herbs and a few tomatoes. Joining them might be one of the best moves you can make, but as Ms. Nelson advises, "keep your day job."

INFORMATION SOURCES

Department of Agriculture

The United States Department of Agriculture (USDA) has Agricultural Extension Service offices spread throughout the 50 states. Local agents frequently give classes on or provide personal assistance with home gardening, raising livestock, soil and water conservation, home economics, and more. Contact your local office (listed in the phone book under "United States Government") and find out which types of vegetables are best suited to your location, type of soil, and climate. Investigate optimal planning dates and gardening methods that can save you labor and money, such as companion planting, mulching, and recyling garbage as compost (all discussed later in this chapter).

Many USDA agents will make free house calls to test your soil and to recommend appropriate plants. Most offices also have a home economist who will give instruction in everything from canning to first aid.

A wide range of publications is available through the Agricultural Extension Service and the USDA. These are highly readable and cover a wide range of subjects in agriculture and home economics. If you have specific questions, stop by the office nearest you to pick up publications and obtain free consultation.

Other Organizations

County agricultural agents or farm advisers (listed in the phone book) and state agricultural experiment stations (usually attached to state universities) are other good sources of information.

Also try the following:

Gardens for All
180 Flynn Ave.
Burlington, VT 15401

The director of Gardens for All aims for a return of at least ten times the cash you put into your garden. The group's newsletter, *Gardens for All* (The National Association of Gardening News), is published quarterly; annual membership and the newsletter are $10.00.

Garden Way Publishing Co.
Storey Communications
Schoolhouse Road
RR 1, Box 105
Pownal, VT 05261

Garden Way offers a free catalog and distributes a line of tools and services; Garden Way Publishing handles books and periodicals. A fine example of their ingenuity is *Carrots Love Tomatoes: Secrets of Companion Planting for Successful Gardening*, for $5.95 plus $2.00 postage.

Rodale Press
33 East Minor St.
Emmaus, PA 18049

Rodale publishes *Organic Gardening* magazine. A year's subscription costs $10.00. Rodale is one of the pioneers of the home gardening movement. Among its books are *The Encyclopedia of Organic Gardening* (1,236 pages, $21.95 postpaid) and *Rodale's Color Handbook of Garden Insects* by Anna Carr ($12.95).

The Progressive Gardening Institute
c/o National Fulfillment Headquarters
P.O. Box 500
Morrison, TN 37357

Their nursery bulb and seed catalog is free for the asking, and brochures on many gardening subjects are available for a quarter apiece or free with an order.

The National Arbor Day Foundation
Arbor Lodge
Nebraska City, NE 68410

Arbor Day got its start in Nebraska City, and the Foundation is its propagator. Naturally, their nursery catalog concentrates on trees, though they do get a bit closer to the ground with grape vines, berry plants, and vegetables.

Free Garden Catalogs

W. Atlee Burpee Co.
P. O. Box 748
Riverside, CA 92502

Butterbrooke Farm
87 Barry Road
Oxford, CT 06483

Henry Field Seed and Nursery
Shenandoah, IA 51602

Gurney Seed & Nursery Co.
Yankton, SD 57079

Joseph Harris & Co.
Moreton Farm
Rochester, NY 14624

Internode Seed Co.
Box 2011, Dept. L
So. San Francisco, CA 94080

J. E. Miller Nurseries
Canadaigna, NY 14424

Musser Forests
Box 340
Indiana, PA 15701

George W. Park Seed Co., Inc.
P. O. Box 31
Greenwood, SC 29447

Sanctuary Seeds
1913 Yew Street
Vancouver, B.C., Canada V6K 3G3

R. H. Shumway Seedsman
628 Cedar Street
Rockford, IL 61101

Stark Brothers' Nurseries and Orchards
Louisiana, MO 63353

Stokes Seeds, Inc.
737 Main Street
Box 548
Buffalo, NY 14240

Thompson and Morgan
P. O. Box 24
401 Kennedy Blvd.
Somerdale, NJ 08083

Vermont Bean Seed Company
Garden Lane
Bomoseen, VT 05732

Also see books listed at the end of this chapter (pages 74–75).

BEGINNING HINTS

- *Restrict your first crops to safe and indestructible bets, such as tomatoes, peas, and squash (especially zucchini).* Branch off into more temperamental species as you get better.

- *When planning your garden, think of planting crops that you can store without relying on energy to do so.* Winter squash, onions, corn, carrots, parsnips, kidney beans, turnips, and potatoes can be stored without canning or freezing. Winter squash, for example, will store for up to six months in a cool place, with no loss of flavor or nutrient value. If they're left outdoors in the fall, the skin hardens substantially and protects them for storage. Zucchini does the same thing and can be stored for up to three months.

- *Avoid overstocking.* Don't order or buy seeds or plants without knowing exactly where they are to go in your garden.

- *A vegetable garden planted within view of the house gets more attention.* At least it will provide a sense of guilt if you can't avoid seeing it.

- *Mulching always makes for a better garden.* It saves watering and weeding. Mulch can take the form of sawdust, lawn clippings, shredded leaves, or cocoa bean hulls spread as a protective covering. Black plastic can also be stretched over the ground with holes cut for the plants to grow through.

- *Many local factories give away fertilizer sludge, which can be used for everything but root vegetables.*

- *Be on the lookout for spring premiums of free plants and seeds from gardening companies.*

- *If you have a yard, landscape it with fruit or nut trees and bushes instead of decorative plants.* Scatter plants around the yard—strawberries along the fence or walk, rhubarb and mint plants on the north side of a building, two or three pepper plants in a flower bed, and half a dozen tomato plants staked in a sunny spot.

- *Consider dwarfed fruit trees.* These have several advantages: (1) They can be grown in a small area that a larger tree would overfill (30 to 40 dwarf trees can be planted in the space usually taken up by three or four regular trees). (2) They produce full-grown fruits (each tree provides at least a bushel) in less time than regular trees. (3) They make for the easiest and most efficient harvesting since no ladders are necessary; they can be spot picked with only the properly matured fruit being harvested each time.

PESTICIDE ALTERNATIVES

Avoid pesticides when possible; they are energy-expensive and generally unhealthful. Try these hints:

- *Plant varieties of seeds that are disease-resistant.*
- *Eliminate hiding and breeding grounds for insects by keeping a neat and tidy garden.*

- *Welcome toad frogs, snakes, spiders, and insect-eating birds.* A single toad can eat up to 10,000 insects in a three-month period.
- *After handling a diseased plant, don't work with a healthy one.*
- *Don't put a diseased plant in the compost heap.*
- *Some plants grow better next to one another and protect one another from predators.*
  — Plant onions and garlic near carrots and beets; the onions and garlic keep Japanese beetles, carrot flies, and aphids away.
  — Place onions near lettuce and beans.
  — Plant radishes near cabbage to keep maggots away. (Conversely, because vegetable aromas can affect fruit, never plant peas near garlic or onions near strawberries.)
- *Herbs also repel garden pests.* Plant them among plants and flowers.
  — Basil keeps flies and worms away from tomatoes.
  — Dill, mint, sage, and thyme keep cabbage moths away from vegetables such as brussels sprouts, broccoli, cabbage, and cauliflower.
  — Anise and coriander repel aphids.
  — Horseradish keeps potato beetles off potatoes.
- *Protect your crops from soil-borne diseases.* Yearly rotations of crops can cut down on these diseases. Crop rotation is especially effective with tomatoes and eggplant. Catalog entries of tomato and cucumber varieties are marked "VFN" to signify their resistance to the soil-borne diseases verticillium, fusarium, and nematodes.
- *Avoid fruit trees.* They inevitably require spraying. Concentrate instead on blueberries and other small fruit, many of which are comparatively pest-resistant. (Note: If buying raspberry stock, make sure the catalog or nursery guarantees it's virus-free.)
- *It's hard to avoid having to spray cabbage, broccoli, and cauliflower.* They're especially susceptible to cabbage worms.

If your plants are being attacked, try to pick the culprits off. If this fails, then:

- *Hose down your plants.*
- *Spray the plants with soap and water or salt and water* (two tablespoons of either soap or salt to a gallon of lukewarm water). Test this first on one or two plants.
- *Make your own organic spray.* Mash or grind four large onions, two bulbs of garlic, four dried chili peppers, and four tablespoons of

cayenne, and place the mixture in a bowl. Add water to a level 1/4″ above the mixture, and let it stand for 24 hours. Strain it through cheesecloth, then add enough water to produce a gallon. Spray affected plants several times a day.

- *Set out a mixture of flour and fresh beer, which attracts and drowns slugs.*
- *Set barriers to stop cutworms and other such pests.* Simply place tin cans with both ends removed around the stems of young plants. Make sure they're an inch or two into the ground.

COMPOSTING

You can conserve energy and money by substituting organic composted fertilizer for fertilizer based on fossil fuels. Many gardeners feel the compost is superior. If you do your own composting, your fertilizer will be free.

- *Almost a quarter of the average American family's garbage is compostable.* Almost all kitchen waste—including coffee grounds, bone meal, eggshells, vegetable scraps, and tea bags—can be composted. Other waste products—hair, vacuum cleaner contents, garden refuse, lawn mowings, wood ashes—can be used as well. Avoid only meat and dairy products because they attract vermin. Both clamshells and eggshells are excellent sources of calcium for your garden soil. Coffee grounds and tea leaves are good for increasing the acid level of soil.
- *Do some kitchen work as you harvest your garden.* Leave tops of carrots, radishes, corn husks, pea shucks and other waste right there in the garden plot. They'll disintegrate and return to the soil, helping to nourish it as they do.
- *If you don't want to build or buy a composting box, you can simply dig a hole, fill it with compost, then plant over it the next year.* For a very small garden you can make compost by gathering together all the rinds, peelings, eggshells, and other eligible garbage from the day's food preparation and pulverizing it in a blender. Pour the blend into small holes next to your tomatoes, peppers, and other plants. If you live in a hard-winter area, keep the kitchen waste outdoors in a garbage can and add to the compost heap when it thaws.
- *The garbage disposal can be converted to a compost producer.* Don't wash the kitchen garbage down the drain. A garbage diverter can enable you to divert this valuable waste and use it in your garden. For information, send $1.00 and a self-addressed, legal-size envelope to Little Jim Dandy Garbage Diverters, Box 447, Bolinas, CA, 94524.

IN THE CITY

An excellent way to cut costs in the city is by cooperative or community gardening, a process whereby vacant lots or portions of public parks are split into gardens that are rented or lent to interested citizens. Excess produce can be traded or bartered, or preserved cooperatively. The cost of heavy equipment can be shared, and the labor can be shared, too. Under-used public-owned land is often available for the asking. Contact your city council representative or the mayor's office for help and information.

If you're not about to join a gardening group, but still want to grow your own, take a good look at your back yard, balcony, or roof. Cherry tomatoes, strawberries, lettuce, and fresh herbs can all be grown easily in tubs. An investment of time is required, but only a small investment of money. Look for scrap wood to use in making planter boxes. Any vacant lot is a source of dirt, though it may need some energizing to bring it up to necessary quality.

Urban areas sometimes don't have local agricultural programs, so you might find yourself at a loss for advice on your soil. But there are reasonably priced soil-test kits that you can use yourself. Write to Sudbury Laboratory, 572 Dutton Road, Sudbury, MA 10776 for a catalog of soil-test kits costing $10.00 and up. Some labs will analyze a soil sample and make recommendations: one is Woods End Lab, RFD Box 65, Temple, ME 14984, which will give you advice based on organic gardening principles.

INDOOR GARDENING

If you have either sunlight or supplementary lighting and are willing to sacrifice a little room, you can have a continuous indoor harvest from October to March. The simplest way is to install an extra-wide sill or a set of shelves on a south-facing window and you're in business. Plants add some pleasant humidity to otherwise dry rooms, and every day you can have fresh salads that would otherwise cost a fortune.

Plants with shallow root systems can be grown in a growing box; plants with deeper root systems, such as cherry tomatoes, broccoli, and green peppers, can be grown in pots. Also try the following plants:

- *Bean Sprouts.* Home-grown sprouts are a wonderful addition to salads, sandwiches, casseroles, and many other dishes. They are simple to grow and are good for you. All untreated beans (and many grains and seeds) can be sprouted within only two to five days. The sprouting process multiplies the protein and vitamins of the bean or seed. Buy beans for sprouting from health food stores or mail order companies. To be sure you get fresh beans, specify that you intend to sprout them. Beans or seeds for planting may have been treated with insecticides and fungicides and thus be unfit to eat. Supermarket stocks may be too old to sprout. Use whole beans; split peas will not work.

- *Gingerroot.* Gingerroot is expensive, so buy just a little and then grow your own ginger plant. Put a healthy knob of fresh ginger in a large pot of good soil. Keep it moist (not wet) and in a sunny place. After about a month your plant may be up to four feet high. Dig up the root; it will have multiplied eightfold. Replant one knob and start the process over.

- *Herbs.* Home-grown herbs are nice to look at, but they're even nicer to eat. Your local garden center has them already potted and ready to grow. You can raise them either indoors or out. Use scissors to trim off what you need to spice up your salad, soup, or spaghetti sauce.

FOOD STORAGE

GENERAL TIPS

Proper storage of food allows you to buy items when prices are down and keep them safely until needed. Clean, dry, cool places are best. Don't store foods under the sink where it's damp and attractive to rodents and other creatures. Keep food away from household chemicals. Don't store over the stove; high temperatures can cause spoilage and reduce quality.

Other tips:

- *Foods purchased in bulk should be stored in glass or plastic containers with tight covers to prevent infiltration by small insects.* Foods most susceptible include cereals, flour, chilies, pasta, dried mushrooms, and nuts. Grains are more perishable than regular flours and should be given special storage attention.

- *Rearrange your kitchen—or another area of the house—if necessary, to allow enough room to store foodstuffs.* Don't be hampered by inadequate space, or by lack of the proper containers.

- *Get in the habit of saving useful containers and wrappers, and invest in a few sturdy storage containers.* Plastic bread wrappers and plastic margarine tubs, for example, make excellent storage containers.

- *Clean and save all cans with plastic lids, such as those that coffee and shortening come in.* Put masking tape around the top edge of the can to seal in the contents you're storing.

- *Store food in glass and it will hold its flavor longer.* Save jars with screw-top lids for this purpose. Another benefit of glass is that you can see at a glance what you've got instead of having to lift foil and plastic tops to peek in (and leave the refrigerator door open while you're doing it).

- *Canning jars are inexpensive and attractive containers.* Use the ones filled with heaviest contents (beans, grains) as bookends for your cookbooks.

- *Get large mayonnaise jars free from delicatessen counters.*
- *You can also store food by placing a bowl or plate over the dish it's in.* This, too, saves on tin foil, Saran wrap, and other costly sealers.
- *Keep leftovers conspicuous so they don't get overlooked.* Or better yet, keep an inventory posted nearby so you'll know what you've got and can plan accordingly. Don't let leftovers spoil in the recesses of your refrigerator.

FOOD DRYING

Drying as a means of preserving fruits, vegetables, and meats goes back to biblical times. Dried food is highly concentrated, is easy to store, and can keep for years. There's no better way to preserve home garden produce or peak-season food buys. Dried food is excellent for camping trips or vacations; it beats the fast-food places on the road for taste and nutrition any day. And dried fruits, nuts, and seeds are perfect for snacks. They are inexpensive, satisfying, and healthful—better than junk food snacks in all ways.

When fruit is dried, some 50 percent of the water is removed while the nutrients remain. It's the moisture that causes decay and bacterial growth; when it's removed, fruits will keep up to six months, and other foods for years. Phyllis Hobson reports in *Garden Way's Guide to Food Drying* that " . . . a selection of dried food on your pantry shelf can save your food budget as much as a $1,000 a year."

Drying costs less than canning and freezing in equipment, energy, and storage space. In addition, drying has the following advantages:

Advantages over Canning	*Advantages over Freezing*
—Nutrients not cooked out	—No freezer "burn"
—No sugar added	—Keeps longer
—No botulism danger	—No power-failure danger
—No jar and lid shortages	—No complicated packaging

Just to see how easy it is, dip thinly sliced apples, bananas, or other fruits or vegetables in a quart of water with four tablespoons of lemon juice. Place the slices on a cheesecloth spread over an oven rack and let the heat from the pilot light (on a gas stove) or oven light (on an electric range) do the drying. It takes 24 hours.

The sun is an excellent source of free heat for drying food. Wood frames with a screen tray to keep insects off can be built from scrap lumber. Four-tray units that can be used in the oven, ten-tray jobs for outside use, and several in-between sizes are available commercially.

Equi-flow Food Dehydrators are manufactured by B&J Industries, 514 State St., Marysville, WA 98270. For lower-priced models, drop a card to Garden Way Catalog, Charlotte, VT 05445. Equi-flow manufactures dehydrators for Garden Way as well. A ten-tray Equi-flow can dry up to 13 pounds of food in ten hours for as little as one penny per hour. Worth investigating.

THE ROOT CELLAR

Home storage of fruits and vegetables can provide a family with fresh produce through the winter. Root cellars can be quite inexpensively installed in a basement, or in an attic, a garage, or underground in a barrel—any place where a stable temperature can be maintained. For starters, send $1.00 to Garden Way Publishing Co., Inc., Charlotte, VT 05445 for Bulletin #1, *How to Build and Use a Root Cellar.*

Here's a list of fruits and vegetables that lend themselves well to common storage:

- Apples (some varieties)
- Beets
- Cabbage
- Carrots
- Celery
- Onions
- Parsnips
- Pears (winter)
- Potatoes
- Pumpkins
- Rutabagas
- Salsify
- Squash
- Turnips.

FOOD PREPARATION

Basically, the key to thrift in cooking is to buy the ingredients and prepare the food yourself. Make your own salad dressing, bake your own bread, and cook your own meals rather than heating up store-bought convenience packages. A lot of people spend more money for convenience because they're on the go and don't mind paying extra for it. But they fail to realize that (1) the extra they pay for convenience is also buying them shoddy nutrition along with chemical preservatives, artificial flavoring, artificial coloring, and other additives that are bad for their health; (2) it often takes no longer to prepare food from scratch; and (3) if they cooked themselves, they could make more, giving themselves the benefit of leftovers. The extra effort is marginal, the personal satisfaction is great, and the yield in terms of health and nutrition is the difference between night and day.

Thinking along these lines, it seems wise to invest in a couple of good all-around cookbooks and some decent equipment—an electric mixer and/or food processor or blender, a cooking thermometer or two that really work (one for the oven and one for the refrigerator/freezer), at least one really sharp knife and a couple of good pots (cooking in cast iron enriches your diet with iron), a hand grater, and a steamer (more versatile than you'd think).

Other basic hints:

- *Minimize waste by serving less.* Most people in this country eat too much anyway. Parents overload their children's plates and then complain when the kids can't get it all down. To avoid having to rake uneaten or picked-over food into the garbage, serve a reasonable helping first, and make the seconds smaller. The U.S. Department of Agriculture says you can save two out of every ten food dollars by adopting this habit.

- *Check out cookbooks that tell you how to make convenience foods at home* (pancake and waffle mix, cake or biscuit mix, granola, self-rising flour, instant cocoa, etc.). Not only will you save money, but you'll avoid preservatives, artificial flavorings and colorings, thickening agents, and other additives. Store these foods in canisters labeled with directions on how to use them. This makes it easier for all family members to participate.

- *Don't overcook.* It wastes energy and causes your food to shrink and lose nutritional value.

- *Plan for leftovers.* Cook large portions that can be warmed up later. Remember that stews, curries, and casseroles taste better as they age because poultry and meat absorb the spices and become more flavorful over time.

- *Use leftovers creatively.*
  - Plan a smorgasbord for a weekend lunch or brunch. Here presentation is important. Be creative and spruce the food up a little. Make open-face sandwiches, cut the edges off a half-eaten pear, add a can of cheddar cheese soup to a fading casserole, put fresh red tomatoes in yesterday's salad.
  - Use leftovers in "brown bag" school lunches.
  - Use them as nutritious snacks (as opposed to junk food).

— Make soups from scraps accumulated in either the freezer or the fridge.
— Grind up leftovers with other ingredients and fry them, make sauces resembling chili or Sloppy Joes, or use them as fillers in other dishes.
— Toss them like a salad.
— Grind them up as baby food.
— If you have a pet, instead of scraping leftover food into the garbage, give it to the dog or cat.

INDIVIDUAL FOODS: PREPARATION AND STORAGE HINTS

BABY FOOD

Puree leftovers to make baby food. Leftovers are cheaper and are better for the baby than commercial baby foods. And when the baby starts right off eating what the rest of the family eats, there'll be no difficult adjustment to be made as the baby grows.

Get a hand-cranked baby food grinder (Sears-Roebuck has them for around $6.00) or use your blender to turn fresh vegetables, meats, potatoes, fruits, and leftovers into tasty baby food. But don't use highly seasoned food. Even salt, which is a common ingredient in factory-made baby foods, has been proven to cause problems. When making baby food in a blender, add some brewer's yeast or wheat germ for more B vitamins. You can also freeze the pureed food in ice cube trays.

Even a leftover spoonful or two of baby food shouldn't be thrown out. Save it in a jar in the refrigerator. When enough is accumulated, feed the baby the leftovers.

BEER AND WINE

You can legally brew up to 100 gallons of wine or beer a year. For wine use grapes, apples, pears, dandelions, peaches, or any fruits. Beer-making is extremely practical and produces natural, healthy results. Beer was brewed even before bread was made, and both have been adulterated through the ages. Naturally fermented beers these days are rare. The process should involve simply brewing water, corn, hops, barley-malt, and yeast. Sugar is often used to provoke fermentation, however, and preservatives, foam stabilizers, coloring, filtering agents, and anti-gushing agents like EDTA are added. Homemade is cheaper and better.

While serving champagne (or any effervescent drink), place the handle of a fork in the bottle to keep the liquid from going flat. The metal doesn't have to touch the liquid, and it slows the bubbles from bursting, keeping drinks sparkling and fizzy through an evening.

Refrigerate leftover wine after transferring it to the smallest airtight container possible to reduce oxygenation. In other words, don't store an inch of wine in the bottom of a bottle; pour it into a small glass jar. You can also leave it unrefrigerated (and loosely corked) until it turns to wine vinegar and can be used as a marinade.

BREAD

Bake your own bread. Savings can really mount up over the years, since good store-bought bread is two or three times as expensive as homemade. And by baking, you'll enjoy a better-tasting product and avoid the preservatives and artificial colors and flavors of most commercial breads.

Breadmaking is *not* difficult. You can see how easy it is by starting with simpler breads like muffins, biscuits, and Irish soda bread. Here's a recipe for a simple bread that requires no kneading.

> In 1 1/4 cups body-temperature water, mix 1 package of dry yeast and 2 tablespoons oil; then add 2 tablespoons sugar, 2 teaspoons salt, and 1 1/2 cups flour. Beat for two minutes with an electric mixer or for 300 hand strokes. Stir in another 1 1/2 cups of flour, then cover the bowl with plastic wrap and let it sit for 45 minutes or until batter doubles its size. Pound it back down to size, beat again—hard—and pour batter into 9-inch loaf pan (greased). Let rise for another 40 minutes. Place in 375° oven until top is brown—about 45 or 50 minutes.

Vary your basic bread recipe by adding chopped sprouts, sunflower seeds, nuts, freshly ground corn or soybeans, caraway or sesame seeds, dried onion flakes, dill, wheat germ, shredded zucchini, chopped fruit or grated lemon rind, poppy seeds, or even grated cheese or ham slivers. And add toppings like poppy, sesame, or caraway seeds before the bread goes into the oven.

Don't be intimidated by the timing of bread making. Work it around your own schedule. The cooler the place you leave the dough to rise, the slower the process. So you can do everything ahead of time and let the dough rise in the refrigerator, or freeze a batch until needed, or make your own "brown and serve" bread that can be refrigerated up to a week. See *Fleischmann's Bake-It-Easy Yeastbook* (available for $1.00 from Fleischmann's, Box 337, Teaneck, NJ 07666). If your yeast batter rises too much while you are busy elsewhere, just punch it down and let it rise again. Yeast breads are better if the dough rises slowly.

Experiment with various combinations of whole grain flours: oats, barley, rye, wheat, corn, rice, and soybean. You may want to double the yeast if you are using the heavier and more nutritious stone-ground flours. Buy yeast by the jar and save 35 percent over the dry yeast sold in packets. (One envelope of yeast equals 2 1/2 to 3 teaspoons or one scant tablespoon, and a jar equals 16 envelopes.) Or buy yeast in a two-pound baker's package and store it in the freezer; it will retain its power for a year.

Rather than rice, pasta, or potatoes, make homemade bread the carbohydrate in your main meal. You'll save money. When fresh bread comes to the table warm from the oven, it's so good you may need no more than butter, a piece of cheese or chicken, and a salad for your meal. Let the bread be the main dish.

Other tips:

- *Add low-cost bran to your breadstuffs to add flavor and fiber.* One cup bran replaces 3/4 cup of flour.

- *Cheap flatbreads open up a whole new dimension in breadmaking.* Many need not be baked in an oven; they can be cooked on top of the stove in a skillet. Try pita breads, tortillas, chappatis, or pizza. Even cornbread can be made quickly and simply: use your waffle iron.

- *Make your own bran muffins, fruit breads, and English muffins for breakfast, and save money.* Oranges, dates, bananas, pumpkin, zucchini, oatmeal, and cranberries are all good in bread.

- *Save the water in which your potatoes were boiled and use as the liquid in bread dough.* It acts as a leavener and helps the yeast grow. It also imparts an attractive flavor.

- *Pulverize stale bread and bread products (old danishes, muffins, etc.) in a blender to make crumbs for pie crusts, breading, apple brown betty, etc.* If you normally discard bread crusts, allow them to dry out and then crush them for crumbs. If you don't have a blender, put the stale bread in a paper bag and roll over it with a rolling pin. Store the crumbs in a tightly covered jar.

- *Garnish vegetables with a crumb topping.* Put crumbs in a skillet with one or two tablespoons melted butter or margarine. Season with herbs, sesame seeds, etc., and toast until golden brown. Sprinkle this over vegetables, cooked or raw. It's especially good on cold sliced tomatoes, zucchini, cooked green beans, and corn.

- *To keep bread fresh, let it cool and then wrap it tightly in foil for 24 hours to develop the flavor.*

- *Seal bread in airtight plastic bags before freezing.* Remove the bread from the freezer a few hours before it's needed. If you slice the bread before freezing it, you can remove slices as you need them.

- *Don't throw away stale bread; freshen it.* Wrap it in a damp towel and refrigerate it for 24 hours. Remove the towel and heat the bread in the oven for a few minutes, or steam it as you would steam vegetables.

BUTTER

Cut down on the amount of butter you use by serving it at room temperature. It's easier to spread, so less is used. Savings mount up.

Another way to save is to stretch your butter, following these four steps:

1) Soften 1 pound (4 sticks) of butter.
2) Mix with any of the following:
   - *Unflavored gelatin and milk:* Soften one packet of unflavored gelatin in 1/4 cup cold milk; dissolve this mixture completely by adding 1 3/4 cups hot milk; cool until lukewarm, then combine with butter and beat.
   - *Vegetable oil:* Blend 2 cups vegetable oil into butter.
   - *Evaporated milk:* Beat softened butter into a cream; slowly add 2 cups evaporated milk, beating constantly.
3) If you prefer salted butter, add 1/4 to 1/2 teaspoon salt for each cup of non-butter ingredient.
4) Refrigerate mixture after blending. The result spreads well, costs less than butter, and has fewer saturated fats.

Butter can be stored in a freezer safely for up to six months, so take advantage of specials. If butter goes bad, soften it to room temperature and mix it well with 2 tablespoons of milk. Then drain off the milk, which will have absorbed the bad taste.

CASSEROLES

To freeze a casserole, line the dish with aluminum foil and freeze. Then lift out the casserole, wrap with more foil, and refreeze. This way your casserole dish is ready for action again.

CHEESE

- *Buy cheese in more economical large blocks and wedges, divide it into manageable portions, and wrap each tightly in plastic.* Hard cheese will keep for several months this way.
- *To keep cheese from drying out, butter the cut side or wrap in a cloth dampened with vinegar.*

- *Don't throw out cheese because it's covered with mold.* Just scrape it off. After all, mold is what made the cheese in the first place, and it's only on the surface. The remainder of the cheese is quite edible.

- *Freeze dried-out cheese ends for grating later and use on pasta, salads, omelettes, casseroles, and cream sauces.* Or dice the ends and use for making cheese sauce.

- *The high cost of milk as compared to the amount of cheese produced is an unavoidable factor, so for the most part cheese-making isn't economically worthwhile.*

- *Grate your own cheese.* It's cheaper and fresher. Block Romano and Parmesan are quite easy to grind with a Moli hand grinder, but any grater will do. The extra you pay for those shake jars or plastic packets of factory-ground cheese simply isn't worth it. Another hint: if you use Parmesan or Romano only now and then, freeze them; it actually makes them easier to grate.

- *Grated cheese can be stored indefinitely in your freezer and takes only fifteen minutes to thaw.*

- *An idea for leftover cheese: run it through a meat grinder with ingredients such as onions or green peppers for cracker spread.*

- *Cottage cheese makes a nice spread for bread.* It's low in fat, low in calories, and low in cost. Its texture can be improved by putting it in a blender. Don't buy expensive flavored cottage cheeses. Flavor them yourself with carrots, celery, or whatever you like.

- *Ricotta works just as well as cottage cheese.*

- *Cottage cheese lasts longer—twice as long—if stored upside down in the refrigerator.* But put a paper towel underneath in case it leaks.

CHOCOLATE

Three tablespoons of powdered cocoa and a teaspoon of melted butter or fat equals one ounce of unsweetened cooking chocolate.

COFFEE AND TEA

- *Avoid cranking up the percolator or coffee maker for a single cup of coffee.* Fill a small, finely meshed strainer with coffee and pour boiling water through it into a cup; then let the coffee steep to the desired strength. Melitta makes a small filter-holder that works nicely for a single cup, and paper towels can be substituted for the expensive filter papers.

- *If you grind your coffee until it is very fine, you don't need as much.* Also, you can pour the water through a second time to get all the flavor out (although some people believe this produces bitter coffee).

- *Refrigerate leftover coffee in a tightly sealed non-metal container and use it to flavor puddings, gelatin, and other desserts.*

- *To save energy and time in reheating coffee, put the leftover in a thermos and dispense as needed.* This also works well for tea.

- *Make tea with solar energy and save on electricity or gas.* Put loose tea bags in a large glass jar, add cold water, cover, and put out in the sun. The tea will brew swiftly. Pour it over ice, refrigerate the jar overnight. It will never get cloudy.

- *Mix leftover tea and fruit juice.* If it's cloudy, add a little boiling water and the liquid will clear.

COOKIES, CRACKERS, AND CHIPS

- *Make excess cookie dough and freeze it in empty frozen orange juice cans.* When you're ready to use it, remove the bottom lid, push out the dough, slice, and bake.

- *Home-baked cookies keep longer if stored with apple slices.* Store-bought cookies keep indefinitely because they're packed with preservatives.

- *Save hardened cookies: place a damp paper towel in your cookie jar overnight to soften and restore freshness.* A large piece of orange rind may be used in the container with gingerbread or spice or fruit cookies and will continue to soften the cookies until it dries out itself.

- *Crumble stale cookies and store for use in pie crusts, as a dessert or fruit topping, or to add a crunchy layer to puddings and gelatin desserts.* Crumbled fresh cookies can also work here.

- *Don't throw away soggy potato chips, cereal, or crackers.* Re-crisp chips under the broiler for a few moments. Be careful not to brown them. Crisp cereal and crackers on a cookie sheet in the oven for a few minutes.

- *Stale potato chips, pretzels, and crackers may be reduced to crumbs and added to your breadcrumb supply for use in meat loaves, toppings, stuffings, and coatings.*

EGGS

- *Always refrigerate eggs; they deteriorate quickly at room temperature.* In one hour on the counter they age as much as in one week in the refrigerator.

- *Eggs are porous and lose moisture through their shells.* They should not be stored on refrigerator doors, but in covered plastic egg containers or glass containers. Never wash eggs before storing. Water destroys the protective film that helps keep out air and odors.

- *Eggs stay fresher if you store them pointed side down.*
- *A blood spot in an egg does not mean it's bad.*
- *Egg whites can be stored in the refrigerator in a tightly covered container for about a week and in the freezer for up to six months.* Yolks last for only two to three days in a closed container under a covering of cold water; for freezing, see below.
- *To freeze eggs, separate yolks and whites, and put one yolk or one white in each section of an ice cube tray.* When they're frozen, unmold them and keep them frozen in a plastic bag. Use them individually as needed, bringing them to room temperature before using. Yolks need to be mixed with one pinch of salt and sugar apiece to prevent coagulation when freezing.
- *Extend scrambled eggs with a variety of additions:* sauteed onions; green peppers; bread crumbs; leftover meats (chicken, ham, etc.); cooked rice; diced, boiled, or baked potatoes; leftover or fresh vegetables (corn, broccoli, etc.); and cheese. Tomato or pizza sauce can be heated and spooned over top. Perk up flavor by simmering first with a little oregano, parsley, or garlic or onion powder.
- *If you want to boil a cracked egg, wrap it in foil first.* And a surefire way to keep eggs from cracking while being boiled is to punch a pinhole in the pointed end.
- *You can get away with substituting a teaspoon of cornstarch for one egg in any recipe.*
- *Leftover egg yolks can be boiled and used as a garnish or beaten slightly and added to bouillon.*
- *You can add leftover egg whites to pancake batter.*

FISH

An advantage to fish is that it's fast-cooking. Be especially careful not to overcook fish, or it will be dry and tough. Remove it from the flame when it flakes easily. Broiling is the fastest and easiest method, taking only ten to fifteen minutes. Baking takes twenty to thirty minutes. Frying is not recommended; it uses more energy in preparation, adds unnecessary fats, and smothers the natural taste of the fish.

Here are some other tips for preparing fish:

- *Fresh fish spoils quickly, so cook it at once or store it well-wrapped in the coldest part of the refrigerator.*
- *The type of fish called for in a recipe can be replaced by the best catch of the day.*

- *Try bonito instead of tuna;* use it in the same ways.
- *Try unusual fishes like blowfish and skate,* which are delicious and cheap. Experiment with unfamiliar varieties of fish. They are often less expensive.
- *There's little waste from fish, so you need less of it by weight than meat.*
- *You can make fish go farther by serving it with a stuffing of rice or spinach, or by making fish chowder.* Extend the protein in fish dishes by preparing them with vegetables and beans, or with cheese sauce, newburg sauce, or with another milk-based sauce.
- *Keep fish in a very cold freezer (0° to −10°F).* Seal tightly in freezer paper or an airtight container. Put waxed paper between individual fish or fillets so that they can be separated. A good way to freeze fish is in a clean milk carton filled with water. (When you thaw the fish, use the water to fertilize your houseplants.)
- *Thawing frozen fish in milk draws out the frozen taste and makes fish taste fresher.* Soak fish in vinegar and water before cooking it; this also freshens it and gives it a sweet, tender taste.
- *Shrimp cooks easily, too.* Never boil shrimp—pour boiling water over them, stir a few minutes, and then cover tightly. Large shrimp average six minutes in preparation; small shrimp three. Soak canned shrimp for 15 minutes in two tablespoons vinegar and a teaspoon of sherry, and they'll lose their canned flavor.
- *Mussels are cheaper than other types of shellfish.* Discard any that don't open and steam the rest in wine. Serve with fresh French or Italian bread to sop up the broth.

FRIED FOODS

- *Always reuse cooking oil.* Oil used for making french fries, for instance, can be reused at least a half dozen times, until it darkens. Let the oil cool, and the sediment will naturally settle to the bottom, making it easy to pour off the clean oil. But keep oils used for different kinds of frying separated and labelled. Don't use fish-frying oil to make french fries!

FRUITS AND VEGETABLES

The three R's of nutrient conservation for cooking fresh fruits and vegetables are:

1) *Reduce the amount of water used.*
2) *Reduce the cooking time.*
3) *Reduce the exposed surfaces by limiting cutting, paring, and shredding.*

The cooking process destroys vitamins (especially vitamin C, which the body cannot store and which must be replenished daily) and uses energy. So eat your fruits and vegetables fresh and raw, rather than canned or cooked at home, whenever possible. Try raw cauliflower, asparagus, green beans, peas, zucchini, and spinach, especially in salads. If you do cook, minimize the cooking time and keep the pot covered to conserve nutrients and energy. Steaming is an especially efficient way to do this.

The skins of all fruits and vegetables are generally quite high in nutrients and provide essential roughage for the digestive system. Scrub carrots and potatoes, for example, but leave the skin on. If you insist on peeling, then do so after cooking, when the fruit or vegetable has absorbed some of the nutrients from its skin.

Vegetables

General Hints

- *Give new textures to raw vegetables by serving them shredded or julienned.*
- *Add variety to low-cost vegetables with new combinations.* Stir-fry Swiss chard with scallions. (Fry the scallions first, cover with chard and let it wilt. Toss, season, and serve.) Try carrots with apples, or cooked sweet potatoes with bananas and green pepper.
- *Steaming is about the most nutritious way to cook vegetables.* It preserves B vitamins, vitamin C, and essential minerals. Steaming is quick and easy, and can be used for both fresh and frozen vegetables. *You can use any of the following for steaming:*
  - An inexpensive aluminum steaming basket (the type that opens up like a flower)
  - A colander or strainer propped up in a large pot
  - A bamboo steamer, which you can buy cheaply wherever Oriental groceries are sold.

    The steaming process:
  - Fill the bottom of a pot with water, which you can flavor with salt, lemon juice, garlic, herbs, or even wine, and bring it to a boil.
  - Cut up the vegetables just before cooking (to preserve vitamins) with the sharpest utensil you have. (*Hint for broccoli:* cut an X incision through the stem up to the flower so that it will be cooked at the same time as the flowers. *Hint for asparagus:* skin the tough, lower end of the stalk with a vegetable peeler so it will be as tender as the upper part.)
  - Add vegetables and cover. Steam until tender. It doesn't take long.

- *The pressure cooker cooks vegetables even faster, with the same advantages as steaming.* Be sure not to overcook.

- *The pot liquid from cooking vegetables is high in flavor and nutrients.* Use it as a broth for soups and gravies or for mashed potatoes, or freeze it in ice cube trays or a plastic container for later use.

  - *Broiling vegetables in bouillon or broth is cheaper than cooking them in butter or oil.* Place sliced vegetables in a pan. Stir in three tablespoons broth made from powdered mix, or use seasoned "pot liquor" you've saved from previous meals. Put the pan under broiler and cook five to ten minutes at medium heat. Stir occasionally to keep the vegetables moist and prevent burning.

  - *Stir-frying vegetables is also quick and nutrient-saving.* Shred or slice vegetables thinly at an angle and stir-fry quickly in a little oil. Add a little meat, cheese, fish, or tofu and pour over brown rice. Try vegetables you've never stir-fried before. Romaine lettuce works quite well in a wok.

  - *Save scorched vegetables by setting the pan in cold water for 15 to 30 minutes and then dumping out vegetables.* (Do not scrape the pot first.)

  - *Make complete use of vegetables.* Don't discard darker leaves, carrot parings, parsley stems, outer celery stalks, or the greens of beets, turnips, or radishes. These are often more nutritious than the vegetables themselves. Beet greens provide more protein, fiber, and vitamin C, three times as much iron, and 150 times more vitamin A than beets themselves. Simmer the trimmings with bouillon cubes to make vegetable broth. Cook greens as you would spinach and season them with butter and spices; or shred or finely chop them or put them through the blender and add them to soups and stews. Chop celery tops for stuffing, stews, and salads, or freeze-dry and crumble them for use as an herb or in celery salt.

- *Don't throw wilted fresh vegetables away.* Pick off the brown edges, sprinkle the vegetables with cool water, wrap them in a towel, and refrigerate them for at least an hour. Or douse them quickly in hot water and then in ice water with a little apple cider vinegar. Revive soggy lettuce by soaking it in a bowl of ice water and lemon juice in the refrigerator.

- *Throw odds and ends of vegetables into a common freezer container and use a handful in stews or soups.* Save leftover onion bits, green pepper, single tomato slices, leftover salad, inner cores of broccoli or cabbage, and broccoli leaves.

- *Keep vegetables from going bad by lining the bottom of your refrigerator's vegetable compartment with paper toweling to absorb excess moisture.* Store lettuce and celery in paper bags instead of cellophane ones for the same reason.

Individual Hints

Beans

There are two basic methods of preparing dried beans (legumes):

- *The long-soak method* makes beans easier to digest and maintains the beans' shape better. Wash the beans and place them in a bowl with two or three times their volume of cold water. Let them stand eight hours or overnight—24 hours to be most digestible—and then cook them slightly.

- Use *the rapid-soak method* when you're in a hurry. Wash the beans, and put them in a pot. Add two or three times their volume in water and bring to a boil. Cook until tender (20–30 minutes).

Since beans are such an excellent protein source, substitute them for more expensive meat in main dishes. Add a little animal protein (milk, eggs, cheese, meat) to supplement the bean protein and add flavor. For example, a combination of cold cooked beans, cheese, cold cooked macaroni, celery, and dry-roasted peanuts tossed with an Italian dressing makes a balanced and delicious light meal. Combine beans with vegetables for economical cold salads or hot side dishes.

Try these other uses for beans:

- *Pop soybeans for a nutritious snack.* Soak them in water for five minutes and proceed as you would for regular popcorn.

- *Leftover beans make great soup.* Puree the beans in a blender or food processor; add broth or milk; heat gently and season with salt, pepper, garlic, or such herbs as basil, oregano, sweet marjoram, thyme, cumin, or chili.

Potatoes

Potatoes make up a complete protein when combined with dairy products. A medium potato with a cup of milk (or 1/3 cup instant non-fat dry milk) supplies nine grams of usable protein. You can drink a glass of milk with your baked potato; melt cheese or yogurt and cheese on top of it; whip potatoes with milk, yogurt, or cottage cheese; or scallop potatoes with milk and cheese.

More hints for preparing potatoes:

- *Serve potatoes with their skins instead of filling up on extra meat.* You'll get the benefit of the vitamins in the skins, and you'll save on calories. You can make french fries, chips, mashed potatoes, scalloped potatoes, and casseroles without peeling.

- *Instead of boiling potatoes, chop them in smaller pieces and steam them to save more nutrients.*

- *Save the potato water used in cooking and use it in breads (see p. 46), or add it along with dry milk, butter, and seasoning to mashed potatoes.* Refrigerate extra for later use.

- *Bake potatoes when you are using the oven for other foods; and when you do, bake extras for later use.* For crisp, attractively browned baked potatoes, wash the skins well, dry them, and rub them with oil before baking. Don't wrap them in foil; the skin loses crispness and the foil is wasted. If you don't happen to be using the oven to bake anything else at the time, bake your potatoes on top of the stove and save energy. Put the potatoes on a heat diffuser pad over a low flame (do not use asbestos, as it has carcinogenic properties) and put a pan upside down over them to hold in the heat. Or place the potatoes in a covered coffee can set on a diffuser.

- *To shorten the baking time of potatoes, insert an aluminum nail or metal fork through each, or boil them 10 minutes in salted water before baking.*

- *Baked potatoes can be recooked.* Dip them in water and bake them at 350° for only twenty minutes. Or slice them, skin and all, and fry them for nutritious hash browns.

- *Save time and energy by broiling potatoes instead of baking them.* Scrub the potatoes and quarter them lengthwise. Dry them and brush them all over with salad oil. Place them on the broiler rack with the skin side up. Salt and pepper, and broil for 15 minutes until brown and crusty. Turn, brush with oil, and broil 10 minutes more.

- *Use leftover mashed potatoes to make potato pancakes or other dishes.* For pancakes, mix the potatoes with an egg, mashed carrot, and a little yogurt or sour cream. Form it into patties and pan-fry. Or put the mixture in a casserole and cook it in the oven. Heat it until it's steaming, then top it with grated cheese. These are complete protein meals. (Any leftover meat or vegetable can be mixed in—diced meat, sausage, chopped onion, peppers, etc.) You can also use leftover mashed potatoes to top casseroles, or to form pie shells to hold sauteed or creamed vegetables or meat bits.

- *Leftover mashed potatoes can be frozen and fried up when you need them.* Shape them into patties and freeze.

- *Don't refrigerate potatoes, sweet potatoes, or hard-shell squash.* Cold temperatures convert the starch into sugar, affecting the taste. Store them at ordinary room temperature in a cardboard box, which will absorb the moisture they give off. The box should be kept in a dark, dry place because light affects the vitamin C content. Remove any potatoes that have started to sprout or go soft. Discard the bad parts of each and cook the remainder immediately.

Onions

- *Keep dry onions from sprouting and going soft by wrapping them individually in foil.* Once an onion has been cut in half, rub the exposed side with butter so that it will keep longer.

- *Don't throw away sprouting onions.* They are homegrown scallions. Use the sprouts in salads, sandwiches, soups, and Chinese foods. You can eat the rest of the onion, too.

- *Do not store onions with potatoes.* The onions will spoil from the extra moisture given off by the potatoes.

- *Onions brown faster if they're fried with paprika.*

Greens

- *Green salads are expensive in the winter.* Go with cooked vegetables and fresh fruit salads instead.

- *Spinach and other greens can be cooked in only the water clinging to their leaves from washing.*

- *To get three meals from one head of cabbage, use the outer leaves for stuffed cabbage, the middle leaves for cabbage soup, and the inner leaves for coleslaw.*

- *Outer lettuce and cabbage leaves may not be attractive but are perfectly edible and full of nutrients.* Cut off blemishes or wilted edges and shred the rest for slaw, sandwiches, or salad. Or put these leaves in the blender and add the bits to soups or stews. If you do discard these leaves, don't remove them until you're ready to use the lettuce or cabbage head.

Fruits

General Hints

- *Fruits that can satisfy a sweet tooth are better than desserts.* A recent school study found that, surprisingly, kids prefer apples to sweets. The sugar in fruit is in its whole and natural form, as opposed to refined sugar, which is devoid of nutrients and adversely affects general health.

- *Slightly damaged fruit works nicely in pies, purees, jams, and other cooked dishes, especially if used right away.*

- *Fruits and berries can be processed (crushed, chopped, etc.) much faster if they are frozen first.* Less juice is lost, because it's in a crystalline form.

- *Smaller pieces of fruit are usually priced cheaper than larger pieces.* The smaller also keep longer. And they're perfect for snacks.

- *Fruits—especially berries—will last longer if you don't wash them until you serve them.*

- *Keep leftover cut fruit appetizing by tossing it with lemon juice before refrigerating.* The lemon juice keeps fruit from darkening; it works with cut bananas, pear and apple halves, etc.

- *The syrup from cans of fruit, if not used at the same time as the fruit, can be used in gelatin desserts, as an ingredient in barbecue sauce or marinade, to baste hams and roasts, to sweeten beverages, or as a base for compote.*

Individual Hints

Bananas

- *Overripe bananas are often marked down in stores.* Use them in banana bread, fritters, pies, pancakes, waffles, cakes, or milkshakes. You can also fry them in a little butter until they're brown and crusty for a great addition to breakfast. Or add a little brandy or liquor to the butter and serve the brandied bananas hot with a scoop of vanilla ice cream for an elegant, but simple, dessert.

- *Use bananas to make a substitute for cream to use on pudding, gingerbread, or cake.* Beat a sliced ripe banana and one egg white with an electric mixer until the mixture is stiff (about five minutes).

- *Refrigerate any ripe bananas you don't intend to eat right away.* Although the skin darkens, the ripening process is slowed down.

- *Don't throw away overripe bananas; freeze them for cooking later or to be eaten as popsicles.* If they've darkened, peel them and beat them slightly; then freeze them for later use in cakes or bread.

Citrus Fruits

- *To get more juice from a citrus fruit, try any of these methods before squeezing:*
  - Roll the fruit across a counter, putting a slight pressure on it with your hand.
  - Warm the fruit in a bowl of hot water for about 15 minutes.
  - Warm the fruit in the oven for a few minutes.

These methods do not change the vitamin content or taste, but nearly double the yield of juice. In addition, lemons will yield more juice if they're stored in the refrigerator in a tightly sealed jar of water.

- *Don't throw away orange, lemon, or lime rinds.* Cut the rinds from the white membranes and chop, blend, or grate them. Freeze them for use in baking to flavor breads, cakes, etc.

- *When a recipe calls for a little lemon juice, simply pierce the lemon with a metal skewer, knitting needle, or knife, and squeeze out the amount you need.* Seal the hole with masking tape.

- *When you halve any citrus fruit (lemon, lime, orange, grapefruit), store the leftover half with the cut side down in a small amount of water in a saucer.*

Other Fruits

- *When strawberries are cheap and abundant, buy extra ones, mash them or puree them in blender, and freeze them.* Use them later (thawed) as topping for desserts or fruit salad, as flavoring in apple juice, or sweetened slightly to top yogurt.

- *Plum tomatoes or tomatoes that are oddly shaped or slightly blemished usually cost less, but the food value is the same.* Slice or chop them for salad, broil them with butter or margarine and basil, or use them in stews, casseroles, or any other cooked dish. If you can buy a lot cheaply, make tomato juice.

- *Rather than can tomatoes when they are bountiful, freeze them raw.* If you prefer them skinless, dip them in boiling water and slip off the skins. Freeze them whole or cut up, seasoned or unseasoned. Use them just like stewed tomatoes. This saves you the extra equipment needed for canning.

- *If raisins are expensive, try substituting prunes, dates, or currants.*

- *Don't throw away the contents of the Halloween pumpkin.* Bake the seeds in the oven to dry, and eat them salted or plain for nutritious snacks. Use pumpkin meat for pies, bread, muffins, custards and puddings. Pie filling can be made ahead of time (but add the eggs only when you're ready to bake) and frozen in plastic bags or containers in pie-sized amounts. You can steam or pressure-cook pumpkin meat and pack it in one-cup amounts to be frozen or used soon.

HERBS AND SPICES

- *Use whole spices and grind or crush them yourself.* The flavor and quality of the spice will be better, and your savings will be considerable, especially if you buy in bulk. Use a hand grater for nutmeg. For grinding and chopping other spices, use an electric blender, or fashion a mortar and pestle by putting the spice in a small custard cup and using the bottom of a small jar or a piece of wood for the grinder.

- *Store herbs and spices in airtight metal or glass containers in a dark, cool, dry place.* Cover the jars or paint the outsides black. Heat, light, and moisture destroy flavor.

- *To keep garlic cloves longer, store them in a bottle of cooking oil.* The garlic will never dry out and you can use the flavored oil for salad dressing or cooking.

- *Fresh gingerroot may be preserved indefinitely if immersed in sherry in a refrigerated covered jar.* Sherry does not affect the ginger flavor, but the ginger adds a pleasant taste to the sherry, which can be drunk or used in cooking.

- *To make your parsley and other leaf herbs go farther, freeze them in a plastic bag, then chop them finely.* Keep these herbs frozen and use pinches as you need them. Or to bring out the best in leaf herbs, crumble or rub them between your palms before adding to foods. This releases the oils.

- *Make your own Chinese five spices flavoring by mixing one teaspoon ground cinnamon, one teaspoon ground thyme, one teaspoon aniseed, one teaspoon ground cloves, and a dash of allspice.*

- *Create your own fines herbes to use in salad dressing, herb butters, batter breads, and sauces, and on vegetables.* Mix equal portions of chervil, chives, tarragon, and parsley in a small, tightly closed jar.

- *Saffron is the world's most expensive spice, but saffron substitute gives rice a gourmet twist at a minuscule cost.* Add about 1/2 teaspoon of turmeric and 1/4 teaspoon of garlic powder per two cups of uncooked rice. Cook as usual; the rice will take on a saffron color as well as a similar taste.

- *Make your own seasoning salts and save.* Mix a quantity of garlic, onion, or another herb with three times that quantity of salt in a blender or food processor.

- *Make your own superior vanilla extract.* Put a vanilla bean in a bottle large enough to completely immerse it, and cover with an inexpensive vodka or brandy. Shake two or three times a day. In two weeks you have the best vanilla extract available.

HONEY

- *Cook with honey instead of with refined sugar.* Not only is it better for you, but your baked goods will last longer and remain moist longer.

— Sauce recipes: Use equal amounts of honey for sugar.

— Regular recipes: Use 3/4 cup of honey for every cup of sugar called for because honey is more concentrated; decrease liquids by 1/4 cup. If there are no liquid ingredients in the recipe, add 1/4 cup of flour per 3/4 cup honey.

- *For homemade sweet spreads to replace processed jams and jellies, crush berries or chop dried fruit and mix with honey, or cook diced fruit with honey until thick.*

- *Crystallized honey, syrup, jam, or jelly may be revived by heating the jar gently in a pan of warm water.* The crystals will dissolve.

- *Minimize waste when measuring sticky liquids such as honey, molasses, or corn syrup by lightly greasing the inside of the measuring utensil; the liquid will pour out completely.*

ICE CREAM

Homemade ice cream and ices save 80 percent of the cost of store-bought and give better nutrition and flavors. You can use a commercial ice cream maker or, more simply, a blender and your freezer.

JUICES

- *Well-diluted drinks quench thirst better and keep down calories and sugar intake—as well as expense.* Dilute fresh and canned juices with three times their volume in water and frozen juices with twice their usual volume.

- *Recycle pickle juice.* Save it to thin salad dressing, soak dehydrated onions, and flavor sandwich spreads, potato or pasta salads, or cole slaw. You can also use it to pickle hard-boiled eggs or fresh cucumbers.

MEAT

- *Refrigerate meat immediately after buying it; bacteria multiply otherwise.*

- *Meats of lesser grades are super for soups, stews, stir-fry dishes, pot roast, and casseroles.* No need to buy expensive cuts for these. And combination meat dishes use less meat and save you money. You can save by combining small amounts of meat with grains and beans. Examples are pork fried rice, chili con carne, spaghetti and meat sauce. The list is endless.

- *"Mixed grill" allows everything to cook together, saving energy costs.* Use budgetwise combos such as thin pork chops, chicken wings, chicken livers, sausage, tomatoes, and mushrooms, thinned with white wine and flavored with oregano.

- *Age beefsteaks yourself.* Rub each side with a cut garlic clove; then brush with cooking oil. Layer the meat between sheets of wax paper, place on a platter, and refrigerate about one week before cooking. If meat is on sale, eat some when you buy and age the rest.

- *If you have meat cut at the butcher or supermarket (you're better off cutting it yourself), ask for the trimmings and simmer them with vegetables for a hearty soup or stockpot.* They can also be used to add flavor to stuffings and casseroles.

- *Many working people feel they only have time to broil steaks or chops. Take a weekend afternoon to cook cheaper, tougher cuts of meat that require longer cooking.*

- *A rule of thumb: the higher the oven temperature, the more the meat shrinks and the tougher it becomes.* Use no more than a 300°–325°F temperature, and consider even lower settings. It's advisable, though, to roast meat at 300° the first hour to destroy bacteria that would otherwise multiply. Then lower the temperature. This saves fuel as well.

- *Vinegar, because of its acidity, makes an excellent tenderizer and does not affect the taste (wine can also be used).*
  — Steak: Rub the meat with a mixture of cooking oil and vinegar and let it stand two hours. Or put it in a plastic bag of marinade for two hours, turning occasionally.
  — Boiled meat: Add a tablespoon of vinegar to the cooking water.
  — Game or tough meat: Mix half a cup of wine vinegar with a cup of heated bouillon and seasoning. Marinate for two hours.

- *To speed up the process for meat that requires a long roasting time, cover the meat with tin foil before putting it into the oven.* Roasting bags, available in supermarkets, do the same thing, and keep the juices closer to the meat while it's cooking, thereby enhancing the flavor. These bags also save you the trouble of scrubbing a roasting pan.

- *Allow a roast to stand 10 minutes before carving to set the juices and seal the flavor.*

- *To extend your ground beef, mix in any of the following and fry:* ground turkey, oatmeal, breadcrumbs or cubes of bread, wheat germ, onion or eggs, grated raw potatoes, beans, rice, vegetables, stuffing mix, vegetable protein (burgers made with this shrink less because the extender absorbs juices from the meat). Or seal two layers of meat together around seasoned bread stuffing, slices of cooked potatoes, beans, cooked vegetables, or seasoned rice. Such fillings can help keep meat juicy. Be sure to close the edges tightly.

- *For quicker cooking, put a hole through each hamburger patty.* It will seal itself during cooking.

- *Unsmoked fresh ham is economical, free of excess fat, and goes a long way.* Season it with salt, pepper, and garlic; surround it with whole peeled onions; and roast it in a 350° oven for 35 minutes per pound. Slice thinly to serve.

- *Use the gelatin that surrounds canned ham.* It is rich in meat juices and flavor. Add it to the pan juices and spoon it over the ham while it's cooking, or use it in a sauce to serve over the ham. Or add it to soup.

- *Bacon is a low-yield food.* Cooking reduces it to three to five ounces per pound. But the leftover fat has some important uses:
  - Use it instead of margarine, butter, or vegetable oil for frying potatoes, chicken, etc.
  - Use it instead of shortening in soups, stews, biscuits, puddings, pancakes, or corn bread. When substituting for shortening, use a quarter less.
  - Melt it with lemon juice as a salad dressing on mushrooms and spinach salad, and cut it with vinegar for other salad dressings.
  - Use it on top of casseroles so that they'll cook better.

- *Make your own sausage patties or links and save money, while controlling the meat quality, the fat content, and the seasoning.* Use any kind of meat. Grind the meat of your choice in an ordinary meat grinder or a food processor, or ask your butcher to do it. Sausage seasoning mixes and casings are available in spice stores and from mail-order firms (like Garden Way Catalog, see p. 34). Or make up your own seasoning mixes; look in recipe books for inspiration.

- *Keep bones for stock.* Freeze them until you've accumulated enough.

- *Instead of using a paper towel to clean a cast-iron skillet, use newspaper.* It works just as well. Salt also works as an abrasive, and it doesn't disturb the seasoned surface. Never use soap of any kind.

- *If you're buying a charcoal grill, buy one with a lid.* Keeping the lid on decreases the cooking time and enhances the charcoal flavor. And after cooking, you can close the lid and vents to extinguish the charcoal so that it can be reused.

- *You don't need to buy charcoal lighter fluid.* Turn a cardboard egg carton inside out so the top and bottom halves are touching. Place briquets in the upper half (as you would eggs) and ignite.

MILK AND MILK PRODUCTS

Buttermilk

For a bottomless supply of inexpensive buttermilk, prepare three cups of powdered nonfat milk in a clean quart jar as per manufacturer's instructions.

Mix with a cup of buttermilk and a pinch of salt. Warm over low heat. Cover, leave out overnight, then refrigerate; you'll have buttermilk. As you use it, repeat the process and you'll never run out. This product contains fewer calories and is fresher than the store-bought equivalent.

Chocolate Milk

Commercial chocolate milk must be made from whole milk; "chocolate drink" is made with partially skim milk. Chocolate milk is cheaper if you make it yourself from milk and chocolate syrup or powder. It's not a good idea to drink chocolate milk regularly, as the chocolate inhibits the absorption of calcium.

Cream

Cream just starting to sour may be restored to sweetness by adding a pinch of baking soda.

Sour Cream

Substitute buttermilk for sour cream on baked potatoes. Yogurt can also stand in for sour cream.

Whipped Cream

Make whipped cream from light cream and save. Mix 1 1/4 teaspoons unflavored gelatin with 2 tablespoons cold water in a small, deep bowl. Set the bowl in hot water to dissolve the gelatin. Add one cup light cream and a dash of salt. Now set the bowl in a larger bowl filled with ice. Whip 5 to 7 minutes, until the mixture holds smooth, then add flavoring if you wish. Use immediately or refrigerate.

For an even cheaper alternative, whip evaporated milk instead of cream for dessert toppings. Thoroughly chill the evaporated milk, the bowl, and the beaters before whipping.

You can also stretch whipped cream by adding one egg white and a few drops of lemon juice.

PASTA

The best reason for serving pasta, aside from the fact that it's cheap, is all the healthy and delicious things you can prepare it with: tomato and/or vegetable sauce, ham, hamburger, chicken, fish, clams, parsley and olives, cheese, cream or butter, different herb combinations, anchovies, etc.

Pasta is relatively cheap, but even the enriched type is nowhere near as nutritious as potatoes, rice, or whole grains. Shop for the most nutritous or buy whole wheat pasta products from a health food store or mail-order firm. This pasta is twice as expensive, but nutritionally it's worth it. Enriched soy macaroni, for example, has more protein than hamburger and with vegetable sauce makes a thrifty balanced meal.

Use leftover pasta in soups or stews, mixed in scrambled eggs, reheated alone, or in a pasta salad served cold with a little leftover meat or fish.

PEANUT BUTTER

- *Extend peanut butter with grated carrots and use it for sandwich filling.* The carrots add crunch, are nutritious, and reduce calories and cost.

- *Thin peanut butter with honey as a substitute for cake frosting or as an ice cream topping.*

PIES AND CAKES

- *Want fresh-fruit pies all year? When fresh fruit and berries are in season, prepare large quantities of pie filling and freeze it in pie pans lined with waxed paper or aluminum foil.* When frozen, the fillings can be removed from the pans and bagged tightly. Anytime you want a pie, just make a crust, put a frozen filling in it, and let it thaw.

- *Pie crusts can also be prepared in advance and frozen.*

- *Frozen, unbaked whole pies keep up to two months; baked, six months.*

- *Don't discard dried-out cake; make it into a pudding.* Put it in the top of a double boiler with half a cup of heavy cream. Cover and warm for 15 minutes.

POULTRY

- *Reduce roasting time for poultry by making a slit halfway through the bird at the end where thigh and leg meet on each side.*

- *Hen, labelled "fowl" in the supermarket, is often fairly tough, and therefore inexpensive.* Tenderize it by soaking it in vinegar for two or three hours.

Chicken

- *Stretch your roasted chicken by stuffing it.* Simply put, stuffings can be made from any grain mixed with seasoning. Use anything you have, such as leftover rice, croutons, or cornbread mixed with celery, sauteed onion, diced liver, or nuts.

- *Chicken freezes well, so stock up during sales.*

- *Chicken livers are one of the best meat-counter bargains.* Divide livers into groups of four, put in small plastic bags and freeze for convenient selection. Paté is also easier to make if the liver is frozen first and then put through the food processor or blender.

- *Freeze chicken innards for stock—when enough pile up or whenever you have time, make soup from them.*

- *There are no restrictions against raising chickens in most towns and cities.* It takes a small outlay of cash and very little time, and it provides protein in the form of meat and eggs. Chickens will eat practically anything—scraps of food, grass, bugs, even oyster shells. Six chickens can supply the average family with eggs, and excess eggs and meat can be bartered. And chicken raising can be most informative for children. (See pages 74–75 for information sources.)

Turkey

- *Self-basting turkeys cost more and aren't necessary.* Either baste them yourself or soak a cheesecloth in oil and drape it over the bird before roasting. The cloth should be removed for the last hour of cooking so that the skin will be brown and crisp.

- *To get five meals from a turkey:*
  — Use the breast for cutlets.
  — Roast the legs.
  — Cube the thighs and back for casseroles.
  — Grind the bits for hash or croquettes.
  — Use the remainder for soup.

RICE

- *Brown rice takes more cooking time but no extra work in its preparation.* It's as nutritious as white rice is not.

- *Even if you're in a hurry for rice, don't choose instant, which is nutritionally empty.* Instead, cook regular rice like pasta: bring a pot of water to a boil, and add salt and rice. Boil it uncovered, and start testing for tenderness after five minutes. Drain the rice in a collander or strainer. It's as instant as instant rice, and still much better for you, though you'll pour off some of the nutrients with the water.

- *Combine brown rice with beans, dairy products, or a little meat for a completely balanced food with all the amino acids.*

- *Do not wash or rinse rice before cooking it because washing can dissolve and drain away nutrients and vitamins.*

- *Don't buy preseasoned rice mixes.* They're very expensive and take just about as long to cook as plain rice (even the frozen immersible packets take 15 to 20 minutes). Flavor rice yourself by cooking it in vegetable or meat broth, tomato juice, or another vegetable juice instead of water. Or use the water in which other vegetables have been cooked. You can also flavor your rice with margarine or butter; chopped dry fruit, nuts, onions, carrots, parsley, peppers, citrus peels; or tamari or soy sauce, cinnamon, dry mustard, dill, basil, thyme, or marjoram.

- *Leftover rice has many interesting uses.* Serve it cold in a salad with a vinegar and oil dressing, or use it instead of potatoes in salad nicoise.

Use it for fritters; have them for breakfast. Make rice pudding or other desserts. Brown rice makes especially good pudding. Leftover rice is also great in scrambled eggs, soups, stews, fried rice, casseroles, and stuffing. So make twice as much as you need when cooking to save time and energy.

SALAD DRESSINGS

You save at least 50 percent of the cost of bottled salad dressings and avoid preservatives, artificial ingredients, and sugar by making your own. Dressing takes five minutes to make and keeps just like the bottled variety you pay so much for. Make up and store large batches.

- *The simplest of French dressings (vinaigrette) is made from three parts oil to one part vinegar or lemon juice, with salt and pepper to taste.* Dijon-style mustard can be added to this for creaminess. Any cookbook will provide dozens of such simple recipes.
- *If you want the dressing to have the taste of an herb, such as dill weed, basil, or tarragon, be sure to let it soak alone in the vinegar before mixing in the oil.*
- *Many people feel olive oil is superior in taste and therefore worth the extra money.* Mix olive oil with another vegetable oil to save.
- *Flavored vinegars can cost as much as a bottle of wine.* Make your own. Put two tablespoons of the clean, dry herbs of your choice in a quart-size wide-mouthed jar. Heat, but do not boil, enough vinegar to fill the container, and pour it over the herbs. Cover the jar with a non-rusting lid, and set it in a dark place at room temperature for two weeks. Strain the vinegar through cheesecloth and funnel it into attractive bottles. Try garlic cloves, sweet marjoram, tarragon, basil, peppercorns, savory, mint, or other flavorings.
- *When your ketchup bottle is empty, add oil and vinegar, shake vigorously and use for salad dressing.*

SAUCES AND GRAVIES

Once you get the hang of it, most sauces can be made from scratch in five to ten minutes.

- *Make white sauce by stirring dry milk powder into a roux of margarine or butter and flour and then adding water slowly.* Stir the sauce until it's well blended and let it simmer for a few minutes over low heat so that the flavors can meld.
- *Use a large salt or sugar shaker for flour to avoid waste when dredging foods.* This will also allow you to thicken your sauces without lumps.

- *Pan juices from roast beef, roast chicken, etc., make good gravy.* After pouring off most of the fat, put the pan on the stove and add water, broth, or wine. Mix this well with the remaining drippings and burnt bits, and then thicken with a tablespoon of cornstarch dissolved in 1/4 cup cold water.

- *That butter sauce you pay extra for in the frozen vegetable bag can be made by adding salt and pepper to taste (about 1/4 teaspoon of each) to four tablespoons of melted butter.* What could be easier?

- *For a fast mock-sauce for vegetables, sprinkle hot cooked vegetables with grated parmesan or shredded Swiss cheese.* Toss well and serve immediately. This method saves energy, too, as the "sauce" is not cooked on the stove.

SODA POP

Make your own. Prepare frozen juice according to package directions, then dilute with an equal amount of plain club soda or seltzer. Or buy soda flavor extracts like sarsaparilla, root beer, cherry, and cream soda from the Garden Way catalog (see page 34) or Nichols Garden Nursery (1190 NW Pacific Highway, Albany, OR 97321).

SOUPS

- *Nothing is more economical than soup*—especially the kind you make from scratch. You can make a large pot of lentil soup for slightly more than it would cost you for one 20-ounce can of lentil soup. You can use all your leftovers and odds and ends, as well as super-nutritious additives such as wheat germ, soybeans, dry milk, and cooking liquid from other dishes (vegetables, boiled meats, etc.). Soup bones can be purchased for very little, or you can use the bones you have taken from your main course meat dish. Using soup as a first course takes the edge off appetites before diners reach the high-priced main dish.

- *Make stock to be used in many different soups, gravies, or sauces by boiling up meat bones* left over from roasts or hams. You can also use ham hocks or any smoked meat bones, or you can purchase lamb neck bones or other soup bones from your butcher. Simmer the bones with some simple seasonings (salt and pepper), and refrigerate or freeze the stock until needed.

- *Inexpensive hot or cold soup can be made from potatoes* (the cold is vichyssoise). Potato plus milk equals a complete protein. Season with onion, parsley, and dill, then sprinkle sesame seeds on top.

- *Make gazpacho by mixing leftover salad with tomato juice in a blender, and top it with yogurt; or blend salad with only yogurt and seasonings for a refreshing cold summer soup.* Season these soups with onion, vinegar,

Worcestershire sauce, garlic, and parsley. Add a little oil if you think it needs it. A slice of stale bread adds body; sprouts add nutrition.

- *Pick up extra canned soups in your favorite flavors when on sale.* Bean combination soups like bean and bacon or split pea with ham are high in protein. One cup has as much as one or two ounces of meat. Canned soups are good in casseroles and sauces and as bases for homemade soups. Or dress them up by adding chopped vegetables, meats, or other leftovers, or a shot of sherry, lemon juice, or chives. Use them as a sauce over fish or steamed vegetable for a quick meal.

- *Soup concentrates made from organic vegetables (no preservatives or artificial additives) can be purchased in health food stores or from mail-order firms like Biorganic Brands, Inc. (Long Beach, NY 11561).* These products are much cheaper than dried soups from the supermarket. Chicken and beef soup concentrates can be purchased cheaply by the pint from companies like Highbar Wholesale Spice Co., Inc. (2919 Long Beach Road, Oceanside, NY 11572).

- *A bouillon cube or packet may be used instead of chicken or beef broth.* It's cheaper but probably saltier, so taste it before salting further.

- *Soups and stews may be thickened with leftover mashed potatoes or instant potato flakes.* These will not lump or stick together like flour or cornstarch. Or use oatmeal—nutritious, delicious, and also cheap. Stir in a tablespoon at a time; let it cook for a few minutes before adding more.

- *Make soups more interesting by beating in an egg or adding any chopped or slivered meat.* Add crunch with thinly sliced water chestnuts or fresh vegetables such as snap peas or Jerusalem artichoke. Or float any of the following on top of the soup: minced chives, sifted hard-boiled egg yolks or whole eggs, bacon or soy bits, croutons, chopped green pepper or onion, yogurt or sour cream, or thinly sliced cucumber, zucchini, onion, or lemon.

STUFFINGS

Why use the prepared stuffings that manufacturers supply? Prepare your own from leftover vegetables (finely diced), dried fruit, stale bread, brown rice, and other whole-grain cereals.

SUGAR

- *Get kids off the sugar habit.* Put sugar in a salt shaker for moderate dispensing.

- *You can make small amounts of powdered sugar in the blender.* Put in two or three tablespoons of regular sugar at a time and blend for a few seconds.

- *Use a dusting of powdered sugar on cakes instead of frosting; it is cheaper and better for you.* Place a paper doily or homemade cut-out snowflake over cake and sprinkle sugar through it to make design.

- *To prevent brown sugar from solidifying, place it in a covered container with a slice of apple, or store it in the freezer.*

- *If your brown sugar does solidify, don't throw it out.* Grate the amount you need, or put it in a food processor. Or dissolve the sugar in warm water with a little butter and vanilla or maple flavoring to make pancake syrup.

SYRUP

- *To make your own pancake syrup, blend 1/2 cup molasses, 1/2 cup honey, 1/2 teaspoon vanilla, and a pinch of salt.* Add walnuts if you like.

YOGURT

- *Making your own yogurt is simple and can save you up to 80 percent of the cost of store-bought.* The yogurt makers are nice but not necessary; all you really need is a warm place or a well-insulated bowl or a thermos. Bring one quart of milk to a boil and pour it into a large mixing bowl. When you can comfortably put your finger in it, add two tablespoons plain yogurt, cover, and put it in a warm spot (on a radiator, over the pilot light, atop the refrigerator) for at least five hours. When your supply gets low, save a couple of tablespoons for the next batch.

- *Homemade or commercial plain yogurt can sometimes be used instead of mayonnaise to save money and calories.* Or use a mixture of half mayonnaise and half yogurt.

- *If you must buy yogurt in the supermarket, then buy it plain in large quantity and add your own flavorings* (fresh fruit, preserves, honey, raisins, nuts). This will save you a bit of money.

WAFFLES AND PANCAKES

- *If you have excess waffle batter, make extra waffles and freeze them.* They can be successfully toasted or revived in a table top broiler-oven.

- *See "Potatoes," page 55, for tips on potato pancakes.*

KITCHEN APPLIANCES

WHAT TO BUY

A full 30 percent of the energy that supports our food system is consumed in the home, and much of that energy is wasted. The hot water heater, refrigerator, and stove are the three largest users of electricity in the kitchen.

When electricity must heat or cool, as in a stove or refrigerator, it is expensive.

- *Portable appliances such as toasters, toaster ovens, electric kettles, electric skillets, broilers, and other small appliances do specialized cooking more economically than the oven or its surface units.* But don't buy these items with the intent to pay for them by the energy you save; that will take a long time.

- *Food processors, blenders, and mixers, however, are items which will pay for themselves quickly. They serve a unique and very useful function while using only a tiny amount of electricity.* When electricity turns a motor, especially for very brief periods of time, as with a food processor or blender, it is less expensive.

- *When you purchase an appliance, you are buying two packages: the new appliance itself and the energy to run it.* Makes and models of larger appliances—especially refrigerators and freezers—can vary widely in their energy consumption. EER (Energy Efficiency Ratio) labels now appear on all major appliances and indicate how much energy will be required to operate the unit. Although energy-efficient appliances may cost more than less efficient models, the difference can pay for itself through lower fuel bills.

- *Purchasing last year's model of a major appliance can reduce your cost substantially unless an energy- or labor-saving improvement has been made.* For example:

  — New thin-walled refrigerators with improved urethane-foam insulation give almost twice as much storage capacity.

  — Refrigerators with energy-saving switches or post-condenser loops decrease the amount of energy consumed in winter when the house is cooler.

  — Electric ignition on gas ranges uses 5 to 10 percent less natural gas than the pilot light.

  — A power-saver surface unit on the stove distributes heat efficiently, matching the size of the pan—four, six, or eight inches.

- *Bear in mind that a frost-free refrigerator uses 36 percent more electricity than one you manually defrost.* Its energy consumption can be cut 16 percent by purchasing a model with a power-saver switch that can turn off the defrost when humidity is low (in winter).

- *Be a wise buyer and don't buy too big a freezer.* A space of three to four cubic feet is enough for each family member, five or six if you shop infrequently or have a garden.

- *The best time of year to buy refrigerators or freezers is the end of July.*

- *In the summer, microwave ovens have the advantage of reducing heat in the kitchen, thus reducing operating expense for the air conditioner or fan.* They use about 1,500 watts per hour, at a cost of around 9 cents an hour. However, bear in mind that the surface element on a stove uses less energy than a microwave for a large quantity of food when cooking times are similar.

- *Call the Consumer Product Safety Hotline toll-free, (800) 638-8326, to check whether the appliance you are considering is satisfactorily rated and trouble-free.*

USING THE STOVE

- *Nearly half the fuel cost to run a gas stove is consumed by the pilot lights alone.* If you own a gas stove, ask your gas company to turn the pilot lights off (do not blow them out) and use a striker or matches instead.

- *In summer, cook during the cooler parts of the day—morning and evening— in order to cut down on the uncomfortable heat in the house. In the winter, this heat can be an advantage.*

- *Don't overcook.* Energy is wasted and nutrients and flavor are destroyed.

- *Turn off the heat a few minutes before the end of cooking;* food continues to cook with stored heat.

Burners

- *Use the highest heat setting to reach the desired temperature; then turn to the lowest setting that will maintain that temperature.* Steady use of a higher setting uses more energy and doesn't cook food any faster.

- *Covering the pots will prevent the escape of heat and reduce energy consumption by 20 percent.*

- *When using the surface of the stove, match the burner size to the size of the pot.* If the heated electric coil extends beyond the pan, or, with a gas stove, if the flame runs up the side, energy is wasted.

- *Keep reflector pans and drip bowls clean.* Bright reflector pans can save up to 30 percent on fuel consumption.

- *When boiling water, start with hot water from the tap and boil it in a tea kettle or a covered pot to save time and energy.*

- *Stir-frying (cutting food in bite-size pieces and cooking over high heat)* cooks food quickly, thereby conserving nutrients and energy, and adds variety to a diet. A wok is recommended for this, though a skillet will do.

- *Pressure cookers and steamers are also energy-efficient and nutrient-conserving appliances for cooking.*

Oven

The oven is the most energy-wasteful way to cook. A large area has to be heated and there is substantial heat loss through the walls and door. *So when you use your oven, make it count.* Make more than you need and freeze the rest in meal-size packages. Keeping your freezer full makes that appliance more efficient anyway.

Other tips:

- *When cooking several foods together, place the food to be removed first (or that requires attention) in front to minimize the time that the oven door is open.* Meat and vegetable dishes should be placed on the bottom rack; desserts and baked goods cook better on the top.

- *While baking or roasting foods for a meal (meat, potatoes, even cakes) bake your frozen vegetables too, rather than boiling them separately.* Place the contents of a standard-size box of frozen vegetables in a casserole with salt and one or two tablespoons butter or margarine. Cover tightly and bake for 30 to 60 minutes, depending on the oven temperature.

- *You can lower the oven setting 25° below the recipe instructions when baking in glass or glass ceramic.* These materials give better heat transfer than metals.

- *Pastries and bread need a preheated oven; other foods such as casseroles and the like do not.* No longer than 10 to 12 minutes is needed to preheat.

- *Covering the bottom of an oven with foil to catch drippings can cause an electric oven to short out and will lower the heating efficiency of a gas oven.*

- *Electric ovens become energy guzzlers when used to heat the kitchen.*

REFRIGERATOR

- *The location of your refrigerator and freezer can make a difference in their operating efficiency.* Keep them away from heat producers and out of sunlight, and try to keep four inches of air space around them so that the motor heat can easily escape.

- *Housing and compressor coils of refrigerator-freezers and freezers should be vacuumed at least three or four times a year.* Dust and grime make for inefficient operation.

- *Keep the refrigerator only as cold as is necessary.* The temperature inside the average refrigerator should be 40°F. A rule of thumb is if the milk stays cold and the lettuce doesn't freeze, the setting is correct. If your unit has an energy-saving switch, use it when condensation forms.

- *When ice builds up in a non-frost-free model, the unit must work harder and uses more electricity.* Always defrost before the ice is 1/4 inch thick.

When defrosting, a good place to store the food is inside an empty dishwasher or washing machine. Throw in a couple of ice cube trays.

- *Refrigerate only those items that actually require it.* Some foods need cold storage only after they are opened; check the labels. Don't overload the fridge, because air must be able to circulate around each container. (The freezer is just the opposite and should be completely filled.)

- *Cool cooked foods before refrigerating.* Hot foods in the refrigerator cause it to work harder and use more energy, lower the temperature of surrounding foods, and build up frost in the freezer compartment, hastening your next defrost. Cool foods faster by putting them in a pan or bowl of cold water.

- *Cover all foods and particularly liquids—especially in a frost-free refrigerator.* Evaporation can dry food out, and the moisture released inside the fridge makes it work harder and frost up faster.

- *An open refrigerator door wastes electricity.* Know what you're going in for when you open the door. If children persist in "window shopping," standing with the door open and looking in, declare the refrigerator off limits until they can learn. The same goes for putting groceries into the refrigerator. Gather all foods to be refrigerated before you open the door.

- *A small open container of baking soda (only 1/2 cup is necessary) eliminates the refrigerator odors which can give your food an unpleasant taste.* Change the soda approximately every two months.

- *Temperatures aren't the same throughout the inside of the refrigerator.* The coldest part is usually at the back of the top shelf and is the ideal place for highly perishable items like milk and eggs. The door racks are the least effective storage space.

- *If you're going to be away for a few days, shift the temperature to a warmer setting to compensate for the door not being opened.* If you'll be away awhile, empty and unplug the fridge and prop the door open.

- *Remove excess store wrapping from food before refrigerating it;* the packaging can act as insulation.

FREEZER

Chances are that home freezers will not save you money. The disadvantages—initial cost, repairs, and the rising cost of electricity—can seldom be offset by food savings unless you live on a farm or do your grocery shopping infrequently. There's also the possibility of food spoilage caused by power failure, and the time and trouble involved in thawing food before cooking it and in defrosting the freezer. If the refrigerator you purchase has a good freezer, then you can reap the benefits of freezing on a small scale. A two-door refrigerator then becomes a must: that separate freezer compartment keeps food much longer than the freezer compartment in a single-door fridge.

- *If you do have a one-door refrigerator, frozen foods should be eaten within three to four days since they are usually stored above 15°F (freezers in the two-door units average 0° to 8°) and lose vitamins rapidly.* In the conventional home freezer, foods will keep up to one year.

- *To make a freezer pay off, you should keep it filled to near capacity, using food frequently and restocking.* This allows you to shop for and store food bargains, and it makes for more economical operation as well: a bulk of food retains the cold better than empty air. If the supply of food in your freezer diminishes, fill plastic or cardboard containers with water and freeze them to keep the freezer full. Besides cutting your electric bill, the ice blocks may be useful on summer outings. Bang the ice against something hard and you've got usable ice chunks.

- *A chest-type freezer is more economical to operate than an upright because less cold air "falls out" when it's opened.* The chest type uses half the electricity of an upright.

- *Be aware of the two major rip-offs associated with buying a home freezer:* the "freezer food plan," in which you are promised (for a price) bargain food for the freezer; and the "bait and switch" in bulk meat buying, in which you are promised one thing and sold an inferior one.

- *Always rotate your stock (as they do in the supermarket).* Store whatever you're adding underneath what is already there.

- *Extra ice trays are essential for a home freezing plan.* When you make up a soup stock or baby food, or have leftover coffee, stew gravy, pan juices, or anything you'd rather not throw out, freeze it in an ice cube tray, and then transfer it to a labeled plastic bag (the cubes won't stick together). As you need coffee ice cubes for undiluted iced coffee or reheated homemade soups, stock, or gravy for cooking, simply grab a few cubes.

- *Empty milk cartons (both quart and half-gallon) make excellent freezing containers.* The tops can be stapled shut again and contents marked outside.

- *When big items are transferred from freezer to fridge a day early, they thaw gradually and cool the refrigerator in the process.*

SOURCES

GROWING YOUR OWN

Backyard Livestock by Steven Thomas. Charles Scribner's Sons, Vreeland Ave., Totowa, NJ 07512. $5.95.

The Bean Sprout Book by Gay Courter. Recipes and instructions for growing this cheap, nutritious food in your kitchen. Simon & Schuster, 1230 Ave. of the Americas, New York, NY 10020. $1.95.

Complete Book of Community Gardening by Jamie Jobb. How people can join together to grow together. Turn your town's vacant lots into productive gardens. William Morrow & Co., Wilmore Warehouse, 8 Henderson Drive, West Caldwell, NJ 07006. $7.95.

The Complete Urban Farmer: How to Grow Your Own Fruit and Vegetables in Town by David Wickers. Viking Press, 625 Madison Ave., New York, NY 10022. $9.95.

The Complete Vegetable Gardener's Sourcebook by Duane Newcomb. Where to find out all about the varieties of vegetables and the seedsmen who supply them. Avon Books, Mail-Order Dept., 250 W. 55th St., New York, NY 10019. $10.20.

Down to Earth Vegetable Gardening Know-How by Dick Raymond. Good charts and excellent information. Garden Way Publishing Co., Inc., Charlotte, VT 05445. $7.95.

Dwarfed Fruit Trees by Harold Bradford Tukey. 1964, 1978. Cornell University Press, 124 Roberts Place, Ithaca, NY 14850. $32.50 (or from your local library or library extension service).

Escarole in the Bedroom: Growing Food Plants Indoors by Jack Kramer. How to garden even if you live 50 stories up. Little, Brown Co., 34 Beacon St., Boston, MA 02106. $5.95.

Good Food Naturally: How to Grow It, Cook It, Keep It by John B. Harrison. One of the best buys, from a man who has worked the same land organically for 36 years. Keats Publishing, Inc., 36 Grove St., Box 876, New Canaan, CT 16840. $3.95.

Minnie Rose Lovgreen's Recipe for Raising Chickens by Minnie Rose Lovgreen. Nancy Rekow and Claire Frost, Editors. Pacific Search, 222 Dexter Ave. North, Seattle, WA 98109. $2.00.

Postage Stamp Garden Book by Duane Newcomb. You can feed four people for a year from a 15-square-foot garden with this book and some hard work. Houghton Mifflin Co., Wayside Road, Burlington, NJ 01803. $5.95.

Raising Small Meat Animals by Victor M. Giammatei. The Interstate Publishers, Inc., 19-27 N. Jackson St., Danville, IL 61832. $12.35.

Tub Farming: Grow Vegetables Anywhere in Containers by Mary Johnson. Turn your balcony, your bathtub, or even your living room into a miniature family farm. Garden Way Publishing Co., Charlotte, VT 05445. $5.95.

MAKING YOUR OWN

Better than Store Bought by Helen Witty and Elizabeth S. Colchie. How to make stuff you usually buy: hot dog buns, marshmallows, even cream cheese and pumpernickel bagels. Harper & Row, Keystone Industrial Park, Scranton, PA 18512. $12.95.

Making Your Own Baby Food by Mary D. and James Turner. Practical advice on feeding your child without the help of Gerber or Beech-nut. Workman Publishing Co., 1 W. 39th St., New York, NY 10036. $3.95.

Making Your Own Cheese and Yogurt by Max Alth. A variety of homemade dairy foods. Harper & Row, Keystone Industrial Park, Scranton, PA 18512. $4.50.

Quality Brewing: A Guidebook for the Home Production of Fine Beers by Byron Burch. Good, cheap suds. From Great Fermentations, 87 Larkspur St., San Rafael, CA 94901. $3.25.

PRESERVING AND STORING

The Ball Blue Book. A guide to canning and freezing from the folks who have been helping America put up its harvest for almost 100 years. The Ball Corp., Consumer Affairs Dept., Muncie, IL 47302. $2.50.

Complete Book of Home Storage of Vegetables and Fruits by Evelyn Loveday. Garden Way Publishing Co., Inc., Charlotte, VT 05445.

The Freezer Book. For those who don't care to can. The Ball Corp., Consumer Affairs Dept., Muncie, IL 47302. $.75.

Garden Way's Guide to Food Drying (How to Dehydrate, Store and Use Vegetables, Fruits and Herbs) by Phyllis Hobson. The best overview on this least expensive way to preserve food. Garden Way Publishing Co., Inc., Charlotte, VT 05445. $5.95.

Home Storage of Fruits and Vegetables (NRAE-7). One of several informative booklets on food and gardening from The Distribution Center, 7 Research Park, Cornell University, Ithaca, NY 14850.

Putting Foods By by Ruth Hertzberg, et al. A basic source for storing and preserving food. Bantam Books., 666 Fifth Ave., New York, NY 10103. $2.95.

VEGETARIAN COOKING

The Book of Tofu by William Shurtleef and Akiko Aoyagi. First of a series of books by these authors about high-protein, low-cost foods from Asia. Available through your bookstore, or order from New Age Foods, Study Center, P.O. Box 234, Lafayette, CA 94549, and ask for information on the other volumes and additional information. $2.95 in paperback.

Forget About Meat Cookbook by Karen Brooks. Advice on vegetarian eating. Rodale Press, Emmaus, PA 18049. $7.95.

The Great American Tofu Cookbook by Patricia G. McGruter. More about this versatile food, with an American slant. Autumn Press, 1318 Beacon St., Brookline, MA 02146. $6.95.

Modern Vegetable Protein Cookery by Joan and Keith Kendig. How to get the nutrition you need without high-cost meat. Arco Publishing, 219 Park Ave. South, New York, NY 10003. $11.95.

Recipes for a Small Planet by Ellen Ewald. Information about the good sense of eliminating meat from your diet, and some high protein recipes to replace it. In paperback. Ballantine Books, 201 E. 50th St., New York, NY 10022. $2.50.

The Unabridged Vegetable Cookbook by Nika Hazelton. An encyclopedic treatment of vegetable cookery. M. Evans & Co., 216 E. 49th St., New York, NY 10017. $14.95.

Vegetarian Epicure by Anna Thomas. Proof that meatless cooking can satisfy the most discriminating tastes. Two volumes. Random House, 455 Hahn Road, Westminster, MD 21157. Vol. 1, $5.95; Vol. 2, $6.95.

MISCELLANEOUS COOKBOOKS AND WAYS TO CUT FOOD COSTS

Bag It! A Guide to Packing Nutritious Lunches. Giant Food, Inc., Consumer Affairs, P.O. Box 1804, Washington DC 20013. Free.

Brown Bagging It: The Lunch Box Idea Book by Adeline G. Shell and Kay Reynolds. Simon & Schuster, 1230 Ave. of the Americas, New York, NY 10020. $3.95.

Joy of Cooking by Irma S. Rombauer and Marion Rombauer Becker. A great all-around cookbook. How to eat an artichoke, make puff pastry, cook a woodchuck, plan a buffet dinner for 50. Bobbs-Merrill, Box 558, 4300 W. 62nd St., Indianapolis, IN 46206. $12.95. (Also now in two paperback formats: a large single volume and a two-volume pocket-sized set from Signet Paperbacks, 1633 Broadway, New York, NY 10019. The two-volume edition costs about $6.00 for both.)

Waste Not, Want Not: A Cookbook of Delicious Food from Leftovers by Helen McCully. Random House, 201 E. 50th St., New York, NY 10022. $8.95.

Yogurt Cookery by Sophie Kay. Good recipes using this healthful and delicious food, which is easy to make at home, too. In paperback. Bantam Books, 666 Fifth Ave., New York, NY 10103. $2.25.

AVOIDING SUGAR AND JUNK FOOD

The Junk Food Junkie's Book of Haute Cuisine by Lucinda Sullivan and Emilie Gibbs. Recipes for recreating the taste of fast food favorites. Perhaps a way to up the nutritional value as you wean your family to better foods. Popular Library, CBS, Inc., 383 Madison Ave., New York, NY 10017. $1.50.

Naturally Delicious Desserts and Snacks by Faye Martin. The one book to get if you want to eliminate sugar and junk food treats from your family's diet. Rodale Press, Emmaus, PA 18049. $14.95.

The Taming of the C.A.N.D.Y. Monster by Vicky Lansky. How to get the sugar out of your sweetie's system. Meadowbrook Press, 16648 Meadow-brook Lane, Wayzata, MN 55391. $3.95.

FORAGING

Start your trek with a trip to the bookstore for Euell Gibbon's classic foraging handbooks, *Stalking the Wild Asparagus* and *Stalking the Blue-Eyed Scallop*. Both from David McKay Co., 2 Park Avenue, New York, NY 10016. $3.95 each.

HEALTH

HEALTH

Health care is the fastest rising expense in our budgets. It's also an area that seems to leave little margin for choice; we turn responsibility over to the experts—doctors, clinics, hospitals—and insist on the best care and health coverage. The cost of health care in America has always been high. In 1981, it passed the $200 billion mark. That averages about $930.00 per person.

There are ways to save, however, and they are presented in this chapter. Included are simple ways to save on health and disability insurance and on drugs and pharmaceuticals. Further on in this chapter is information on the benefits of health maintenance organizations; on getting the best service from doctors; on reducing the cost of hospital stays and surgery; on avoiding quackery; on senior citizens' health care and nursing homes; and on funerals.

SELF-CARE

First and foremost is self-care: the better care we take of ourselves and the more knowledgeable we are about ourselves, and about health, nutrition, medicine, and medical procedures, the less we need to rely on outside help.

THE FIRST STEP: PAYING ATTENTION

The sporadic attention of a physician or health worker is no substitute for the first line of good health care—the attention you pay to yourself and to those close to you.

The very best way to cut your medical costs is to take care of yourself.

- *Don't smoke.* If you do smoke, stop. If you can't stop, cut down. (The American Cancer Society, with offices in most larger cities, sponsors quit-smoking clinics free of charge.)
- *Reach and maintain a proper weight.* But as long as you're not suffering from high blood pressure or some other weight-related health prob-

lem, it may be better to keep a steady though high weight than to yo-yo up and down.

- *Watch your diet* for fats, sugar, salt, and additives. Avoid excessive alcohol and stay clear of caffeine and junk foods.
- *Keep active and maintain a program of regular exercise.*
- *Schedule a regular health checkup*, though not necessarily a full checkup each year. Regular tests for blood pressure, cholesterol, cervical and bowel cancer, and glaucoma can be supplemented at less regular intervals by a full physical.

It's important to know yourself—your medical history, the things that stress you or make you relax, and the conditions that make you sick or make you well. Educate yourself: be aware of basic nutrition, find out about vitamins, learn basic first aid and emergency procedures, and attend health fairs and take advantage of their free literature and lectures. Make it a point to know when and where free medical services—inoculations, blood pressure tests, etc.—are available. And keep your medicine cabinet well stocked.

Your state of health is a complex, holistic balance that depends as much on prosaic elements like the clothes you wear as on elusive factors such as job satisfaction.

For instance, did you know that repeated vaginal yeast infections are very hard to treat if the patient wears pantyhose without a cotton crotch? Ordinary pantyhose prevent air circulation, and that can keep a yeast infection raging.

Similarly, a pair of jockey shorts and a bicycle seat might be being delaying a long-awaited pregnancy. Sperm production requires a temperature lower than that of the rest of the body. Jockey shorts and bike riding can raise the temperature of the testicles enough to cut sperm production below the level required for easy reproduction.

Annoyance ailments like skin rashes, stress headaches, and muscle tension often find their origin on the job. Daily confrontation with purposeless work, anxiety-creating management, unreasonable work rules, and other kinds of stress can also contribute to more serious diseases, such as ulcers, colitis, hypertension, and heart disease.

As part of self-care, you owe it to yourself to pay attention to environmental factors. The Love Canal tragedy was the most publicized instance of an environmental health problem. People in this upstate New York neighborhood realized that there was a pattern of illness to which doctors were oblivious. The health care profession was treating sick individuals, but what really needed treating was a neighborhood poisoned by chemical wastes.

Again and again, inattentive members of the health profession are being confronted by aware and concerned lay people. "Black lung" and "brown lung" are familiar examples from the mining and textile industries. New examples include the chemically induced sterility suffered by workers in chemical and fertilizer plants, the cancers of uranium miners, the hearing losses of all those exposed to unhealthfully high noise levels in the workplace, and the "Agent Orange" struggle between Vietnam veterans and government agencies.

There is no way we can expect our doctors to step in and protect us from these health threats. The only protection is awareness and cooperation with our neighbors, our co-workers, and our families.

SELF-TESTING

On a simple level, you can and should monitor your own health with simple self-care tests. Primary among them are:

- *Blood pressure testing.* In conjunction with your doctor, you can have a hand in maintaining and adjusting your blood pressure by home monitoring. (A kit costs about $25.00. *Consumer Reports* has published ratings of those available.)

- *Home pregnancy tests.* The instructions have to be carefully followed and the test gives a false negative one time in five, but it is 97 percent accurate in *positive* results. As long as you follow instructions and don't trust the negative result very much, home pregnancy testing can provide you with a fast, private affirmation of pregnancy.

- *Breast self-examination.* You can learn how to do this fast and simple test for lumps or other growths that may be cancerous by asking your doctor or by attending a women's clinic or health fair.

- *Testicular cancer examination.* Especially important for men under 35, this is a simple exam that you can learn from your doctor.

- *Skin cancer exams.* A periodic examination of your beauty marks and moles can reveal precancerous and cancerous changes.

There are also home tests for bowel cancer, home Pap tests, do-it-yourself strep throat cultures, and tests for urinary tract infections. They can all save you money, but you should consult your physician about procedure and usefulness before you begin a program of using them. (As in all health matters, a second opinion is a good idea. Bear in mind that some doctors are opposed to anything that keeps a patient out of their office, so get a second opinion if your physician is overly opposed to self-testing.)

THE ASSERTIVE PATIENT

In addition to this kind of hands-on self-care, a generally assertive consumer's attitude toward health can help you stay healthy, recover more quickly, and avoid excessive costs.

Some Guidelines

- *The assertive patient works with the doctor to find a treatment that is satisfactory to both sides.* That can range from insisting on being shown how to test at home for a urinary tract infection, at $1.00 a test instead of $25.00, to insisting that the doctor consider a lumpectomy instead of a radical mastectomy.

- *Being an assertive health consumer can mean seeking out alternative health care,* such as chiropractic treatment for that painful back instead of drugs and/or surgery. Relaxation and meditation might be a better means to controlling hypertension than a permanent regimen of powerful drugs.

- *You are not a machine, and the doctor is not a deity.* The entire health care profession and the treatment it delivers benefit when the patient enters into an active partnership with the physician.

- *The field of self-care is as wide as your own life experience.* It can lead you to a yoga ashram or meditation center or to your union headquarters or local OSHA (Occupational Health and Safety Administration) office. (For the OSHA office nearest you, write to the Department of Labor, Washington, DC 20210.)

- *The most important thing to consider is that you must ultimately take responsibility for your own health care.* If you're not satisfied with your doctor's attitude, if you sense that your illness is not being resolved, if you find that your health problem is shared by neighbors and co-workers, then it is up to you to do the research, knock on doors, and pester the institutions until you get the help and response you need.

Dealing with Doctors

You can keep your health costs down and the quality of your health care up by learning how to deal with your physician:

- *Find a family doctor and see him or her regularly.* The doctor's familiarity with your medical history will help you save time and money in diagnosis and treatment.

- *Be frank with your doctor about fees and your budget.* It may be possible for the doctor to adjust the charges to meet your insurance benefits or your pocketbook. This is especially recommended when you're dealing with a specialist.

- *If your doctor makes house calls, you should use this service only when an illness confines you to the home.* Go to the office so that the doctor can do a full examination. An office visit will probably cost less. And when you call to make the appointment, ask if you should fast for a period before the visit or if you should bring a urine or stool sample—it may save you a second appointment.

- *See if you can get the advice you need by phone.* If you have a regular family doctor, he or she may be able to advise you on minor problems without an office visit. But don't abuse this courtesy, or trouble the doctor for routine appointments or information requests that can be handled by the nurse or receptionist.

- *Do what your doctor tells you.* A simple adjustment in your life-style can save years of debilitating illness and thousands of dollars in lost wages and medical bills.

Questions to Ask When Your Doctor Gets Out the Prescription Pad

- *Is there an alternative therapy or a change in diet or living style that is equally effective?*

- *Will this drug's effect be altered when combined with other drugs you're already taking?* Drugs can interact in your system with extremely problematic results. The same applies if you often take aspirin, antihistamines, or other over-the-counter drugs. Tell the doctor everything you're taking.

- *Are there any possible side effects and/or adverse or allergic reactions to this prescription?* Some drugs cause problems as aggravating as the disease. If you are allergic to any drug, let the doctor know.

- *Are there any special instructions you should follow?* Is it all right to drink and smoke? Some things like coffee, milk, or alcohol can have adverse effects.

- *Does he have any "starter" supplies he can give you?* Doctors often receive free samples from drug firms and are glad to pass them on to you.

- *Has this drug been in use for some time?* Don't be a drug company's guinea pig. Drugs that have been in use longest are generally safer because their dosages and side effects are more fully established. Doctors are frequently visited by drug salesmen whose concern is to sell drugs, not to cure you.

- *What is the most reasonably priced drug outlet in the area?* Surprisingly enough, the American Medical Association is recommending that doctors provide this information.

- *Is the drug, by any chance, available over-the-counter?* If it is, you can save the fee a pharmacist automatically charges when you walk in with a prescription form.

- *Can the doctor prescribe a generic—or cheaper—form of the drug you require?* Brand-name drugs often cost twice as much as generic ones. (See pages 88–90.)

Getting to Know Your Pharmacist

Pharmacists have six years of training and clinical work behind them; they are also professionally licensed. Don't overlook the advantages of their advice and friendship. They can be a valuable part of your health maintenance network. Your pharmacist can:

- Fill an emergency prescription for you on a Saturday night when your doctor's out of town.
- Give you a discount if you're going to require a large quantity of a drug over a long period of time.
- Tell you how long drugs last and how to store your medicines for maximum life. (Proper storage varies for different drugs, and storing properly may mean preserving on-hand supplies rather than paying for a new prescription.)
- Advise you on what over-the-counter medications you can take for minor ailments, so you don't have to consult your doctor.
- Give you exact details on how to take a medication and answer any miscellaneous questions you might have forgotten to ask your doctor.
- Warn you if you're combining medications you shouldn't be, assuming that he or she is familiar with the drugs you've been taking.

YOUR MEDICINE CABINET

It's three in the morning. The crab rolls your husband ate for dinner are having their revenge, your cold has you breathing through your mouth like a stranded carp, and little Emmeline's poison ivy is tormenting her to tears. Where do you go for help?

If you're like most of us, you head for the medicine cabinet and thrust aside old prescription vials, contact lens solutions, and the toothpaste, looking for some simple remedies for these everyday problems. And if you're like most of us, your chances of finding just what you need are slim.

Some Organizing Hints

Taking the time to organize your medicine cabinet can turn it into a useful source of first aid and a money-saving family health center.

1) *Get rid of all your old prescriptions.* Keep only the ones for hay fever, high blood pressure, or other chronic or repeating problems.

2) *Check the label and/or container of over-the-counter remedies for the expiration date.* Throw away those that are too old or almost too old.

3) *Throw away any unlabeled containers, as well as any containers whose contents show signs of deterioration:* discolored pastes or creams, liquids that have formed a sludge at the bottom of the bottle, crumbly tablets, etc.

4) *Mark potentially dangerous drugs,* such as tranquilizers or prescription pain-killers, with some sort of marker that you'll recognize even in the dark— for example, a piece of sandpaper or a velcro dot from the sewing chest.

5) *Reserve your cabinet for things you use in the bathroom.* Move drugs and remedies to a high shelf in another cabinet. Best of all, especially if you have kids, is a cabinet you can lock. You'll also need another shelf for bulky items like a vaporizer and a heating pad.

6) *Drugs really don't keep well in the warm, moist air of the bathroom.* They stay freshest and most potent in a cool, dry, dark place. Some should be stored in the refrigerator. Ask your pharmacist about proper storage when you pick up any prescription.

What to Stock

Now that you've got the cabinet cleaned out, begin stocking it. Here's a list:

- Aspirin
- Antacid, such as Maalox, Di-gel, or Mylanta
- Kaopectate for diarrhea
- Antiseptic swabs or spray for cuts and scrapes
- Antibiotic spray or lotion
- Band-aids in an array of sizes
- Eyecup and eyewash (best for removing irritants)
- Burn ointment or spray: use for minor burns after they've been put under cold water. (Large burns require medical attention. Don't put anything on them.)
- Nasal spray
- Nonsuppressive cough syrup
- Calamine lotion or hydrocortisone for rashes
- Athlete's foot remedy
- Sunscreen and suntanning lotion
- Insect repellent
- Poisoning remedies: syrup of ipecac to induce vomiting, activated charcoal to absorb poison in the stomach, epsom salts. (First call the poison control center in your community for specific instructions.)

- Miscellaneous: tweezers, cotton balls and gauze pads, elastic bandages, an ice bag and a hot water bottle, a nonpetroleum lubricating cream like K-Y jelly, some lamb's wool or adhesive foam for blisters, and—last but far from least—a thermometer.

CUTTING MEDICAL COSTS

In addition to dealing assertively with your doctor (see pages 83–86), there are a number of things you can do to lower your medical bills.

FREE AND LOW-COST HEALTH SERVICES

Don't forget these useful ways to cut your medical costs:

- *Immunizations for your children and yourself are available through your local health office.*
- *Teaching clinics offer low-cost or free services.* You'll be treated by students under close supervision by their professors, so your care will be meticulous and carefully reviewed. This can be a particularly good way to get low-cost dental care.
- *Check community and voluntary agencies for services* ranging from birth control and free blood pressure exams to VD treatment, drug and alcoholism programs, and mental health care.
- *Donating blood to a nonprofit blood bank or to the Red Cross insures that you and members of your immediate family will be able to get free or low-cost blood when and if you need it.* With whole blood costing up to $50.00 a pint, you gain an important safeguard while serving the community.
- *Visit your local health fair.* Experts in health care offer lectures and perform demonstrations of everything from taking your own blood pressure to doing your own pregnancy test. You can often receive free tests for diabetes, hypertension, glaucoma, tuberculosis, hearing afflictions, and other problems. You may also find a wealth of information on health topics including nutrition, chronic illness, and community health programs.

CUTTING DOWN ON DRUG COSTS

Generic Drugs

Using generic drugs can save you money. *Generic* refers to the original name given a drug during its screening and testing period. Once it's past that, it hits a medical marketplace with a commercial name and a higher price, although it may still be available under its generic name. For example, order the tranquilizer Librium and you pay $10.75 per hundred, while the generic equivalent Chlordiazepoxide goes for $7.25. You can start relieving your anxieties right there in the drugstore.

Notes About Generics

- The decision to substitute should be the doctor's, although you and the pharmacist can decide yourselves in every state except Indiana, Louisiana, and Texas.

- With generic drugs, the question of bioequivalency (whether or not the drug is absorbed into the body the same way as the brand-name) can arise. Three-quarters of generics are bioequivalent, and often a lack of bioequivalency won't make a difference anyway. But be sure to ask your doctor or pharmacist.

- Who manufactures generics? Not unknown, fly-by-night pharmaceutical companies; 90 percent of the generics are produced by the same company that makes the brand-name drug. Also, *all* drug manufacturers are under the control and inspection of the Food and Drug Administration.

For more information, write to Consumer Information Center, Dept. 44, Pueblo, CO 81009, and ask for their free pamphlet, *Generic Drugs: How Good Are They?* (Item # 572).

Generic Price List

Below is a comparative shopping guide to generic and non-generic drugs from *Family Circle* magazine.

BRAND-NAME DRUG (what it's for)	PRICE PER 100	GENERIC EQUIVALENT	PRICE PER 100	AMOUNT SAVED BY BUYING GENERIC
AMCILL, 250 mg. capsule (antibiotic, fights infections such as pneumonia, sore throat, VD)	$10.25	AMPICILLIN	$ 8.50	$ 1.75
ACHROMYCIN-V, 250 mg. capsule (antibiotic, fights infection of mouth, gums, teeth, urinary tract, etc.)	$ 5.25	TETRACYCLINE	$ 3.25	$ 2.00
POLYCILLIN, 250 mg. capsule (antibiotic, fights infections such as pneumonia, sore throat, VD)	$20.50	AMPICILLIN	$ 8.50	$12.00
DARVON COMPOUND, 65 mg. capsule (analgesic, relief of pain)	$ 9.50	PROPOXYPHENE COMP.65	$5.25	$4.25
HYDRODIURIL, 50 mg. tablet (a diuretic, often prescribed for congestive heart failure, high blood pressure, kidney dysfunction)	$6.25	HYDROCHLOROTHIAZIDE	$3.25	$3.00
V-CILLIN K, 250 mg. tablet (antibiotic, for bacterial infections)	$11.50	PENICILLIN V	$7.75	$3.75

Brand		Generic		
LIBRIUM, 10 mg. capsule (tranquilizer, relief of symptoms of anxiety, tension)	$10.75	CHLORDIAZEPOXIDE	$7.25	$3.50
ERYTHROCIN, 250 mg. tablet (antibiotic, effective for infections of upper and lower respiratory tract)	$17.50	ERYTHROMYCIN	$11.25	$6.25
ANTIVERT, 12.5 mg. tablet (antiemetic, antivertigo agent for relief of motion sickness or middle-ear infection)	$9.50	MECLIZINE	$5.50	$4.00
LOMOTIL (antidiarrheal, used for treatment of diarrhea)	$12.50	DIPHENOXYLATE HCL	$6.75	$5.75
BENADRYL, 50 mg. capsule (antihistamine, to relieve seasonal allergies, stuffy nose, itchy eyes)	$9.50	DIPHENHYDRAMINE HCL	$4.25	$5.25
ELAVIL, 50 mg. tablet (antidepressant, prescribed for depression)	$20.25	AMITRIPTYLINE HCL	$13.50	$6.75
EQUANIL, 400 mg. tablet (tranquilizer, for relief of anxiety, tension, to promote sleep in anxious patients)	$9.50	MEPROBAMATE	$3.25	$6.25
APRESOLINE, 25 mg. tablet (antihypertensive, commonly prescribed for high blood pressure)	$8.50	HYDRALAZINE HCL	$4.00	$4.50
DILANTIN, 100 mg. capsule (anticonvulsant, controls epileptic seizures)	$4.75	PHENYTOIN	$3.25	$1.50
ISODRIL, 10 mg. tablet (antianginal agent, for relief of heart, chest pain associated with angina pectoris)	$7.75	ISOSORBIDE DINITRATE	$5.75	$2.00
PREMARIN, 1.25 mg. (estrogen drug, given for symptoms accompanying menopause)	$10.25	CONJUGATED ESTROGEN	$6.50	$3.75

Other Tips for Saving on Drugs

- *Shop around!* Savings of 20 percent or more can be obtained from discount drugstores, for instance.

- *If you have the time to wait, order drugs by mail:* you can save 50 percent, even with postage. You must send your doctor's prescription along with your order. Note: the savings in buying drugs by mail are greatest on prescription drugs and far less on nonprescription ones. Write for catalogs and compare prices, postage rates, and so on.

  Mail-order sources:
  NRTA–AARP
  1750 K St. NW
  Washington, DC 20006

(For members of the National Retired Teachers Association or the American Association of Retired Persons only. Membership fee is $3.00 per year and you have to be over 55. Their drugs are completely reliable. Also see page 208.)

Pastors
126 S. York
Hatboro, PA 19040

Pharmaceutical Services, Inc.
6427 Prospect Ave.
Kansas City, MO 64132

Federal Prescription Service, Inc.
2nd and Main Streets
Madrid, IA 50516

Getz Prescription Co.
916 Walnut St.
Kansas City, MO 64199

- *Learn to read the labels* in a drugstore and buy according to specific contents. Some drugs, like aspirin, have the same chemical composition, but vary widely in price.

- *Know if your insurance covers drug costs.* Some policies do, and this type of coverage can be good protection against the high drug costs a chronic condition can entail.

- *Don't buy a nonprescription drug in a large quantity unless it's really needed.* Often it will go stale before you use it up.

- *Stop buying useless pills.* This is the best way to reduce drug costs. Cold remedies, for example, do *not* cure colds. Doctors can prescribe antibiotics or give you a shot of penicillin; pharmacists can recommend a decongestant; and aspirin can be a temporary help, but not much. The cure is rest, liquids, and protection from exposure. Many ailments simply have to run their course. Take it easy and let them.

REDUCING THE COST OF YOUR HOSPITAL STAY

- *Choose the right hospital.* If you already have a personal physician, you'll probably choose the hospital he or she is affiliated with. But if there's no particular reason to prefer one hospital over another, or if your physician is affiliated with more than one, take these two steps in making your choice.

  — *Choose a hospital that is a teaching institution with a research program.* You'll get the widest range of treatment and services there. And because their funding comes from other sources than you, you save.

— *Choose by finding the hospital with the lowest per diem charges* if there are no teaching hospitals to be considered. You may find that the prices vary by as much as $50.00 a day. Don't mistake bigger for better. You may find better service and more attention at one of the smaller hospitals.

• *Try to arrange any admission to the hospital for a Tuesday.* Studies have shown that the one factor most influencing the length of hospital stays isn't the severity of the illness but the day of admission. Tuesday admissions generally have the shortest stay. Avoid entering the hospital on a Friday because you'll just be spending Saturday and Sunday waiting for laboratories and technicians to resume their weekday schedules. (Of course, this advice pertains only to elective surgery. You can't try to postpone treatment for an acute illness like pneumonia or kidney stones.)

• *Arrange with your doctor to have your routine lab tests done before admission.* As long as your insurance covers this arrangment, it can save you a day of hospital charges, conserve an insurance benefit day, and give you added time at your job or at home with your family. This arrangement also relieves the pressure to hurry tests and treatment which results from the necessity to maintain turnover in hospital-bed occupancy.

SLICING SURGERY BILLS

There are two main ways to save on surgery costs:

1) *Get a second opinion.* In New York, one quarter of elective surgery recommendations were discouraged by the second opinion. Most Blue Cross/Blue Shield plans consider this so important that they cover second- and even third-opinion consultations.

2) *Choose outpatient surgery.* If you are fairly young and in good general health, you enter the hospital in the morning, have your surgery, recover under supervision for several hours, and then return home. There are more than three dozen surgical procedures that can be done on a walk-in basis. They include D & C's (dilatation and curettage), abortions, vasectomies, skin grafts, biopsies, removal of cysts and other superficial growths, and cataract operations.

This approach saves you time, money, insurance benefits, and psychological wear and tear, especially when the patient is a young child.

IF THE BILL IS JUST TOO HIGH

A surefire way to avoid a bill that's too high is to get the anticipated fees and charges straight *before* you begin. But sometimes this is not feasible.

Hospitals

If your hospital bill is too high, there's not much recourse. The charges are generally accepted by private insurers and Blue Cross/Blue Shield plans, and they probably won't change because a private individual finds them too steep.

You can try complaining to the hospital administrator, or the state hospital association, but this is more likely to prove an exercise in bureaucracy than a path to a reduction of your bill.

Private Doctors

On the other hand, if a private doctor has overcharged you, you may have a better chance to negotiate a reduced bill.

1) First talk to your doctor directly. Don't bother with the receptionist or bookkeeper. Only the doctor can lower the bill.
2) If he refuses to talk to you, or if he offers an inadequate explanation for the high charges, tell him that you're taking your case to the local medical society. You'll probably have to submit details of your complaint in writing to the local grievance committee, and perhaps you'll even have to present your case in person.
3) The committee will compare your bill to the average charges for similar treatments and procedures. Even if the committee recommends a reduced bill, however, the doctor is not bound to comply.
4) Should that happen, you can take your complaint and the medical grievance committee's findings to the state board of medical examiners or office of professional licensing. These bodies sometimes deal with fee disputes.
5) Otherwise you may have to see a lawyer who will advise you on the prudence of pursuing your complaint in court.

AVOIDING QUACKERY

Americans spend millions of dollars every year on various kinds of quackery. The occasion may be as minor as paying $3.00 for a "stop-smoking" kit, or as harmful and tragic as paying thousands to try a useless cure for cancer.

If you're struggling with a weight problem, losing your hair, suffering from arthritis, or in the grips of a cigarette addiction, you may be tempted to seek some kind of miracle help from an outsider. However, our advice is this: you should probably keep your money in your pocket.

Recognizing Quackery

If you find yourself genuinely interested in the advertising, consider these marks of the professional quack:

- The advertisement hails the product as a "new scientific break-through," a "secret cure," or something similar.
- The ad includes testimonials from "satisfied" users. (These may be either totally false, or from well-meaning people who have no understanding of the basis for their improvement, which may have been anything from a natural remission to a placebo effect.)
- The ailments to be cured are ill-defined or widely varied.
- The product is a weight reduction aid that promises results without any diet or exercise.
- It claims to cure baldness, cancer, arthritis, or alcoholism, to develop the bust, or to help you to stop smoking without pain.

What to Do if You Get Taken

If you have been taken in by quackery, there's almost nothing you can do to recoup your losses, but your actions can insure that others don't get conned.

- *Notify the government.* The FDA deals with harmful and mislabeled foods, drugs, and health articles. Write to the Food and Drug Administration, Rockville, MD 20857.
- *The U.S. Postal Service deals with those who use the mails for fraudulent promotions*—either to advertise or to take orders. Write to the Inspector in Charge, Special Investigation Division, U.S. Postal Service, Washington, DC 20260.
- *For false advertising claims in general, contact the Federal Trade Commission,* 6th St. and Pennsylvania Ave., NW, Washington, DC 20580.
- *Also check with local consumer agencies and the State Attorney General's office* for the current scams and false promotions in your area.

Our Advice

If you are having a hard time resisting an ad, talk to your family doctor and check with the Better Business Bureau for advice on the product or device before you send your check.

HEALTH-CARE COVERAGE

Hospital costs and doctors' fees have risen more than three times faster than the Consumer Price Index over the past ten years. It is worth your while to investigate health insurance and its alternatives to be sure that you can cope with the high cost of health care if and when you need it.

HEALTH INSURANCE

Evaluating Your Health Coverage

The first step to saving money on health care is to take a look at your medical history and your life-style to determine the kind of care you may need. For example, if you are a woman of childbearing age, the policy should cover pregnancy-related services. If you are a senior citizen, that coverage is superfluous and an obvious place to save. If you spend a lot of time driving, or if you're in the prime age category for auto accidents (18 to 30), major medical insurance to cover the exorbitant costs of serious accidents should be a high priority in your coverage.

Types of Health Insurance

Health insurance falls into three general categories:

1) *Basic.* The basic health insurance package includes three specific types of insurance:

   - *Hospital care.* The cost of the room, nursing care, and small medical supplies is covered for a set period of time that may be as short as 21 days or as long as a year or more.
   - *Surgical expenses.* The various operations covered by the policy are specified by a list of maximum payments.
   - *Physicians' expenses.* The cost of doctors' in-hospital visits during your illness is covered to a specified maximum.

   This basic coverage is provided in both Blue Cross and commercial policies. Blue Cross coverage has been expanding in some communities to cover outpatient care, preadmission testing, dental care, and nursing home stays.

2) *Major Medical.* The basic hospital care package sometimes is inadequate to cover the costs of serious accidents or illness. That is where the major medical coverage kicks in. These plans provide maximum benefits of $250,000.00 or more, but they also have deductibles and co-insurance provisions—in other words, you have to cover a percentage of the costs of your hospital stay.

Both basic and major medical coverage are often offered in two forms:
- *Indemnity*, which pays a fixed dollar amount against your claim (so make sure it is adequate to cover rising medical costs).

- *Service benefits*, covering all services, regardless of the cost or where they're incurred.

3) *Disability Insurance.* This insurance replaces the earnings you lose when you are disabled by sickness or injury. Disability insurance shouldn't be overlooked, especially in families where there's only one breadwinner. A family can be ruined faster through permanent disability of the income producer than through his or her death. Even Social Security workers' compensation doesn't come to the rescue until a person has been laid up for five months.

Ways to Save on Health Insurance

- *Get into a group plan.* If you are planning to join a new company, take their health coverage into account. Join a union, investigate fraternal organizations, or see if any club or organization you belong to has group health insurance for members. You can save 15 to 40 percent of the cost of individual health insurance through a commercial insurer by joining a group. You'll be safe from cancellation as long as you're with the group. Another benefit is that you won't need to pass a physical to join. You probably won't have to worry about being covered for a pre-existing condition, such as a kidney problem, although there may be a waiting period before you can collect benefits for services relating to that problem.

- *Consider coverage for a lower number of hospital days.* If you're not in a group plan, take a look at the number of days your plan provides for. The average hospital stay is about seven days. In fact, only three in every hundred hospital stays last more than 31 days. There's a good possibility that you can reduce the number of hospital days in your policy without jeopardizing your coverage.

- *Keep your insurance updated.* A policy that seemed adequate three years ago may now be seriously outdated because of the continuing upward spiral of hospital costs. If your co-insurance factor called for you to pay 20 percent of hospital costs up to a maximum of $100.00 a day and 100 percent of the amount over $100.00, and the average stay in your locality now costs $150.00 a day, you are faced with average hospital costs of $70.00 a day. So check your insurance periodically to be certain that it is keeping pace with costs in your community.

- *Don't overinsure yourself.* A maximum of $250,000.00 in major medical benefits is likely to be sufficient. This figure may change within a few years or may be inadequate if your family has several members in a hazardous occupation where there is a chance of simultaneous injury, but for most people at the moment, $250,000.00 provides enough protection.

- *Take the highest deductible you can afford.* If you can cover the first $1,000.00 in medical expenses, elect the bigger deductible and take your savings on the lower premium.
- *Don't replace your old coverage—supplement it.* The older policy probably reflects the youth and good health you enjoyed when you first bought it. It makes more sense to buy an additional policy than to start from scratch with a large policy that calls for premiums based on your current age and condition.
- *Make sure your policy has a conversion clause* that enables you to change jobs or marry without waiting periods or fear of a lapsed or invalid policy.
- *If you lose your job, take out a short-term policy* to insure you against illness until you find new employment. A six-month policy is not unreasonable if you find a job almost immediately; many employers have a three-month waiting period before the group health insurance becomes effective.
- *Pay your policy on a quarterly or annual basis* rather than monthly. Insurance companies give you a better break the more you pay in advance. Monthly billing means more paperwork and less interest for them.
- *Make sure the policy is noncancellable.* It is important to know that the insurer cannot drop your policy because you submit a run of expensive claims.
- *Pay the extra cost for a "waiver of premium" benefit.* This allows you to forgo premium payments while you are sick or disabled.
- *Read your policy from time to time* to remind yourself of what is covered and what is excluded. This can save you an unpleasant shock when it is time to pay the bill.

What to Do if Poor Health Excludes You

If you can't get regular insurance because of poor health, try the following:

- *Find out if your state has an open enrollment period for Blue Cross/Blue Shield* when the plan must accept all comers, regardless of their state of health. Call your state insurance office or department.
- *Investigate Medicaid.* Coverage under Medicaid varies widely from state to state. Generally, Medicaid helps pay for medical services for those

who cannot afford to pay for insurance and/or health care. Contact your Medicaid or welfare office to find out if you are eligible. If you qualify, begin looking for a doctor right away; don't wait until you're ill. Doctors will accept Medicaid in payment for their services from their regular patients but often try to avoid doing so from nonpatients. In fact, some refuse because they have to wait as long as six months for the government to pay the Medicaid bills.

HEALTH MAINTENANCE ORGANIZATIONS (HMOs)

One of the fastest growing health care alternatives is the Health Maintenance Organization (HMO). These are groups of doctors and health personnel who provide health care on a prepaid basis.

If you work for a company with more than 15 employees, and if there is a federally approved HMO in the area, your firm *must* offer you the choice of traditional health insurance or membership in the HMO.

Reasons to Consider Joining an HMO

- *The HMO coverage is more comprehensive than traditional health insurance coverage.* Non–hospital services include unlimited doctors' visits, checkups, eye exams, lab tests, X-rays, maternity care, emergency care, and even such specialized services as hemodialysis.

- *All the health services are united in one organization*, making it more likely that you can get timely, coordinated care.

- *The economics of the system put the emphasis on good health.* HMO profits are largest when members are well because HMO medical personnel are paid a flat fee regardless of services rendered. Health care professionals not affiliated with HMOs make their money *only* when you are sick. So doctors in HMOs have more of an incentive to keep you healthy, and their emphasis is on preventive medical care.

- *An HMO can give you up to a year of hospital care*, including room and board, drugs, tests, ambulance service, anesthesia, X-rays, therapy, and all surgical and doctors' fees.

Potential Drawbacks of HMOs

- *HMO membership is more expensive than traditional insurance.*
- *Not all HMOs are federally approved.* Quality varies widely from community to community.
- *Your choice of hospital and doctor is restricted to those in the HMO plan.* You may not always be in the care of the same physician on every visit. And you may run into trouble with HMO coverage if you travel frequently and are hurt or taken ill away from your HMO facilities.

- *You may need to pass a physical in order to join an HMO.* Check with your HMO office to see if there is an annual period of open enrollment when anyone can join, no matter what their state of health.
- *Your specific HMO may not offer the full range of medical services and specialists.*

Questions to Ask About the HMO You're Considering

- *Do the actual costs of HMO coverage compare favorably with the actual costs of your current coverage?* That is, add up your current insurance premiums, out-of-pocket expenses, deductibles, and exempt services. Then figure the monthly costs of the HMO and check carefully for any exempt items in the HMO plan. Compare the benefits and costs of the two alternatives.
- *Does the HMO cover drugs bought outside of its hospital pharmacy?*
- *How do current HMO subscribers like the plan?*
- *At what hours are the HMO facilities available, and are the locations convenient to your home and job?*
- *What are the age limits on coverage?* Does a newborn child have coverage from birth? At what age do teenagers and young adults in your family become ineligible for the HMO coverage?
- *Is a full range of medical facilities available?* It's too late to find out your HMO doesn't have a burn unit after your child has been scalded in a kitchen accident.
- *Will you be assigned to a regular doctor or can you choose a doctor from among the staff?*

For further information about HMOs, contact the Group Health Association of America, 1717 Massachusetts Ave. NW, Washington, DC 20036.

HEALTH CARE AND SENIOR CITIZENS

Aging never has been easy, although in the past the elderly were more integrated into the family structure and were generally cared for at home. Today it's different.

- The longer lifespan of our burgeoning population means more and more elderly to be cared for.
- Our society is more mobile than ever before; families are spread all over the nation.
- Houses are smaller, not large enough to accommodate three generations.

- More women have jobs.
- Children grow up unaccustomed to dealing with grandparents.
- Some of the financial responsibility of dealing with old people has been shouldered by health insurance companies and government programs like Medicare and Medicaid, lessening the concern on the part of families involved.

BENEFITS FOR THOSE OVER 65

Supplemental Security Income (SSI)

The goal of SSI is to assure enough income to sustain the lives of those over 65 and the blind of any age. SSI differs from welfare in that SSI recipients can be collecting Social Security or other benefits and compensation, and they can have personel assets—savings, a home, car, etc.—and still be eligible. SSI supplements the recipient's income from these sources. Qualified single individuals can get up to $228.65 per month; for couples it's $327.74 monthly. In most states, receiving SSI also makes you eligible for Medicaid, even when you already have Medicare (see next section). SSI recipients are also eligible for special extra funds in case of emergency.

For more information, phone your local Social Security office. You'll find them listed in the white pages under U.S. Government. Inquire about your eligibility and ask what documents you need to bring along when you apply.

Medicare: Some Helpful Facts

- Medicare is federal health insurance for people over 65 and is applied for at your local Social Security office. (Medicaid is administered on a state level. State rules vary, but those who are on welfare or SSI are usually eligible.)
- Apply two to three months before you reach 65 to obtain the best rate. The cost increases otherwise.
- Medicare consists of two parts:
  — Part A: Compulsory hospitalization insurance.
  — Part B: Optional supplementary medical insurance to cover physicians services and other medical services not covered by Part A.
- Hospitals do their own filing. You are usually charged a deductible amount which is equal to the average cost of a day's hospitalization. Medicare completely takes care of 60 days of hospitalization (less the deductible) and you pay part of the costs from day 61 to day 90.
- If you subscribe to Part B, there are two ways to pay doctor bills.

— "Assignment Method." Doctors will send 80 percent of their bill to Medicare and wait the six months or so to receive payment; you pay the remaining 20 percent and whatever deductible applies.

— "Direct Payment." The doctor bills the patient; the patient pays the doctor and applies for reimbursement from Medicare. Medicare in turn remits 80 percent of what it considers a "reasonable charge." When there is a variance between the "reasonable charge" and the amount billed, you can lose.

● The Medicare program (and Medicaid as well) is fraught with fraud, and the program is billed billions of excess taxpayer dollars. Many doctors and hospitals increase the number of services in order to increase their income. If you feel services rendered were unnecessary or the hospital and doctor's statements reflect services you did not receive, don't hesitate to report them.

● The Social Security department publishes a booklet entitled "Your Medicare Handbook," which explains how the system works.

NURSING HOMES

If you are selecting a nursing home, get ready for some big expenditures. Like the cost of gasoline, the cost of nursing-home care has skyrocketed. Nursing home revenues in the last 20 years have increased a whopping 3,000 percent. Nursing homes get over half of their money from Medicaid; private sources account for around 43 percent; and Medicare pays a little over 3 percent.

Types of Nursing Homes

Home care or another alternative to a nursing home is often better for an older person and also saves money (see pages 103–105). However, if it's impossible to keep a friend or relative at home, let the person's condition determine where he or she goes. There are three categories of nursing homes:

1) Those for folks who can pretty well take care of themselves and can come and go on their own, but need some supervision of diet and medication as well as someone nearby in case of illness or accident. These places are often referred to as "retirement homes." In many cases, home health care can do just as well.

2) Those for people who cannot manage on their own and need daily nursing and medical supervision.

3) Those for people requiring 24-hour care, most of whom are confined to wheelchairs or bed.

What to Ask a Nursing Home Director

- *Does the home have Medicare's certification? And what are the home's other accreditations?* Medicare and Medicaid will not reimburse a nonaffiliated institution. When an elderly person is hospitalized for three days or more and requires subsequent skilled nursing or rehabilitation services, Medicare will assist in paying up to 100 days of convalescence. And Medicaid will spring for part of the nursing-home bill if a patient cannot afford it. Make sure any nursing home you consider is eligible for these benefits, even if you don't presently require them.

  Criteria for Medicare certification are minimal, so look for other accreditations as well. All states require licensing, but the standards vary. About the best seal of approval is given by the Joint Commission on Accreditation of Hospitals, which periodically evaluates the building and medical and nursing services (see page 105).

- *What is the ratio of nurses and aids to patients? And are there any assurances as to the quality of the staff?* A ratio of one to three should be considered good. Staffing is the most costly item in a nursing home, but an understaffed home is unsatisfactory. And since it's the aids who take care of the patients, you should know about their qualifications. Ask if their work is periodically evaluated and if there is ongoing training available for them.

- *What professional services are available and at what cost?* The cost of a doctor is not included in the monthly rate, and licensed institutions require that their patients be seen by a doctor once a month. A private family physician can be used only if the home is located close enough to his or her practice; in most cases the nursing home's own physician will attend. Inquire how much their doctor charges per visit. And what about dental service, eye care, podiatrists, etc.—what's their cost?

- *Does the home offer rehabilitation and therapy programs?* You might be needing them.

- *What are the additional charges?* A nursing home's basic rate includes room, board, and routine nursing service. Get a clear picture of how much laundry, hair care (does a beautician visit the facility?), special diets, and other incidentals will run.

- *Are there social-service personnel to provide social and recreational programs that encourage projects and relationships with others?* This is important.

Further Considerations

- *How are you going to pay for a nursing home?* Investigate if your loved one is eligible for any government financial help or has any private health insurance coverage to assist with the expenses. If the elderly person can qualify, Medicaid will pick up part of the tab; also, some Blue Cross/Blue Shield programs now have nursing home care added to their coverage. Or maybe now is the time to sell a home or other property.

- *When you visit nursing homes, take note of your impressions from the minute you walk in the door.*
  - Do the patients seem in good spirits?
  - Is any small-group activity visible?
  - Is the place relatively clean without being cold and antiseptic?
  - Are there volunteers tending to patients?

  One of the best times to visit is at mealtimes:
  - Are patients visiting with others or morosely eating their meals? (After all, meals are the major social events of the day.)
  - How's the food?
  - Check the kitchen. Is it hygienic?

  Visit several homes; each has a different feel.
- *Location is important.* The more convenient a nursing home is to visitors the better. Visitors are very important to an older person.
- *What about the layout?*
  - Are there any areas besides the designated recreation area where patients can congregate?
  - Are there nice spots outdoors for pleasant days?
  - Is there a vocational shop? (Some establishments have cottage industries for their members.)
  - Is there a separate TV lounge?
- *In general, does the place work to keep patients in touch with reality or does it seem to encourage regression?*

ALTERNATIVES TO THE NURSING HOME

A nursing home means an extremely difficult emotional adjustment and can easily run into five figures annually. Fortunately the pressing need for services to the elderly has led to the creation of some unique alternatives to retirement and nursing homes:

Home Health Care

With home health care, both services (medical, dental, social nutritional, nursing) and therapy (physical, occupational, speech) are administered in the patient's home on a routine basis. If emergency assistance is required, then the patient is taken to a full-care institution until he or she can return home.

It's been estimated that workable programs could have kept at home two-and-a-half million elderly people who are presently in nursing and retirement homes. That many hospital and nursing-home beds could have been freed for those who really needed them. In addition, there's an immense psychological benefit to the senior citizen who can remain at home in familiar surroundings. And home health care, of course, can be very financially advantageous to the individual.

- *Your doctor should determine if home care is a viable alternative.* (If he says no, get a second opinion.) You can locate a home health-care program by consulting your doctor, hospitals in your area (many public and voluntary hospitals have social workers affiliated with them), visiting nurse associations, the department of health, or agencies such as Kelly Home Care Services, Medical Professional Pool, and Upjohn Home-makers. (Also see page 105 for more sources.)
- *It often takes more than one agency to provide all the necessary services.* These are examples of relatively specialized nationwide programs:
  - Tele-Care: A system in which volunteers make daily check-up calls to those living alone
  - Meals on Wheels: Delivers hot, well-balanced meals to the elderly at home
  - Nutrition Plan for the Elderly: Brings the elderly to the meals; senior citizens can work as volunteers in their own program.

Day Care

Patients who need either rehabilitation services or social and recreational orientation are picked up, taken to a facility where they spend the day and are given one meal, and then returned home. These facilities operate on a nine-to-five basis, and day-care patients go anywhere from two to five days a week.

Foster Homes

Another alternative is a program that solicits citizens to take elderly people into their homes. Foster homes can provide a family atmosphere for elderly persons who cannot live alone. Add home health care to the foster home situation and a nursing home can be postponed quite indefinitely.

Selection of who goes where is the decision of all concerned; patients and families meet and decide. And the administering institutions—usually local hospitals—send social workers and nurses on routine checks.

The Lifeline System

An estimated 3,000 elderly and disabled in 110 communities and 25 states are equipped with a Lifeline System. When the system is activated, a signal is transmitted to nearby hospital or emergency centers, which in turn phone the patient. If there's no answer, a predetermined "respondent"—friend, neighbor, or relative—goes to the residence and calls for emergency help if it's necessary. Also, each Lifeline unit is set with a timer that must be reset twice daily. Failure to do so also activates the alarm. For more information, write to Lifeline Systems, Inc., 51 Spring St., Watertown, MA 02172.

SOURCES OF INFORMATION FOR SENIOR CITIZENS

There are a multitude of goods and services available to senior citizens—from instruction on filling out Medicare forms to "care wagons" that provide free transportation. Here are some excellent sources of information:

American Association of Homes for the Aging
1050 17th St. NW
Washington, DC 20036

American Association of Retired Persons
1909 K St. NW
Washington, DC 20049

American Health Care Association
1200 15th St. NW
Washington, DC 20005

American Nursing Home Association
1200 15th St. NW
Washington, DC 20005

Joint Commission on Accreditation of Hospitals
875 N. Michigan Ave.
Chicago, IL 60011

National Council of Senior Citizens
1511 K St. NW
Washington, DC 20005

National Council on the Aging
1828 L St. NW
Washington, DC 20036

National Geriatrics Society
212 W. Wisconsin Ave.
Milwaukee, WI 53203

FUNERALS

The cost of the average funeral is now about $2,300.00. It can be much less. To avoid pointless expenditures that sap your family's finances at the very time you need security most, you must do some planning.

MEMORIAL SOCIETIES

If you are committed to keeping funeral expenses at a minimum for yourself and your loved ones, one of the best arrangements is with a memorial society. These groups have arrangements with local funeral directors to provide services to members at a fixed rate for stated services. A one-time membership fee brings you a list of funeral directors and their list of charges for various services, ranging from simply bringing the deceased to a medical school, to a full funeral and in-the-ground burial. You can find out about memorial societies in your area by writing to the Continental Association of Funeral and Memorial Societies, 1828 L St. NW, Washington, DC 20036.

WHAT TO DO IN ADVANCE

- *Make your wishes for your funeral arrangements clear to your family members.* It's a good idea to discuss this subject openly, no matter how scary it may seem at the moment.

- *Leave a separate statement of the kind of arrangements you want with your lawyer or with a friend or with your insurance policies—not with your will.* You want people to know about your wishes right away, not when the will is read, several weeks after the funeral.

- *Consider prepaying funeral arrangements,* especially if there's good reason to anticipate a death. Funeral costs are rising like all others, and by prepaying you can also be assured of getting what you want. Your survivors won't be in shape to deal with arrangements as economically as you.

- *Make arrangements with relatives and neighbors to step in if there is a death in the family.* A bereaved spouse is easy pickings for an unscrupulous funeral director. A clear-headed neighbor can save the family a good deal of money and lots of unnecessary fuss.

- *Consider the two least expensive options—cremation and donation of the body to a medical school.* (You can arrange to have the remains cremated and delivered where you like.)

DEALING WITH FUNERAL DIRECTORS

- *Don't believe everything that the funeral director says.* In New York State, for instance, it is not necessary for a body to be embalmed, whether a funeral or wake is planned. In fact, it is not even necessary to have a coffin; people of some religious persuasions prefer to be buried in a shroud.

● Other common misstatements of fact include:

— *Insisting that a coffin is necessary for cremation* (not true except in Massachusetts).

— *Telling you a vault is needed.* This device prevents the earth from settling, a process by which an unsightly depression can develop over the grave. You can arrange to have the cemetery fill in the depression, if one develops, at a much smaller cost than the charge for a vault.

— *Telling you that the mahogany number with the brass handles is the least expensive coffin they have.* Insist on a plain pine box if that's what you want. There are even some traditions that encourage family and friends to build it.

● *If you doubt that what the funeral director claims is mandated by statute, call the local health department.*

● *Don't be intimidated by the funeral director and the complexity of the available arrangements.* Remember that funeral directors are essentially salesmen. Approach them with about the same level of caution that you would a used car salesman. If you sense an effort to manipulate you through guilt or continued attempts to switch your attention to a high-priced arrangement, or if only a package funeral is offered, with services you don't need, then don't hesitate to move on to another funeral home. There *are* ethical funeral directors, and when you are fortunate enough to find one, you'll be able to make most of the arrangements you want with a minimum of resistance.

WHAT YOU MAY BE ENTITLED TO

Don't forget to claim the benefits you may be entitled to. If the deceased was covered by Social Security, there's a flat payment of $255.00 available. Honorably discharged veterans of the military service—even peacetime service—are entitled to burial in a national cemetery (if space is available), a grave marker or headstone, and a $300.00 allowance towards the burial expenses ($450.00 if the burial is to be in a cemetery other than a national or government cemetary, and $1,000.00 if the death was service-connected).

In addition, check with the employer of the deceased for any unclaimed benefits. There may be coverage for funeral expenses if the deceased belonged to a trade union or fraternal organization. There may be liability or automobile or disability insurance coverage if the death was connected to an accident. If you are really desperate, the county may provide arrangements for indigent people.

SOURCES

PREVENTION THROUGH SELF-CARE

Family Circle Guide to Self-Help. A guide to 450 self-help groups for gamblers, phobics, child abusers, mental patients, and other people with specific needs. Ballantine Books, 455 Hahn Road, Westminister, MD 21557. $2.25.

Health for the Whole Person. A comprehensive overview of the holistic medicine movement, from family care to homeopathy, chiropractic to hospice. For those interested in more than AMA medicine. Westview Press, 5500 Central Ave., Boulder, CO 80301. $12.95.

I'll Quit Tomorrow: A Practical Guide to Alcoholism Treatment by Vernon Johnson. For those who must intervene in someone else's alcoholism problem. Harper and Row, Keystone Industrial Park, Scranton, PA 18512. $9.95.

Medical Self-Care is a quarterly publication we emphatically recommend. Here's a super guide for those who want to take an active part in obtaining better health for themselves, and save money while doing it. Write to P. O. Box 717, Inverness, CA 94937. A sample copy is $4.00.

Medical Self-Care, edited by Tom Ferguson, M.D., is the source book for the above publication. Also includes a fine reference section for other books and publications. Summit Books, 1230 Ave. of the Americas, New York, NY 10020. $8.95.

Prevention: The Magazine for Better Health. Another highly recommended magazine. Usable advice from a long-time source in the field. Focus on nutrition and what we all can do for our health. Available from Rodale Press, 33 East Minor, Emmaus, PA 18049. Twelve issues for $7.97. Well worth it.

The Tooth Trip: An Oral Experience by Thomas McGuire, D.D.S. Everything you need to know about your dental health. Available from Random House, 455 Hahn Road, Westminster, MD 21157. $4.95.

Total Fitness in 30 Minutes a Week by Laurence Morehouse and Leonard Gross. For 30 minutes, what do you have to lose by trying? Pocket Books, 1230 Ave. of the Americas, New York, NY 10020. $2.45.

HEALTH AND ENVIRONMENT

Environmental Defense Fund Newsletter. Keep healthy by keeping informed and by keeping the world you live in healthful. Environmental Defense Fund, 475 Park Ave. South, New York, NY 10016. $15.00 for a year's subscription.

Household Pollutants Guide. From the Center for Science in the Public Interest comes this invaluable book about the dangerous substances in our own homes. A must, especially if you have small children. Doubleday & Co., 501 Franklin Ave., Garden City, NY 11530. $3.50.

The Human Body: A Comprehensive, Illustrated Guide to the Body and Its Func-

tions by The Diagram Group. A thorough reference for all who want to promote and safeguard their own and their families' health. Highly readable. With more than 2,000 drawings, charts, and diagrams. Facts On File Publications, 460 Park Ave. South, New York, NY 10016. $24.95.

The Life You Save by Lewis Miller. Pointers on how to economically make it through the maze of America's health care system and get the best possible health care. A Berkley paperback, 200 Madison Ave., New York, NY 10016. $2.25.

The Medicine Show by the Editors of Consumer Reports Books. Consumers Union's practical guide to some everyday health problems and health products. As with everything from Consumers Union, this is a valuable and worthwhile publication. Usually available to subscribers (see page 225), but write to Consumers Union, Mount Vernon, NY 10550.

WHEN YOU'RE SICK

Cold Comfort: Colds and Flu: Everybody's Guide to Self-Treatment by Hal Bennett. A great book for when you're sick with either, with good advice and information. Pricey, but pass it on. Crown Publishers, 1 Park Ave., New York, NY 10016. $8.95.

Emergency Medical Guide by John Henderson, M.D. A great price for a comprehensive guide to all sorts of medical self-help situations, from snake bite to painful menstruation. McGraw-Hill Co., Princton Road, Hightstown, NJ 08520. $4.95.

Guide to Free Medical Information by Arthur Liebers is a 128-page reference book on where to go or write for the latest information on everything from acne to cellulite to hemorrhoids to sickle cell anemia. It lists addresses, phone numbers, and ordering information, and has sections on food and diet and why you should quit smoking, among others. Available from Delair Publishing Co., Inc., 420 Lexington Ave., New York, NY 10017. $2.95.

Healing at Home: A Guide to Health Care for Children by Mary Howell. A course in basic pediatric medicine that also guides parents to help their kids develop their own self-care skills. Beacon Press, Harper and Row, Keystone Industrial Park, Scranton, PA 18512. $5.95.

How to Be Your Own Doctor, Sometimes by Keith W. Sehnert, M.D. A primer of basic medicine in plain language. Take control of your health. Grosset & Dunlap, 51 Madison Ave., New York, NY 10010. $5.95.

The People's Hospital Book: How to Increase Your Comfort and Safety, Deal With Nurses and Doctors, Obtain the Best Total Care. Available from Crown Publishers, 1 Park Ave., New York, NY 10016. $8.95.

Take Care of Yourself: A Consumer's Guide to Medical Care by Donald M. Vickery, M.D., and James Fries, M.D. A clear, step-by-step rundown of common medical complaints, when to treat them at home, when to see a doctor. Addison-Wesley Co., Jacob Way, Reading, MA 01867. $6.95.

WOMEN

Birth Without Violence by Frederick Leboyer. A continuation of the movement to make the birth process better for mother and baby. Alfred A. Knopf, Inc., 455 Hahn Road, Westminster, Md 21157. $9.95.

A Cooperative Manual of Birth Control by Margaret Nofziger. If devices, chemicals, pills, and surgery aren't for you, maybe this man-*and*-woman natural birth control strategy is. The Book Publishing Co., 156 Drakes Lane, Summertown, TN 38483.

Our Bodies, Ourselves. The Boston Women's Health Collective published this book as a big pamphlet in 1971. Ten years later, it's a million-seller classic, and still an inspiration. A masterpiece. Simon & Schuster, 1230 Ave. of the Americas, New York, NY 10020. $6.95.

AGING

Over 50: The Definitive Guide to Retirement by Auren Uris. Don't wait for middle age to get this excellent guide for everyone who plans on getting old. Chilton Book Service, Chilton Way, Radnor, PA 19089. $17.95.

What Do You Want to Be When You Grow Old? by Harris Dienstfrey and Joseph Lederer. Revisionist information on growing old—the myths, stereotypes, and potentials. Bantam Books, 414 East Gold Road, Des Plaines, IL 60016. $2.75.

ILLNESS AND DISABILITY

Access: The Guide to a Better Life for Disabled Americans by Lilly Bruck. Eighteen percent of the population of this country has some kind of disability. This book tells where you can find help and information if you or a friend are among them. Random House, 455 Hahn Road, Westminster, MD 21157. $6.95.

Nursing at Home: A Practical Guide to the Care of the Sick and the Invalid in the Home by Page Parker and Lois N. Dietz, R.N., M.P.H. What you should know if you're sick at home or taking care of someone who is. Crown Publishers, 1 Park Ave., New York, NY 10016. $16.45.

Source Book for the Disabled. Practical advice on how to design and implement independent living, for disabled people and those close to them. An exceptionally valuable resource. W. B. Saunders Publishing, West Washington Square, Philadelphia, PA 19105. $14.95.

The 36-Hour Day: A Family Guide to Caring for Persons with Alzheimers Disease, Related Dementing Illnesses, and Memory Loss in Later Life by Nancy L. Mace and Peter V. Rabins, M.D. Sympathic, practical guide to care of persons with these problems. The Johns Hopkins University Press, Baltimore, MD 21218. $14.95 hardcover, $6.95 paperback. Moneyback guarantee offered.

DEATH AND DYING

The American Way of Death by Jessica Mitford. This exposé of the inner workings of our funeral industry is both highly entertaining and informative reading. Lets you know what you can avoid and gives information on memorial societies and other sane, economical alternatives. Available in paperback from Crest Books, 1515 Broadway, New York, NY 10036. $2.50.

Common Sense Suicide by Doris Poterwood. A sensible, sensitive discussion of the ultimate human choice. Dodd, Mead & Co., 79 Madison Ave., New York, NY 10016. $6.95.

A Hospice Handbook: A New Way to Care for the Dying, edited by Michael Hamilton and Helen Reid. The movement to help the dying person find medical and spiritual care, and help for the family as well. Erdmans Publishing Co., 225 Jefferson Ave., SE, Grand Rapids, MI 49503. $4.95.

PERSONAL
GROOMING

PERSONAL GROOMING

SAVING MONEY ON GROOMING PRODUCTS AND SERVICES

SHAVING

Electric shaving is no bargain when you consider the cost of an electric razor, tune-ups, new parts (heads, etc.), and preshave powder or liquid. Using a safety razor is not ideal either; there's an endless supply of expensive blades and aerosol foam.

First off, invest in a shaving brush and mug and shaving soap. You can figure on only $.39 every three to four months for soap, and when you wet your brush with hot water, the lather you work up is hot.

Secondly, to solve the razor blade problem, pick up a new or used straight razor and a strop (your barber should have extras of both lying around and will probably be glad to instruct you in their use). Supplement those with a stone and you're in business. Total outlay is $15.00 to $20.00 for up to 10 years of the best shaving obtainable. You get long, clean, wide strokes—as opposed to raking your face raw with a double-edged blade or getting a rash from your electric shaver.

- *Out of shaving cream? If you have a shaving brush, use regular soap.* If you don't, borrow some cold cream. It makes a good substitute.
- *When you're traveling, use a tube of shaving cream and your brush instead of carrying a bulky aerosol can.*
- *Don't worry about rinsing your shaving brush;* the soap that's left on it can be used tomorrow.

THE HAIRDRESSER

- *Shampoo your hair at home before you go to a professional hairdresser for a cut and styling.* And if you have a casual wash-and-wear cut, then forget the blow dry and setting. Savings can total up to 50 percent.

114

- *Check specials.* Some salons, especially those in department stores, have specials during slow periods—working hours, early in the week, January and February (the best months for "perm sales"), and August through October (traditionally "make-over package" time). And don't be embarrassed to give your hairdresser (or your special salesperson, for that matter) some self-addressed postcards so he or she can notify you of sales or specials.

- *If the hairdresser offers you treatments with special products, don't give the go-ahead until you find out what it does and what it will cost.* If you agree that the product is special, chances are you can purchase it and take it home to use. The cost of the product itself is usually 10 percent of the treatment.

- *Just as beauty salons are now taking men, so barber shops now cater to women and can sometimes do the same job as a beautician for 25 percent less.* And they've been known to throw in the blow dry for free.

- *Just as you can get good dental work done at a dental school, you can be a "model" at a beauty or barber school.* Many schools let only the advanced students work with volunteers. And they are supervised by their instructors, which means you're getting double attention. If you're nervous about trusting your hair to a novice, request to be the instructor's model; he or she will often need one. Also, there are advanced hairdressing schools giving refresher courses for licensed stylists; you're assured of quality work there. Check your Yellow Pages.

MAKEUP

- *The cheapest cosmetics come from mail-order houses; next best are cut-rate drugstores.* Also, many department and chain stores have their own brand names at a lower price, and the manufacturer is often the same one that makes a more popular and expensive product.

- *There is very little difference in the various brands of a cosmetic, except the price—and that can have over a 300 percent variance.* After all, cold cream is cold cream and, as Consumer Union News reports, it doesn't work as well as Crisco.

- *Buying in quantity can net you savings—two for the price of one, eight for the price of six.* Also, the gifts that come with purchases can mean savings, but *only* if you need the gift. Don't buy because its a bargain.

- *Buy cosmetics on sale*—after Christmas, for example.

- *Cosmetics and perfume makers often give away free samples and "trial sizes."* Take advantage of these.

- *Many cosmetic companies have "demonstrators" working in department stores and salons who will beautify you for free.* They are usually paid on commission, so take advantage of them when you are in the market for at least some eyeliner or lipstick. You'll be able to see how a product looks and therefore avoid buying one that's not right. You can also learn to apply it and obtain some other makeup hints.

- *If a lipstick breaks, take a few minutes to mend it instead of throwing it away.* Pierce the broken-off end with a toothpick (like an hors d'oeuvre) and heat it with a match until it's soft enough to be pushed back into place. Leave it in the refrigerator for a couple of hours, and it's ready to use again.

OTHER GROOMING PRODUCTS

- *You'll be wasting your money if you use the same dandruff shampoo over and over.* Your scalp can become resistant to one brand, so alternate.

- *Avoid Q-tips.* Take it from one of the authors who learned the hard way and got this information from an ear specialist. Q-tips are unnecessary and can cause serious injury to the tympanic membrane and to the inner ear. Ear wax is a natural product that protects the ear. In a healthy ear, wax migrates; as it moves toward the outer ear, it dries out, flakes off, and is either washed or blown away.

Children

- *Diaper your baby!* Pampers and other disposable diapers are an ecological and financial disaster. They create litter, waste paper, and constitute a health hazard because they're thrown into the garbage uncleaned. They also cost more to use than real diapers. Remember: Every time you buy a box of disposable diapers, you're paying for an enormous advertising campaign.

- *If you still prefer disposable diapers, here's a small hint: whenever you ruin the adhesive tape on a disposable diaper, use masking tape instead of throwing the diaper out.*

- *Lining up the kids and giving them haircuts can often be easier than carting them to the barbershop and having them wait their turn.* And at $2.25 to $4.50 per barber shop cut, home haircuts are always cheaper. When kids are small, cutting their hair is no chore. Through the years you can save time and a bundle of money. And, remember, no damage is irreparable; hair always grows back.

MAKING YOUR OWN GROOMING PRODUCTS

It's easy to drop a bundle of cash on grooming products and beauty aids; visit any cosmetics counter in any department store and check the prices. The do-it-yourself charts that follow offer you a fine selection in beauty aids for a fraction of what you'd pay on the retail market. Any woman (or man!) who has spent over $10.00 on a jar of any kind of cosmetic cream will thrill to the idea of making more or less the same thing in a blender for virtually pennies. Remember: Many cosmetic ingredients actually cost less than their bottles.

Note: Only small batches of these cosmetics should be whipped up because they do spoil easily. This is, in fact, another of their advantages: Unlike expensive, store-bought cosmetics that last only because they're laced with chemical preservatives and additives, these are all-natural.

A WORD ABOUT FACE MASKS

Face masks are cosmetic substances that moisturize, cleanse, stimulate, tone, refine, smooth, heal, or perform several of these functions. Typically, they are applied to the face and neck, allowed to dry, and then rinsed off. Masks are easy to make at home (see chart). They can be used as often as you wish, although every day seems excessive. There are various types of masks.

1) A *cleansing mask* may contain abrasive particles or hard-drying substances such as egg white or wax. This type of mask smooths the skin and lifts out impurities.

2) A *mud pack* or *clay mask* absorbs excess oils and smooths the skin.

3) A *gel* forms a continuous watertight film over the face, and helps the skin replenish and retain water. It temporarily makes fine lines less noticeable.

4) The effects of *herbal, vegetable,* and *fruit masks* vary, depending upon what plant is used.

5) A *medicated mask* contains healing agents to treat surface skin problems or ingredients to stimulate circulation and remove dead skin cells.

6) A *stimulating mask* stimulates circulation in skin, makes the face pink and glowing, and may also remove dead skin cells.

HOMEMADE GROOMING PRODUCTS AND BEAUTY AIDS

FACE

Masks (Masques)

For best results, cleanse, wash, and even steam your face before applying masks, and pat on a little oil around eyes. Never put the mask around the tender eye area unless a recipe specifically tells you to. After applying, lie down (if possible) for ten or fifteen minutes, and elevate your feet. Remove masks gently with warm or tepid water and then stimulate circulation and close pores by spraying or bathing face with refrigerated mineral water or astringent. (You needn't use expensive imported mineral water; try local brands for economy.)

Oatmeal

Use cooked oatmeal; instant oatmeal, mixed with warm water; or ground-up raw oats moistened with water, milk, buttermilk, yogurt, or honey and water. Works well with other mask ingredients such as mashed fruits or herbs. Good for stimulating circulation and removing blackheads. For enlarged pores, mix oatmeal with buttermilk; let the mixture stand in the refrigerator overnight, strain and discard excess liquid, and apply residue to face for half an hour. Rinse the mask off and pat your face with ice cubes.

Egg

Egg Membrane

Remove the contents of three raw eggs and carefully peel off the membrane from inside the shells. Smooth the membranes all over your face, especially lined areas. Let them dry; then peel off.

Egg Whites

Use straight from the egg or beat until stiff. Apply to face and neck; let dry; and remove with warm water and then a cold rinse to close the pores. Tightens and stimulates skin and refines pores. You can add a couple of drops of lemon juice to the whites to remove oiliness.

Buttermilk

Good for enlarged pores and also a mild bleaching agent. Use plain or mix with oatmeal, cornmeal, whole wheat flour, or mashed fruit.

Honey

Tightens, hydrates, and has healing properties too. Apply honey all over your face and neck; tap lightly all over with your fingertips as the honey dries and gets "tacky," so that the skin is lifted up slightly and massaged with each touch. Let the honey dry completely. Rinse off.

With Cornmeal

Mix cornmeal and honey together and apply to face. When the mask is tacky, apply a layer of yogurt on top of it. Take a warm bath and remove the mask when rinsing.

With Egg

Whip a couple of eggs and add a couple of grains of alum. Apply and leave on for 15 to 20 minutes. Rinse and dry your face; then cover with honey. Leave on for 5 minutes, rinse, pat dry, and spray on astringent.

With Milk (Skim)

Melt honey; add milk. Apply warm to face and bosom. Massage gently and rinse off with warm water.

With Parsley (Chopped)

Blend together in blender. Apply.

With Peach or Apricot Pulp

Good for razor-burned skin or acne. Apply cooked, mashed peaches or apricots. Sit in a hot bath and steam for 15 to 20 minutes to help the honey penetrate before washing it off.

Almond Meal

Make almond meal in your blender from whole or slivered almonds (or buy it ready-made). Mix with buttermilk or yogurt, or mix with mashed cucumber pulp and lemon juice for an astringent effect. Almond meal has a slight abrasive quality that removes dead skin.

With Aloe

Mash gel from aloe vera leaves (or buy bottled gel) with almond meal and about a tablespoon of any cold-pressed oil. Use egg white instead of oil for a tightening effect.

With Mayonnaise and Alum

Mix two tablespoons almond meal with 2 tablespoons mayonnaise (health food variety or home-made is best), 1/4 teaspoon alum, and 1 drop peppermint or vanilla extract for scent (optional). Massage into face, leave on 10 to 15 minutes, and rinse off. Good for dried out, chapped, or wind-burned skin.

With Rosewater and Honey

Add rosewater and honey to almond meal to make a paste. Apply to face and neck. Scrub in until tacky and let dry. Rinse off and apply astringent.

Brewer's Yeast

Some people are allergic to yeast. If you are not, and do not have delicate or sensitive skin, a brewer's yeast mask will stimulate and draw impurities out of your skin.

With Witch Hazel

Mix 1/2 cup brewer's yeast, 2 teaspoons witch hazel, and 1 or 2 drops of vanilla or peppermint extract for scent (optional); add enough water to form a paste. Apply and leave on your face for 10 minutes. Rinse off with warm water and then with cold water to tighten pores. Follow with aloe vera gel to soothe and moisturize.

With Yogurt or Mayonnaise

Mix yeast with mayonnaise (to reduce stimulation), or yogurt (to increase stimulation) and scent extract. Follow directions above.

Vegetable, Fruit, and Herbal Masks:

Cucumber
SLICED

Slice cucumbers and layer them all over your face to tighten and refresh. Lie down for 15 minutes.

With Herbal Treatment   Slice the cucumber in long strips, press them all over your face, and cover with a steaming-hot, moist washcloth or strips of fabric soaked in steaming herbal solution (sage, basil, camomile tea, lavender, or other herbs steeped in boiling water). Lie down for 10 minutes.

With Milk   Dip the slices in skim milk (raw, if you can get it) before applying them to your face.

MASHED

With Cream   Mash cucumber and strain out the juice. Mix the juice with an equal amount of heavy cream. Apply and leave on for 15 minutes. Moisturizes and refreshes.

With Honey and Witch Hazel   Mash cucumber with 1 teaspoon each honey and witch hazel in a blender. Apply for 10 minutes. This is good for sunburn.

With Powdered Milk   Mash cucumber and mix with powdered milk to form a paste. Soothes and refreshes.

Applesauce   Warm the applesauce. (Fresh homemade is even better; leave out the sugar or use honey instead.) Mix applesauce with wheat germ to make a paste that is good for dry skin. Mix applesauce with cooked oatmeal for a soothing, healing mask.

Avocado-Buttermilk   Mash an avocado with a small amount of buttermilk (or powdered milk). You don't want the mixture too runny. Leave on for 15 to 20 minutes. Tissue off; then massage the residue of rich oils into your face with the avocado pit or your fingers.

Avocado-Mint   Mash fresh mint leaves in a blender; then blend thoroughly with an equal amount of ripe avocado. Wash your face and leave it slightly damp. Then apply the mask and massage it into your face with the avocado pit using circular upward movements. Remove with tissue; rinse your face in lukewarm water and spray with astringent. Or rinse with mint tea, which has astringent qualities.

Banana Mash a ripe banana and apply it to your face, or mix it with powdered milk and apply. Mixed with a little lanolin, banana puree has a smoothing effect when applied generously to the neck region.

Cabbage Soak leaves in hot water or vegetable oil for an hour to soften. Apply to your face and leave on for half an hour. Remove the leaves; rinse your face lightly and rub it with cucumber slices. Spray on an astringent. This mask is good for acne.

Carrot Slightly cook carrots and mash them, or scrape raw carrots into a pulp. Mix with yogurt in blender and apply. This helps clear up pimples and acne.

Citrus Fruits Slice lemons, oranges, or grapefruits thinly. Lie down and apply the fruit all over your face; leave it on for 10 to 15 minutes. A warm, moist washcloth can be laid on top of the fruit to help penetration. Stimulates and acts as an antiseptic. Citrus peels can also be ground and mixed with powdered milk to make a paste. (Citrus can destroy the skin's natural defenses against the harmful rays in sunlight—so wash your face before you go outside.)

Mint Chop and mash any kind of fresh mint leaves. Mix this with cream or fine oil (wheat germ, sesame, almond), but don't use too much or it will overpower the refreshing qualities of the mint. Leave the mixture on your face for 15 to 20 minutes.

Strawberries or Other Berries Mash and apply the berries. You can also add powdered milk or buttermilk. Reduces oiliness, softens, and smooths.

Papaya Papaya cuts grease, so it is good for oily skin. Mash a ripe papaya and apply for 15 minutes.

Prunes A prune mask nourishes and cleanses; with oatmeal, it will also heal. For a prune and oatmeal mask, cook the oatmeal first. Pour a small amount of boiling water over dried prunes to soften them. Blend together the prunes and oatmeal with a ripe fig (optional) in a blender, and apply to your face. Take a warm bath (you can throw in some herbs if you like) and soak for 20 minutes. Then rinse off the mask and shower.

Tomato

Mash and strain out seeds and peel. You want to use the pulp from the firm part of the tomato. Rub over your face, or mix with oatmeal or powdered milk to form a thick paste. Apply and leave on for 10 to 15 minutes. This is good for oily skin.

Watermelon

Slice watermelon very thin. Saturate it with lemon juice and refrigerate until cold. Apply to face and neck for 15 minutes.

Gels

Gel Peel-Off

For normal to dry skin. Mix 2 tablespoons pectin, a pinch of alum, 1 teaspoon zinc oxide paste, 1 or 2 drops vanilla or almond extract for scent (optional), to gel consistency. Apply to face, let dry 10 to 15 minutes, gently peel off, and rinse face with lukewarm water. Pat dry.

Gelatin Dessert

Make one package of lemon-flavored gelatin dessert, substituting lemon juice for half of the required liquid. Cool in the refrigerator until the mixture jells enough to coat face. Apply to face, leave on for 10 minutes. Remove with cool water.

Mud Packs

For Acne-Troubled Skin

Mix 2 teaspoons Fostex (or other medicated cleanser) with 2 teaspoons Fuller's Earth into a paste. Refrigerate. Apply cold paste all over face. Let dry 10 to 15 minutes. Remove by splashing face with lukewarm water. Pat dry.

For Normal to Oily Skin

Mix 2 teaspoons calamine lotion with 1 teaspoon Fuller's Earth. Apply to face; let dry 10 to 15 minutes, and rinse off. Or use a mixture of 2 tablespoons alcohol, 2 teaspoons Fuller's earth, and 1 teaspoon scent extract (like vanilla or peppermint).

For Dry Skin

Mix 4 teaspoons mayonnaise (health-food type is best), 1 teaspoon Fuller's Earth, and 1/2 teaspoon kelp (seaweed) powder into a paste. Apply and leave on 10 to 15 minutes. For very dry skin or lines, brush egg yolk over your face before you apply the mask.

With Yogurt and Honey

Mix 3 teaspoons yogurt, 1 teaspoon Fuller's Earth, 1 egg white, and 1 teaspoon honey. Apply; leave on for 10 minutes; rinse off. Or substitute one pinch of bicarbonate of soda for the egg white, and if skin is dry, coat face first with a light layer of cream or fine oil. You can also cover the mud pack tightly with damp strips of cotton gauze or rags, or a damp washcloth. Lie down for 10 or 15 minutes; then remove the mud pack gently with warm water.

Wax

Paraffin mask

Melt paraffin wax over low heat until liquid. Apply generously to your face and neck with a clean makeup or paint brush. The wax should be warm but not so hot as to burn. Heat a large spoon in hot water or by resting it on a heating pad until it is warm. Run the back of the spoon over the mask, pressing gently and concentrating on lines, wrinkles, and trouble spots. Reheat the spoon as necessary. Let the mask cool and solidify and then pull it off in big chunks. Rinse your face with cold water and follow with astringent. If your skin is dry, coat your face with light layer of fine oil or moisturizing cream before applying the mask.

Moisturizers

Apply a moisturizer after cleansing your face, or after rinsing or spraying your face with water, mineral water, or half mineral water and half astringent mixture. Moisturizers work by sealing in the moisture (water), so they are more effective when applied to a damp face.

Day or Nighttime Moisturizer for Normal Skin

Shake together in a bottle 2 tablespoons sesame oil, 1 tablespoon olive oil, 2 tablespoons almond oil, 2 tablespoons avocado oil, 200 I.U. vitamin E (mixed Tocopheral), 100,000 U.S.P. units vitamin A, and 4,000 U.S.P. units vitamin D. Store the mixture in the refrigerator in an opaque or colored glass container to protect it from light. It may be used under the eyes and all over the face and neck. Any of these oils may be used separately on dry skin, and you can also try cod-liver, safflower, sunflower, wheat germ, and apricot oils.

Mineral Water

Spray on face several times a day to moisturize and refresh. Save and reuse spray bottles that come filled with commercial products, or use your plant mister.

Petroleum Jelly

Apply to damp face. Splash water on your face until oiliness of petroleum jelly disappears. Pat dry.

Water

Splash face with warm water ten times. Follow with ten cool water rinses. Gently blot dry and apply your regular lotion moisturizer. Do this at least once a day to keep skin moist. Be sure not to use hot water.

Nighttime Moisturizers

For Dry Skin:

Dissolve 1 tablespoon dry gelatin in 1/4 cup cold water; then add 3/4 cup boiling water. Cool and put in a blender with 1 cup fine oil, such as cold-pressed peanut, safflower, sunflower, olive, almond, or mink oil; or lanolin; or a mixture of these (mineral oil and corn and cottonseed oils are not recommended). Also add 2 tablespoons castor oil, 1 tablespoon cod liver oil, 4 tablespoons lecithin, 2 teaspoons kelp or seaweed, 2 multiple vitamin tablets, and 200 to 400 I.U. of vitamin E. Blend all the ingredients together until smooth (15 to 30 seconds). You may have to crush the vitamin tablets in a mortar and pestle or wrap them in a dish cloth and pound with mallet. Puncture the vitamin E capsule and squeeze out the contents. Apply the blended mixture to the face and throat ten minutes before going to bed at night. Refrigerate the excess in a colored or opaque bottle to protect it from the light.

Dry Skin with Marks or Scars

Use same basic recipe, but add 100 mg vitamin B₂, 100 mg vitamin B₆, 100 mg vitamin B₅, 20,000 I.U. vitamin A, 800 I.U. vitamin D, and one tablet of inositol.

Dry Skin in an Over-Stimulated Environment

For skin that has been exposed to too much heating or air conditioning. Add 2 teaspoons glycerine to basic recipe and sleep with a humidifier or vaporizer in your bedroom.

Mature Dry Skin with Enlarged Pores

Add 2 teaspoons ascorbic acid (vitamin C) to basic recipe.

Problem Dry Skin with Bumps

Add 2 teaspoons ascorbic acid and two aspirin tablets to basic recipe. This will encourage mild skin peeling, which helps bumps under the skin to surface so that you can treat them.

Sun-damaged Dry Skin

Add to basic recipe the gel from one aloe vera leaf (or 1/2 teaspoon dried aloe vera powder or 2 tablespoons bottled liquid aloe vera gel), and two 1,000 mg PABA tablets.

Wrinkled or Sagging Dry to Normal Skin

Add 2 teaspoons ascorbic acid (vitamin C) and 2 egg whites to basic recipe. For a lighter lotion, whip the egg whites first.

For Oily Skin:

Dissolve 1 tablespoon gelatin powder in 1/4 cup cold water; then add 3/4 cup boiling water. Cool and add to blender with 1 cup bubbly mineral water, 2 teaspoons glycerin, 2 teaspoons seaweed or kelp, 2 multiple vitamin tablets, and 200 mg vitamin C. Blend until smooth, about 15 to 30 seconds, on low speed. If blender will not pulverize the vitamin tablets by itself, crush them first and then add them. Apply the mixture to your face and throat ten minutes before going to bed at night. Refrigerate the excess mixture in a colored or opaque bottle to protect it from the light.

Mature Oily Skin with Pimples and Breakouts

Add 4 tablespoons vodka to basic recipe. If skin is breaking out because of stress and anxiety, add 100 mg vitamin B₂ and 100 mg vitamin B₆ to basic recipe.

Oily Skin with Enlarged Pores	Add 2 teaspoons ascorbic acid to basic recipe.
Oily Skin with Lines and Sagging	Add 2 teaspoons ascorbic acid and 1/2 teaspoon alum to basic recipe.
Oily Skin with Marks or Scars	Add 100 mg vitamin B_2, 100 mg B_6, 200 mg vitamin B_3, 2 inositol tablets, 20,000 I.U. vitamin A, and 800 mg vitamin B to basic recipe.
Problem Oily Skin with Bumps and Wrinkles Around Eyes and Mouth	Add 2 teaspoons ascorbic acid and 2 aspirins to basic recipe. These ingredients will encourage mild skin peeling so that oil-clogged bumps will surface and can be treated.

For Combination of Skin Types:

Dry Skin on Cheeks; Oily Skin on Forehead, Nose and Chin	Use same recipe as for Nighttime Moisturizer for Dry Skin (page 125), but add four tablespoons vodka. If skin is mildly oily on forehead, nose and chin, use this lotion over entire face. If skin is very oily, do not use on forehead and nose.
For Dry to Normal or Slightly Oily Skin	Mix equal amounts of petroleum jelly and Nivea lotion, and apply to face every night ten minutes before going to bed. For oiler skin, apply only to cheeks, neck, and problem dry areas. Do not use if you have acne.

Daytime Moisturizers to Wear Under Makeup

For Dry Skin	Make the lotion for normal skin (see below); then mix in equal amounts of petroleum jelly and Nivea lotion until you get a consistency you like. Apply sparingly.
For Normal Skin	Mix 4 ounces Aquacare, 2 percent urea lotion, and 1 teaspoon zinc oxide ointment (Lassar's Paste) together with milk. Add 1 egg white and whisk again. Smooth modest amounts on cheeks, forehead, and chin before applying makeup. Refrigerate excess.
For Oily Skin	Whisk together 4 ounces of Nivea lotion with 1 teaspoon zinc oxide ointment. Add 1 egg white and whisk again. If skin is very oily, apply only to cheek and neck area.

Skin Cleansers and Conditioners

Acid Balance	Apple cider vinegar and warm water	Apply to skin and let dry. Pat on with cotton balls or spray on. Corrects facial acid balance.
Aftershave or Soothing Cleanser	Quince seeds with witch hazel, lavender, or rosewater	Soak quince seeds in lavender water, rosewater, or witch hazel water to form a gel. Use as a non-stinging and healing aftershave, or as a cleansing cream.
Astringent	2 oz. isopropyl alcohol, 2 oz. distilled water, 1/4 teaspoon 2 percent salicylic acid (or Fostex medicated cleanser)	Ask your pharmacist to make you the 2 percent salicylic acid solution. Mix all the ingredients together. Add a few drops of vanilla or peppermint extract for scent if desired. Apply with a cotton ball or spray on the face with a plant mister or recycled plastic spray bottle. Use after cleansing or moisturizing your face or using a mask. For very dry skin use more water and less alcohol. Refrigerate the extra.
	1 oz. camomile, 3 tbsp. witch hazel, 1/2 tsp. cider vinegar, 1 oz. peppermint (the herb)	Boil the ingredients in eight ounces of water. Strain, cool, scent with peppermint extract, and refrigerate.
	Witch-hazel water	Dilute to strength that seems most comfortable for your skin. A stronger solution works best on oilier skin.
Beauty Scrub	Almond meal, oatmeal, or cornmeal with buttermilk or yogurt	Moisten the meal with buttermilk or yogurt and scrub your face (and body too) with the mixture.

	Almonds, honey, cold cream	Grind almonds in a blender to make almond meal. Add 1 teaspoon honey and mix with small amount of cold cream. Scrub face with mixture. Stimulates circulation and helps get rid of blackheads.
Blemishes	Celery or lemon juice or apple cider vinegar	Cut the celery and dab its juice on blemishes three times a day to dry them up. Or use lemon juice or apple cider vinegar in the same way.
Cleansing Cream	1 egg yolk, 4 tbsp. mayonnaise (health food type is best), 1 tbsp. carrot juice, 1 tbsp. yogurt	Beat the egg yolk into the mayonnaise. Blend with carrot juice and yogurt. Cleanses, moisturizes, and conditions. Contains natural vitamin A and lecithin. Refrigerate extra, and if you're making a lot at once, add a few drops of compound tincture of benzoin (a natural preservative), available at herb and spice stores.
	Crisco	Use like cold cream.
	1 oz. olive oil, 4 oz. Crisco, 5 to 10 drops tincture of benzoin (natural preservative available from herb and spice stores)	Mix the ingredients into a homogenous cream. Massage into your face. Tissue off. Remove the residue with astringent, or leave it on overnight.
Dead Skin Remover	Miracle Whip (*not* mayonnaise)	Apply to skin; as it starts to dry, massage dead skin away. Also works on elbows, feet, and knees.
	Sea salt mixed with cold cream or Crisco	Massage mixture into face for five minutes. Cover face with gauze and steam face for five minutes over pot of boiling water and herbs (optional). To do this, make a tent with towel over your head and the pot. Rinse or spray with mineral water afterward.

Deep Cleanser	Kelp powder with cold cream or Crisco	Mix kelp with cold cream, creamy cleanser, or Crisco to make a gritty cream. Work it into the skin with a soft bristled face brush or sea sponge. Massage for five minutes. Rinse the cream off and spray your face with mineral water.
Pore Cleanser	1/3 licorice or fennel, 1/3 comfrey, 1/3 mint leaves or camomile tea (for oily skins add lemon peel or witch hazel); also try other herbs such as thyme, rosemary or lavender)	Boil about 2 tablespoons of mixed herbs with 1 quart of water in a covered pot and steep for 3 minutes. Tie back or cover your hair and drape a bath towel over your head and the uncovered pot. Keep your face at least eight inches or more from the hot pot, close your eyes, and steam for ten minutes or so until the steam starts to cool. Follow by rinsing your face with warm water and then cool water or astringent to close the pores. Don't go outside right away.
Pore Refiner	1 oz. cold cream, fresh bran or shredded wheat	Mix cold cream with bran or wheat until a grainy texture is achieved. Gently massage into your face. Rinse off with splashes of warm water. Follow with astringent. Removes dead skin and deep-cleans pores. Use once a week after cleaning your face. For oily or acne-troubled skin, use two to five times a week.
Scars, Skin Texture	Vitamin E oil capsule	Puncture the capsule and apply the contents to your face and throat before taking a hot bath. Allow ten minutes or so for the oil to penetrate before washing your face. Or apply before going to bed and leave on all night. Improves skin texture; firms and smooths the throat. Can be used anywhere on the body to diminish scars. If you have oily skin, be cautious about this treatment as you're adding oil to oil.

Skin Tonic or Freshener	Apples, honeydew melons, and pears for dry skin; grapes, oranges, and cantaloupes for normal skin; lemons, tomatoes, and strawberries for oily skin	Wash your face; then take a slice of fruit and pat it briskly all over your face and neck. Pat dry. Nourishes and refreshes.
	1 oz. each fresh lemon and lime juices	Shake the juices with eight ounces of water or mineral water and refrigerate. Use cold. Pat on with cotton balls or spray on with a plant mister. Use on dry to normal skin.
Soapless Cleanser	Dry to Normal Skin: 1 oz. cold cream, 1/2 tsp. any acne cream cleanser like Komex or Pernox.	Mix the ingredients and apply cleanser to your face; remove with cotton balls or tissue. Rinse with warm or lukewarm water. **Blot** dry.
	Normal to Oily Skin:	Same as above, but increase acne cream to 1 tsp.
Wrinkle Cream	1/4 cup chopped cucumber, 1 egg white, 2 tbsp. mayonnaise, 2 oz. fruit kernel oil (almond, apricot, peach, etc.), vitamin E capsule	Blend the cucumber, egg white, mayonnaise, and oil. Apply morning and evening. Tissue off excess. At night apply contents of one vitamin E capsule to wrinkled areas ten minutes before going to bed. Leave on all night.

HAIR

Conditioners

1/4 to 1/2 cup mayonnaise	Apply to dry, unwashed hair. Cover hair with a plastic bag for 15 minutes. Rinse thoroughly and shampoo. Health-food mayonnaise (or homemade) is best.
1/4 teaspoon olive, sesame, baby, or corn oil	Massage into scalp. Soak a towel in very hot water, wring out, and wrap around your head for at least 20 minutes. Rinse.
2 egg whites, shampoo	Separate two eggs. Beat the whites till lightly stiff and mix well with a small amount of your favorite shampoo. Shampoo half of this mixture into your hair and leave it on for 5 minutes. Rinse. Shampoo in the second half of the egg white mixture. Rinse well. Note: Rinse water that is too hot will cook eggs, making them difficult to remove.
2 well-beaten egg yolks	Rub the egg yolks into wet hair after washing. Leave on for 1/2 hour. Rinse off with lukewarm to cool water (see above).
Petroleum jelly	Warm the jelly and apply to your hair. Cover your head with a plastic bag or cap, leave the jelly on for 20 minutes, and then wash it out with shampoo. For more effective treatment, keep the jelly warm with a hair dryer while it is on the hair; or cover the plastic cap with a thin towel and drape a heating pad over it for 10 to 20 minutes; or take a hot bath and soak for 20 minutes while the jelly is on your hair. Then wash it out.

Sun- or Chemical-Damaged, Over-Bleached, or Processed Hair	1 egg, half an avocado	Beat the egg frothy in a blender and add the avocado. Apply to hair, massage into scalp, and cover with a plastic shower cap or plastic bag for 20 minutes. Rinse off using cool water, gradually increasing to warm, so you don't accidentally cook the egg while it's still on your hair.
Dry Hair (Hot-Oil Conditioner)	Olive oil or other fine vegetable oil (soy, safflower, almond, etc.); or 1/2 wheat germ oil, 1/2 other vegetable oil	Heat the oil until it is very warm. Section your hair and work the oil into your scalp until the whole scalp is covered. Comb through your hair and cover it with plastic wrap or a plastic bag. Sit under a hair dryer for 45 minutes; or cover your head wrap with a thin towel and drape a heating pad over it for 30 minutes, using a low setting. Rinse well afterwards.

Other Hair Products

Dry Scalp	Glycerin and apple cider vinegar	Mix glycerin with a small amount of apple cider vinegar. Apply the mixture to your scalp for ten minutes. Rinse.
Dry Shampoo	Bran, dry oatmeal, baby powder, or cornstarch; *or* 1 tbsp. salt mixed with 1/2 cup cornmeal	Apply from a large-holed shaker or old baby powder container. Work through the hair with your fingers and brush out thoroughly.
	Egg whites	Beat the egg whites until foamy. Brush your hair. Apply the foam with your fingers and massage it into your scalp thoroughly. Let dry and brush out with a clean brush.

Encourage Hair Growth; Keep Gray Away	Nettle, sage, and walnut leaves	Add the herbs to boiling water and steep. Cool the liquid and rinse it through your hair. Store it in the refrigerator; it will keep indefinitely. Sage encourages growth; nettle and walnut leaves add lustre and color. The herbs may also be used separately. Experiment to find the best strength for you.
Highlighting Rinses	Camomile tea	Make a strong solution. Rinse your hair with it to accent highlights in all hair colors.
	1 or 2 tbsp. lemon juice mixed with water	For blondes. Lightens and brightens.
	Apple cider vinegar mixed with water, *or* black coffee or tea	For redheads and brunettes. Don't rinse out the coffee or tea.
Odor Remover (from Processing)	Tomato juice	Pour tomato juice through your hair to get rid of processing odor. Rinse.
Rejuvenators	1/2 cup yogurt, 1 beaten egg yolk, 1/2 tsp. kelp powder, and 1 teaspoon grated lemon rind	Mix the ingredients and apply to dry hair; leave on for 10 minutes, comb through, shampoo, and rinse.
	2 tbsp. mayonnaise, 1 tsp. kelp powder	Follow directions above.

Setting Lotion	Beer, *or* 1 tsp. sugar or plain gelatin dissolved in 1 cup water with 1/4 tsp. lemon juice, *or* prepared Jello	Use beer at room temperature straight from the can, or dilute it slightly. Leaves no odor when dry. For a firmer set, use the sugar, gelatin, or Jello. Add 1 teaspoon light cologne for scent if desired.

EYES

Bags and Dark Circles	Casaba melon, potato, or pear	Place a thin, fresh slice of casaba melon, raw potato, or pear under each eye while resting for 10 minutes.
Eye Cream	Odorless castor oil, or vitamin A and D capsule (oil)	Apply around eyes before going to bed. Allow 10 minutes for the oil to sink in. (For vitamin capsules, puncture capsule and squeeze out contents.)
	Petroleum jelly and zinc oxide	Mix 4 ounces of petroleum jelly and 1 ounce zinc oxide. Pat on around eyes 10 minutes before going to bed and leave on all night. Also use as a throat cream, following same directions.
Eye Protector	Petroleum jelly	Apply a dab of jelly to eyebrows and eyelids and smear outward toward your cheeks to prevent stinging from salt water, chlorinated water, or shampoo.
Redness and Puffiness	Cucumber slices	Lie down and relax with thin slices of cucumber over your eyes. Try soaking the slices in milk (raw, if you can get it) before applying.

Swelling	Moist, cool tea bags soothe the eyes and reduce swelling and the aftereffects of weeping and tears. Lie down if possible
Cold used tea bags	
Catnip and black tea	Steep the catnip with black tea. Cool. Spoon the moist catnip and tea leaves onto two cloth squares and fasten the ends with rubber bands to make two bags. Lie down and apply to your eyes for 10 to 15 minutes to reduce swelling and bags.
Tired Eyes	
Weak camomile tea	Make ice cubes from weak camomile tea. Rub cubes around tired eyes before applying make up.
Wrinkle Treatment	
Carrot and castor oil	Blend 1 carrot and 1 teaspoon castor oil to make a mush. Refrigerate for an hour. First apply plain castor oil under your eyes; then apply blended mixture over the entire eye area. Lie down for half an hour; then remove cream with splashes of warm water.

MOUTH

Breath Fresheners	Chew on any of these to freshen your breath. No sugar or artificial flavoring!
Clove, cardamom seed, fennel seed, anise seed or greens, or cinnamon stick	
Mouthwash	Though commercial mouthwash is probably cheaper, this works without the alcohol and sugar in store-bought brands
Lemon juice	
Tooth Cleanser	Removes plaque, yellowing, and other stains.
Mashed strawberries	
Tooth Powder	Use like commercial tooth powder.
Plain baking soda	

SKIN

Bath Treatments

Exfoliating Bath

Epsom salts and sea salt, *or* cornmeal, *or* 1/2 avocado mashed with 1/2 cup sea salt

For face alone, mix equal amounts (1 to 2 teaspoons) of epsom salts and sea or table salt in a cup of warm water. Rub into your face with your fingertips (avoid eye area). Rinse and apply astringent. *For body,* bathe in warm water solution of epsom and sea salts. Rub skin all over with loofah or rough washcloth. *Or* scrub skin with avocado-salt mixture. *Or* scrub yourself with a loosely woven bag filled with cornmeal. After any of these treatments, bathe or shower again, and follow with a cool rinse. Dead, flaky outer skin layer washes away.

Herb Bath

Equal quantities of sage, rosemary, lavender, and basil

Mix the herbs and use about 4 ounces per bath. Boil, steep, and add to the bath water. If you're in a rush, you can throw them dry into a hot tub and let the water cool enough to be comfortable before you get in. You can also make up your own herb mixture, or throw in a handful of oatmeal, or add a few drops of fragrant oil, if you have any.

Milk Bath

Skim milk powder

Mix dry milk with warm water in the tub. Use enough powder to make at least three quarts of reconstituted milk. You can bathe in it as is, or add herbs (brew first and let steep before you add), camomile, jasmine, dried-out flower petals (save those wilted bouquets), lavender, etc. Or add sea or table salt with a dash of bath oil, soak, and use a loofah to remove dead skin. Or add one cup of honey and one cup of strong herb tea (camomile, peppermint) for a relaxing bath.

Mud Bath	Sterilized potting soil, dry milk powder, and mineral water

Combine the water and milk powder to form a creamy paste. Add the soil a little at a time, adding mineral water as needed to keep a pastelike consistency. Apply generously all over the body with a shaving brush or soft-bristled paint brush. Leave on 15 to 20 minutes; then shower.

Oatmeal Bath	1/2 lb. oatmeal

Moisten the oatmeal. Stand in an empty tub and rub yourself all over with the oatmeal. Scrub with a loofah or rough washcloth. Add warm water and soak in the oatmeal and water. Blot yourself dry, or rinse lightly and air dry. Soothing and good for itches and sunburn.

Salt Bath	Sea salt

Make a paste with moistened sea salt and scrub yourself all over with a loofah. Don't worry if it stings—this is a curing treatment. Take a warm bath and let the salt dissolve off your body into the water. You can also skip the scrub and just add a cup of sea salt to the bath water. You can also mix the salt with half as much bicarbonate of soda and some powdered Irish moss (if you can find it). Scent with a few drops of bath oil or other fragrant oil. Bathe as usual. Invigorates.

Other Skin Treatments

Baby Powder	Cornstarch

Cornstarch is absorbent and cooling and can be used as a body powder for babies and adults. Dried and powdered flower petals (orange, rose, etc.) can be added for scent. Recycle old bouquets or buy dried flowers in an herb and spice store.

Black-and-Blue Marks and Warts	Raw potato	Grate the raw potato and place the pulp on black-and-blue marks. Hold in place with a bandage. The marks will disappear in a few hours. A slice of raw potato tied over a wart with a loose bandage and left on overnight will help to dry it up. Rub the potato over the wart every night before bandaging. Keep up this treatment until you notice results.
Cellulite and Throat Massage	Avocado pit	Massage problem areas with the avocado pit. Roll it in a circular motion. Helps cellulite and neck wrinkles.
Cellulite Wrap	2 oz. almond oil, 2 oz. olive oil, 1 oz. Vaseline; camomile, thyme, and rosemary, or sage, seaweed, kelp, and marjoram	Mix and melt the oils and Vaseline over low heat until warm. Add scent if desired (one teaspoon peppermint, almond, or vanilla extract). Massage into the body and shower off. Dampen a large bath towel with herbal brew made by steeping the herbs in boiling water. Wrap yourself in the hot, wet towel, taking care it is not hot enough to burn you. Over this, wrap a plastic sheet or drop cloth. Lie down and cover yourself with heavy blankets. Put a cool washcloth on your forehead. Rest for 10 to 15 minutes.
Freckles	Horseradish and buttermilk	Grate 1 tablespoon horseradish. Mix with 2 tablespoons buttermilk and let stand for a couple of hours. Strain and apply to freckles to diminish them.
Rough, Discolored Elbows	Lemon and heavy cream	Halve the lemon and scoop out most of the pulp. Add heavy cream to the lemon shells and put one shell over each bent elbow. Lemon juice bleaches out discoloration, and the cream will soften the rough skin.

Rough Elbows, Knees, or Heels	Avocado skins	Use the inside of the skin, which contains a rich oil. Rub on your elbows, or anywhere there is rough, horny skin. Be sure to rub long enough—until your skin feels smooth and any greenish color has disappeared.
	Avocado and sea salt or table salt	Rub on a mixture of half avocado meat and half salt.
Sunburn	Apple cider vinegar, or cucumber slices, or yogurt mixed with lemon juice, or wet tea bags, or paste of baking soda and water	Apply to afflicted area
Sunburn, Burns, Bug Bites, Cuts, Scratches, Bruises	Aloe vera gel, PABA	Use juice from aloe vera leaves, or buy bottled juice. Apply aloe vera directly to the afflicted area. Soothes as well as heals. Crush a tablet of PABA (1,000 mg) and blend with aloe for overnight sunburn relief.

HANDS AND FINGERNAILS

Callused Hands and Brittle Nails	Olive oil and sage	Heat the ingredients together, and soak your hands in it. Use it on feet too.
Chapped or Raw, Rough Hands	2 heaping tbsp. almond meal or oatmeal, 1 tbsp. honey, 1 egg yolk beaten frothy	Mix ingredients together. Variations on this formula include adding cornmeal, vinegar, or milk. Make a paste, smear it all over your hands, and then cover with a pair of old gloves (kid is recommended, as it doesn't leak and the paste doesn't dry out). Go to bed, leaving the gloves and paste on until morning.

Chapped Hands	Almond oil and crystallized honey; pine bath oil or pine needles and oil	Mix the ingredients in equal amounts and apply thickly to hands. Put on a pair of kid or cotton gloves when going to bed and wear them all night. In the morning, soak your hands in a solution of pine bath oil and hot water (or steep some pine needles in boiling water and add a drop of fine oil).
Hand Lotion	Petroleum jelly	Because of petroleum jelly's stickiness, cover hands with rubber or cotton work gloves after applying. You can try this treatment when you're planning to garden, wash dishes, etc. Or apply before going to sleep at night and wear an old pair of dress gloves (kid are best) to bed. The pressure of the gloves relieves arthritis pains, too.
Manicure Soak	Juice of 1/2 lemon in 1 cup of warm water, *or* solution of mild soap or dishwashing liquid	Soak your nails for five minutes. Rinse, dry, and push the cuticles back.
Nail Polish Liquifier	Boiling water or nail polish remover	If nail polish gets too thick, loosen the cap and place the bottle in a pan of boiling water (the water should not be higher than the opening of the bottle) for a few minutes; or add a few drops of nail polish remover, screw cap on tightly, and shake. (Note: The refrigerator is the best place to store fingernail polish.)
Nail Polish Easy Opener	Petroleum jelly	Smear around the top of the bottle and inside the cap, so the top won't stick.

Nail Shine without Polish	Dry soap or lemon peel	Apply to nails and buff. Lemon peel works well after manicure soak (see page 141).
Nail Strengthener	White iodine	Paint on unpolished, uncolored nails.
Stained Fingers and Nails	Lemon and white wine vinegar	Rub the lemon rind and pulp vigorously over stained or discolored areas on your fingers and fingernails. Rinse with white wine vinegar. Works well on nicotine stains.

FEET

Callus Reducer	1 tbsp. avocado meat and 2 tbsp. cornmeal	Mash the avocado and cornmeal in your hands. Rub the mixture over and around your hands and feet, massaging the fingers and toes one at a time.
Corn Remedy	Onion or garlic clove	Roast the onion or garlic. Apply it to the corn while still hot and secure it in place with a soft bandage. The corn should loosen in 2 or 3 days. Repeat if necessary.
Dead Skin Remover	3 oz. epsom salts, 3 oz. bicarbonate of soda, and 3 oz. table or sea salt	Mix the ingredients together and massage into your feet and legs for 10 minutes. Rinse off and soak feet in herbal bath.
Foot Baths	6 oz. epsom salts, 3 oz. boric acid or bicarbonate of soda, and 6 oz. pine oil, bath oil, or cologne.	Mix the ingredients in a basin of warm water, and soak your feet.
	3 parts cider vinegar to 1 part lemon juice.	Add to a basin of warm water, and soak.

	Any combination of lavender, pine needles, sage, mustard seed, witch hazel, rosemary, comfrey, or bran	Boil the ingredients and steep for a few minutes. Pour into a basin and add cool water until temperature is comfortable for your feet, and soak your feet. Add more hot water from time to time. Try other herbs too if you have them.
Foot Massage	Dried peas or beans	Fill a pair of socks with some dried peas, lentils, or beans. Wear them for a few minutes a day, and walk around the house in them. Also rub your feet briskly with a scrub brush or loofah, when you bathe or shower.
Foot Powder	Equal amounts of talcum powder (or cornstarch) and bicarbonate of soda, 1 tsp. witch hazel, 1 tsp. cologne or peppermint extract	Mix all ingredients together.
Tired Feet	Cayenne (red) pepper	Sprinkle a little cayenne pepper in your shoes to stimulate feet.
Tired, Aching Feet	Safflower, wheat germ, or olive oil; *or* baking soda, *or* avocado pit	Massage feet with warmed oil, moistened baking soda, or an avocado pit. This feels wonderful. (Even if you've never done a foot massage before, you can't go wrong no matter what you do.) Follow with a long soak in a foot bath, or wrap your feet in hot, wet towels for 10 minutes.

DEODORANTS

| *Antiperspirant* | 2 tbsp. alum, 1 pint warm water, 1 or 2 drops of cologne or after-shave lotion | Mix and store in spray bottle. |

	Witch hazel	Spray under the arms or dab on with a cotton ball.
Cream Deodorant	2 tbsp. baking soda, 2 tbsp. petroleum jelly, 2 tsp. talcum powder or cornstarch	Heat the mixture in a double boiler over low heat and stir until it becomes a smooth cream. Cool before using. Store excess in refrigerator.
Dry Deodorant	Orange and lemon peels	Dry the peels and grind them together into a powder, using a mortar and pestle or food processor. Dust the powder under the arms for that natural scent.

DOUCHES

Herb douche	1 oz. vinegar	Mix vinegar with 1 or 2 quarts of warm water.
	Alum, comfrey, mint, peppermint, wintergreen, rosemary	Mix any combination of herbs and steep 1 or 2 tablespoons in 1 quart of boiling water. Add 1 quart of cold water. Cool further if necessary and douche as usual.

MAKEUP TIPS

Blusher Extender	Broken or used-up blusher	Crumble broken cakes of blusher and pry out corner bits of used-up blusher; crush until the blusher is the consistency of loose powder. Store in a container with a tight-fitting top and apply with a cotton ball or fluffy powder brush.
Lipstick Extender	Used lipstick tubes	Scoop out remainders of lipstick in bottom of used tubes and melt compatible colors together over a low heat in a small metal pan or measuring cup. Pour into empty gloss pots or pillboxes and chill

	overnight. Apply with a lipstick brush or your fingertip, or thin with petroleum jelly and use as a tinted gloss.
Makeup Setter	Mineral water	After makeup is applied, spray on a mist of mineral water, or soak a wet tissue or cotton in mineral water and dab it on. This sets the makeup and makes it last longer.
Mascara Extender (for Dried-Out Tube Mascara)	Hot water	Cover the tube with hot water for two or three minutes. The heat will soften the mascara, and you may get another week or two of use.
Perfume Saver	Petroleum jelly	Apply perfume over a tiny smear of petroleum jelly. Added oil holds the perfume longer.
Red Nose	Lemon and orange peels	Boil the peels and bathe your nose in the water to reduce redness.
Rouge (Organic)	Beet and glycerine	Juice a small beet; or grate it, or pulverize it in blender, and then strain and squeeze out the juice from the pulp. Mix 1 teaspoon beet juice to 1 teaspoon glycerine. Pat it on your face. Refrigerate the extra.

SOURCES

How to Cut Your Own or Anyone Else's Hair by Bob Bent is a no-disaster, easy-to-follow manual for home haircuts. A haircut-and-a-half at home and the book pays for itself. Available from Simon and Schuster, 1230 Ave. of the Americas, New York, NY 10020. $5.95.

How to Look 10 Years Younger by Adrien Arpel. Warner Books, 75 Rockfeller Plaza, New York, NY 10019. $8.95.

3-Week Crash Makeover/Shapeover Beauty Program by Adrien Arpel. Simon and Schuster, 1230 Ave. of the Americas, New York, NY 10020. $7.95.

For do-it-yourself-at-home beauty advice, both of these books by Adrien Arpel are well worth the price. Don't be put off by the cutesyness and limp wit of the text. Ms. Arpel has sound common sense to offer on the often outrageously expensive subject of beauty. Besides simple home remedies, she includes such luxuries as do-it-yourself herbal wraps (for deep moisturization and tightening of the skin), cellulite treatments, plasma facial packs, and acupressure—the sort of gourmet beauty treatments usually available only to the wealthy. The books also include diets, exercises, hair tips, camouflage dressing, illustrated examples of make-overs, and a very interesting discussion of underwear.

CLOTHING

CLOTHING

Of the three traditional necessities of life, clothing represents the most variable expense. In fact, probably no area of personal spending is as amenable to good management as clothing.

Everyone has a different philosophy about the importance of clothes and fashion. Some shun trendy garb as stubbornly as others seek to be up to the minute. The way each person chooses to economize in this area will be dictated by his or her ideas and priorities. But regardless of one's fashion "philosophy," there are ways to save on buying clothes and ways to maintain and recycle clothes to extend their value.

MAKING THE RIGHT SELECTIONS

BEFORE YOU BEGIN

- *Know yourself.* Know your level of fashion, what kind of clothes you feel comfortable wearing, what looks good on you. If you find yourself wearing the same few things over and over again while other garments go unused, or if you never seem to have the right thing to wear, you're probably in the dark about your own taste and style. And that's wasteful. Nowadays almost everything is fashionable and acceptable—there's no one correct hemline or width. But your clothes must work well for you.

- *Know your wardrobe.* Take all the clothes out of your closets and drawers and refresh your mind about what you own. You may find things you'd forgotten, or discover combinations of skirts, tops, belts, etc., that you hadn't thought of. And you'll get an accurate idea of what you really need.

GENERAL GUIDELINES

- *Buy quality.* Quality should be one of the main criteria in selecting clothing, especially those garments you will wear most frequently.

149

You do pay more for high-quality clothing, but that difference is much less than the replacement cost for a cheaper article that starts wearing out immediately. With clothing, a durable quality item is the more economical alternative.

- *Avoid extremes.* Too many people follow the dictates of the fashion business and find they're always struggling to keep up with what's "in." Consequently, they "never have anything to wear." The lesson here? Don't buy fashion extremes that will put you "out of style" next season. A conservative approach means you'll be able to wear the clothing comfortably year after year. Always ask yourself: "Can this be worn enough times to justify the cost?"

- *Avoid frills.* No-frill items are cheaper and more useful. A coat with a fur collar, for instance, is more expensive and cannot be worn as frequently as a coat without one.

- *Avoid "designer" labels.* They *always* cost more. You're paying for a name instead of workmanship. And sporting a label or insignia displayed prominently on your clothes only provides free advertising for the designer and takes individuality away from you.

- *Buy in quantity whenever possible.* Items like pantyhose, socks, and men's undershorts and undershirts are more economical when purchased in packages of three or four than when purchased individually.

- *Look for versatility.* Make each garment as useful as possible. Buy clothes that span more than one season and more than one function. For instance:

  — A medium-weight, mid-range color wool suit can be worn in winter *and* summer.

  — Long-sleeved shirts can be worn all year. In the summer, roll up the sleeves.

  — Instead of single-pieced dresses, jump-suits, or leisure suits, buy separate tops or bottoms (pants, blazers, skirts, sweaters, shirts, etc.) that are interchangeable.

  — Raincoats with detachable linings make for year-round use.

  — When buying a suit, let your choice be guided by how well the suit can be broken up and the components worn with other items in your closet. This also applies to three-piece garments like tweed suits with matching coats. A recent innovation in men's suits is a four-piece vested suit that includes a suit coat, reversible vest, and two pairs of slacks. This arrangement can provide six different looks and is available from some of the finer suit makers.

- *Read labels.* Tucked away here and there on a garment are tags, labels, and stickers that will tell you everything you need to know about an article of clothing. The U.S. Government requires the following information:

  — The generic name of the fiber (cotton, nylon, etc.) and the percentages (if 5 percent or over) of each fiber of a combination fabric

  — The manufacturer or seller's name(s)

  — The originating country of the fiber and garment

  — Care instructions.

  The fiber and the care instructions should be particularly important in your decision to buy.

- *Be aware of guarantees.* These now accompany certain lines of clothing and inform you approximately how long an article of clothing should last. Save your receipt and guarantee tag. If the article wears out before it's supposed to, take it back. Stores will honor these warranties.

QUALITY CHECKLIST FOR READY-TO-WEAR CLOTHING

Inside Work

- Seams should be evenly sewn and close together, preferably 10 or more stitches to the inch.
- Stitches should look identical on both sides of the seam; if not, they'll pull out.
- Hems should be properly bound with fabric tape and sewn neatly and securely. Look for at least a two-inch-hem, deep enough to permit lengthening.
- Clothing intended for heavy wear should have double stitching and reinforcement at points of wear.
- Zippers, snaps, and trimmings should be firmly attached and correctly placed.
- Lining (usually a sign of good workmanship) should be well-installed and made of a nonstretch or nonshrink material.

Outside Work

- Buttonholes should be reinforced, especially at the ends. A sure sign of poor quality is buttonholes not sewn through on both sides of the cloth. Buttonholes placed horizontally have a tendency to stay buttoned better than their vertical counterparts. And the well-tailored shirt has buttons below belt-buckle level.

- Print, striped, or plaid patterns should be matched where seams meet. This is a real test of quality.
- A garment should be cut on a true bias (diagonal) or straight along the grain or weave of the fabric; if not, it won't hang properly.
- Top stitching or any other conspicuous stitching should be smooth (no puckers), even, and neat.
- Fabric should be resilient. Bunch up some in your hand and press tightly. If it doesn't return to its original shape quickly, pass it up; it won't wear well.

FABRICS

100 Percent Natural

Nothing quite beats the feel of a 100 percent natural fabric. An all-cotton shirt breathes and is supremely comfortable. But when you buy one, be ready for a higher purchase price and for the necessity of either ironing it or sending it to the laundry (the going rate for cleaning and pressing exceeds a dollar in many parts of the country).

Garments made of high-quality fabrics are also more likely to be well constructed and well tailored. A suit maker is not going to expend the extra time for good workmanship on a cheap fabric.

100 Percent Artificial

At the other extreme are the 100 percent artificial fabrics—polyester double-knits. They're the cheapest, and are easy to maintain. But they're hardly worth buying. Doubleknits are cold in winter and scorching in summer. The workmanship tends to be of low quality, and the styles are quite faddish, preventing their use in seasons to come (if they could hold up that long). Stains are more difficult to remove from polyester, and polyester is suscep-tible to permanent damage from excess heat. Mending is also difficult as polyester doesn't hold a seam as well as a natural fabric. And last but not least, several allergies, especially those resulting in headaches and itching, are attributed to polyester garments.

Wash and Wear

The perfect solution should be a wash and wear mix—enough natural fabric to give an all-natural look and enough polyester to make the garment easy to maintain. Unfortunately, poor-quality wash and wear clothes don't wear as well as one would hope. The fabric pills around collars and sleeves after being worn only a few times. But with good-quality wash and wear clothing, the money you can save on maintenance alone (compared to all-natural fab-rics) will purchase you a new garment when the old one wears out.

CARE REQUIREMENTS

Consider what's involved in maintaining the garment. A "Dry Clean Only" item can mean a steady flow of cash to your local cleaners, plus the trouble and gas involved in dropping it off and picking it up. "Wash separately" means trouble as well, unless you've got a machine load of similarly colored clothing that happens to be ready for washing at the same time.

Buying clothes is like buying an appliance or a car. You're purchasing two packages: the garment itself, and the cost of maintaining it.

A rule of thumb should be: Learn to pass up clothing that isn't colorfast, shrink-resistant, and permanent press.

TIPS ON SIZES AND COLORS

- *If you buy standard small, medium, large, and extra-large sizes, you save.* The price goes up when a manufacturer has to provide more exact sizes, like the sleeve and neck sizes of sport shirts.

- *Always try clothing on.* Sizes vary in ready-made clothing, and a bargain that doesn't fit right is no bargain.

- *Remember, it's easier to take in a garment than it is to let it out.* Buy larger if you can't get the right fit.

- *Buying clothes that are too small for you on the assumption that you'll be losing weight is bad planning and poor economy.*

- *Bear in mind that light colors require extra maintenance.* Pale slacks are easily soiled when you sit on a dirty surface or cross your legs and smudge them with freshly-polished shoes.

- *Avoid buying anything snow white that must be dry-cleaned.* Since dry cleaning fluid itself isn't white or clear, garments work their way to pale gray.

- *Avoid trying to keep colors and sizes in your head when you shop.* If you need to match a color, bring a swatch or the garment itself; for size, bring written measurements or the person. Otherwise, chances are you'll be buying something that won't quite work. If it was on sale, then it will be another bargain hanging unused in your closet.

SHOPPING STRATEGIES

WHERE TO BUY

For the best values, you should buy from a variety of places.

- *Chain stores* give good deals on old reliables such as jeans, undershirts, sneakers, pajamas, and work clothes. Like supermarkets, the larger retailers commission major manufacturers to produce goods for them, so you can save up to 20 percent.

- *Catalog and mail-order houses* also stock reasonably priced clothing. The distributor doesn't have the high cost of a retail outlet, and this saving can be passed on to you.

- *Foreign mail-order houses* can provide savings, even after you pay the postage and handling. Many people don't realize that great savings can be obtained on high-quality merchandise by ordering it from abroad. Some examples are hand-knitted sweaters and yarn goods from Scotland and Scandinavia (many major stores publish catalogs); shoes and other leather goods from Belgium and Italy; and tailored silk suits, jackets, etc., from Hong Kong.

- *Department stores* require that you keep three things in mind.

  — Merchandise of a similar quality may be carried in more than one department and at a different price. Check before you buy.

  — A department store basement isn't always a bargain basement.

  — Merchandise displayed near elevators, escalators, and entrances is to tempt impulse buying and is usually not on sale. (Supermarkets and other retail outlets use this same tactic with end of aisle displays, etc. Don't fall for it!)

- *Irregulars outlets* offer tremendous savings. When an article of clothing doesn't meet the manufacturer's quality-control standards, it is pulled and eventually finds it way here. Do check the merchandise closely; often the irregularity is barely noticeable.

- *Factory outlets* are an excellent source for reasonably priced clothing. Some even sell their own irregulars or seconds. These are sold "as is" and cannot be returned, so check that the size is right, that the zippers are properly installed and working, and that the seams are well sewn.

- *High-fashion discount outlets* in or near big cities offer samples, display goods, overstocks, and overruns of top designer clothing at substantial savings. But some of these places supplement the high-quality merchandise with low-quality goods. It often takes a few visits to find the quality you need, since the better merchandise is always snatched right up.

  Check your newspaper or yellow pages for locations. Look under "surplus" or "factory outlets." If you know of factories in your area, phone and ask them if they sell samples or seconds.

- *Thrift shops* are treasure troves for clothes. They're sponsored by everyone from the Junior League to the Salvation Army. Children's clothes are especially a bargain here, and it makes sense to buy this way since kids outgrow clothing so quickly. Women's clothing is also abundant because of changing fashion and variety. Men's clothes, on the other hand, tend to last longer and are therefore not always as plentiful.

Find thrift and secondhand shops in the yellow pages. Incidentally, the thrift shops in nicer neighborhoods tend to have the nicer cast-offs.

- *Garage and estate sales* also have good-quality merchandise for reduced prices. Check the classified section of the local newspaper for announcements.

- *The lost and found departments* of transit companies, airlines, department stores, and many organizations often sell unclaimed clothing. Make inquiries as to when they're offered for sale. Schools and other organizations turn clothing over to charity groups. Remember: a lost article of clothing is usually up-to-date and not badly worn.

WHEN TO BUY

- *The key to wardrobe savings is planning.* You must know what you need and buy it at the proper time and proper sale price. Don't impulse shop! Don't purchase anything, even on sale, unless you'd planned to buy it anyway.

- *You can save 30 to 50 percent by restricting your purchases to sale items.* The three major storewide clearance sales are after Easter, after the Fourth of July, and after Christmas. There are also back-to-school and fall-fashion sales in August and October.

- *Shop as early in a sale as possible.* Find out when the sale will be and what will be on sale. If you can, pick what you want in the lull before the sale, then return on sale day to buy.

- *Many mail-order houses and retail outlets have two types of clothing sales.*

  — *Seasonal sales* usually offer substantial savings on merchandise in season, such as back-to-school blue jeans.

  — *Clearance sales* come after the peak demand periods and offer huge savings (up to 50 percent) because profit is not the motive. These sales are intended to clear the company's stock of slow-moving or out-of-season merchandise to make room for new inventory.

- *Don't be misled by sale advertising.* Wording such as "Special Purchase" or "Huge Stocks Purchased for This Event" can indicate the sale stock is *not* part of the store's regular inventory and is quite possibly of lower quality. Move in when you see notices like "Regular Stock Sale" or "Store-Wide Clearance." These almost always mean that the store's normal stock is reduced in price.

- Be warned: *One gimmick most common in cities is a phony "Going Out of Business—All Stock Must Go" sale.* Some retailers keep these signs in their windows for months on end. Another trick to mislead customers are signs such as "Going Out for Business" that customers misread.

- On the other hand, *some stores mark down certain merchandise but don't advertise it because such a small quantity may be on sale.* If you're browsing, always check to see if there's a sale table or some item marked down.

- *Visit discount stores frequently since inventories are constantly changing.* Merchandise is still neatly displayed early in the day, so go then.

- *Timing is especially important in men's clothing because styles change slowly.* Because a garmet will last for a few seasons, don't buy before the season at full retail prices; shop the sales in mid-season or late in the season and save.

- Below is a clothing bargain calendar from *Sylvia Porter's New Money Book for the 80's* (see page 223):

  — Back-to-school clothes: August, October
  — Bathing suits: after Fourth of July in July and August
  — Children's clothing: July, September, November, December
  — Coats (women's, children's): April, August, November, December
  — Costume and fine jewelry: January
  — Dresses: January, April, June, November
  — Furs: January, August
  — Handbags: January, May, July
  — Hats (children's): July, December
  — Hats (men's): January, July
  — Hosiery: March, October
  — Housecoats: April, May, June, October, November
  — Infants' wear: January, May, July
  — Lingerie: January, May, July
  — Millinery: February, April, July
  — Men's and boys' suits: April, November, December
  — Men's shirts: January, February, July
  — Piece goods: June, September, November
  — Shoes (boys' and girls'): January, March, July
  — Shoes (men's and women's): January, July, November, December
  — Ski outfits: March

— Sportswear: January, February, May, July

— Toiletries: January, July

TIPS FOR DISCOUNT SHOPPING

Though shopping for bargain clothes requires time and stamina, the search can pay off, especially if you go about it right. Here are some hints.

- *Dress for the occasion.* Wear clothes that can be easily removed so you can try things on. Many discount outlets don't even have dressing rooms, so wear leotards and you can just slip the clothes on.

- *Know the layout of the store.* Discounters always organize their merchandise in certain ways—by size, by category, by price, or by designer. You'll want to head straight for what you're after if there's a crowd, and there often is.

- *Be flexible.* Discount shoppers have to make their needs general instead of specific. For instance, instead of hunting for a size 9 light blue blouse, you'll be more successful if you look for a top to go with both your blue plaid skirt and your jeans.

- *Check the store's policy on returns before you buy.* "All sales final" means just that; you'd better really need what you're considering.

- *If you see something you already bought on sale for a cheaper price at another store, make note of it and go back to the first store.* Some discounters— like Loehmann's and Syms—will refund the difference or give you credit.

OTHER BUYING TIPS

Credit Plans

Do not tie yourself into high-interest revolving charge accounts. A charge account can come in handy because charge customers often receive advance notice of sales, but don't consider an account unless you can avoid being charged interest. Interest payments will negate the savings you earn by shopping the sales.

Barter, Exchange, and Cooperative Buying

One or two friends who share your size and taste can share your wardrobe— and you theirs. This can be especially beneficial with things like coats, formal wear, and expensive accessories. You can decide with your friend (or friends) which items are open for exchange or sharing. You might even occasionally decide on purchases together: you help your friend choose her winter coat, which you'll borrow, and she'll come along when you buy a long gown.

Buying Children's Clothes

- *When shopping for children, take them along.* If they don't like their clothing, they're not going to want to wear it.

- *It's also an excellent idea to put the kids in charge of some of their wardrobe.* Set them up with a clothing allowance, and let them select and buy agreed-upon items. You'll probably notice how well they care for the articles they buy themselves—or at least they'll tend not to lose them.

- *If you have recipients for "hand-me-downs," buy for quality that can be passed along.* If you don't, buy inexpensive items a size too large, and let the child grow into them; it won't take long. When the garments no longer fit, give them to a charity.

Buying Shoes

Most people buy three or four pairs of shoes annually, not including sneakers, thongs, bedroom slippers, and other footwear. Include those and the national total comes to more than a billion pairs a year, costing the average family more than $175.00 a year. This cost can be cut if you follow these shopping tips:

- *Winter and summer seasonal sales are two very important times to buy shoes.*

- *Don't economize on shoes you'll be wearing often,* like work or hiking shoes. Where's the economy if they wear out quickly and aren't comfortable?

- *Darker colors and simple, traditional styles are relatively inexpensive and more versatile.* They can be worn so many places and with so many things.

- *Consider shoes with crepe or composition soles and heels.* They're no more expensive but more serviceable than leather, and they provide a nice, cushioned walk.

- *Buy reputable brands from reputable retailers and hold on to your receipts.* If you have trouble or if the shoes fall apart on you, return them. An honest retailer stands behind his product.

- *Inspect the merchandise.* Check the stitching. The seams should be smooth and not too close to the sole edge. The edges should be evenly trimmed. The linings should be smooth and soft; there should be no roughness or sharp protuberances. And the leather should be of good enough quality to last the miles you'll be walking.

- *Insure the proper fit.* The foot is composed of 26 little bones that take 20 years to grow into their proper position. Don't stuff your feet or your child's feet into ill-fitting or hand-me-down shoes. Wearing poorly fitting shoes is playing double jeopardy. The shoes will wear out faster, and you just might incur a podiatrist bill.

- *Shop for shoes after you've been on your feet a few hours.* Our feet swell by as much as 5 percent during the day. When deciding to buy a pair of shoes, walk around in them *for several minutes.*

- *Try each pair of shoes on.* No article of wearing apparel should be bought by size alone. Sizes vary from style to style and from manufacturer to manufacturer. When you try on a pair of shoes, stand up and check that the big toe doesn't reach the tip of the shoe, that the little toe lies flat (not scrunched up), that the heel is snug, and that the sides are not bowed out.

Shoes for Children

- *For savings and for your baby's healthy feet, don't buy an infant shoes until it starts walking.*

- *When buying children's shoes, buy a half-size larger and economize only on style.* A sturdy, well-fitting shoe is essential.

- *Improperly-fitting socks can also play havoc with babies' and children's feet.* Make sure they're not too tight.

MAKING YOUR OWN

Today there are over 45 million sewing machines in use. Sewing is a craft that can provide good mental exercise and a lot of creative satisfaction. It can also be quite profitable. Even on a small scale, you save. A simple wraparound skirt with no buttons or zippers can be put together for $4.00 or $5.00; the same piece ready-made would run you $20.00 to $25.00. A sewing machine pays for itself even if used for simple projects like mending, making alterations, plain sewing (such as seaming fabrics to make curtains), or buying old clothes and remodeling them. Mothers often teach their children how to sew and let them make their own clothes.

The savings usually lie in women's fashions. Few women are willing to undertake a man's jacket, and ready-made children's clothes are produced in large enough volumes to allow for reasonable prices. Women's garments with extensive hand operations are where you can hit the jackpot on savings.

HOW TO LEARN TO SEW

You can take a sewing class, definitely the most effective means of learning, from any of the following:

- *Your local United States Department of Agriculture Cooperative Extension Service.* ⌐

- *The adult education program at a local high school, community college, YWCA, or technical school.* These institutions usually sponsor more advanced programs as well, and it's not a bad idea to take one as your proficiency develops.

- *Sewing schools sponsored by distributors of sewing machines.* Classes are given as a premium for purchasing or an incentive to buy a machine. But watch it here—these classes can cost twice as much as an evening class at your local high school or Cooperative Extension Service. Shop around.

- *A friend.* Barter for lessons; you can offer to bake bread, run errands, and so on.

BUYING A SEWING MACHINE

Some Tips

- *Taking a sewing course first can provide an idea of what type of sewing machine is right for your needs.* Rent a machine in the interim. It'll be worth it.

- *Sewing machines are built to last.* Avoid those machines with plastic parts and you can count on at least 20 years of service from a new machine. Don't hesitate to buy a second-hand machine; they usually come with warranties (especially from a reputable supplier) and can give excellent service.

- *It's better to stick to a major brand.* Their warranties, repair services, and trade-in values are better. Check *Consumer Reports* for their ratings.

- *Take advantage of demonstrations offered by sewing-machine manufacturers.* Make sure you see the machine operate on various fabrics, not just on stiff cotton, which always shows a machine at its best.

- *Always inquire what kinds of instructions or classes come with the sewing machine you're thinking of buying.* One manufacturer has a learn-by-doing instruction book and provides fabric and operating supervision, making sure you'll know how to operate the machine to its fullest advantage.

- *There are several advantages to a cabinet machine:*
  — The machine is easier to get at, so you might be more inclined to use it.
  — It makes sewing more comfortable.
  — The cabinet protects the machine—less risk of dropping, knocking over, etc.

- *But portables are always cheaper.* If a salesman says a cabinet is necessary so dust won't get into the machine (an argument often used), don't believe it. If your portable doesn't have a dust cover, make one.

- *If you buy a machine that doesn't function properly, take it back right away.* Complaints are easier to handle on a new machine than on an old one.

Traps to Avoid

- *Inexpensive foreign-made machines are often passed off as domestic makes* (complete with stenciled American names and concealed foreign-origin markings). Reading *Consumer Reports* can enable you to avoid this.

- *"Rebuilt" machines often aren't.* Trust only the major suppliers for rebuilt equipment.

- *"Repossessed" machines are often new cheap machines.* The "unpaid balance" you pay is just about what the machine is worth.

- *"Good for today only" specials keep you from comparison shopping.*

- *A misleading ad may imply a price includes a zigzag or stretch stitcher to get you into the store.*

- *You may be offered a service contract at a reduced price,* but good machines should need almost no servicing.

- *Rebate checks or other discounts are often negated by originally inflated prices.*

SEWING MACHINE MAINTENANCE

A clean sewing machine lasts longer and works better. Use the crevice attachment of your vacuum cleaner to clean around the bobbin, and keep a soft brush around to give the machine a clean sweep after each use.

The huge amount of service a sewing machine can give, when compared to the tiny amount of maintenance it requires, makes for one of the most efficient service-to-maintenance ratios of any electric home appliance or machine. Usually only a little oiling is required here and there over the years— so do it! Check your manual for the manufacturer's instructions.

PATTERNS: SOME ADVICE

- *Set up a check list to aid you in selecting a pattern.* Pull a half-dozen of your favorite and least favorite garments out of the closet and try them on. Make *written notes* of your design preferences and non-preferences. List everything from necklines, collars, armholes, and darts to pockets, slacks cuts, lapels, and length. This will make you aware of the component parts of a design and enable you to end up with clothes that feel good and look good on you.

- *Some branch libraries have pattern-lending files.* You can also swap patterns with friends—the advantage here being that you can see firsthand what you're going to end up with.

- *Sewing centers always have pattern sales.* Do your choosing in advance. Write down the numbers of your favorite patterns. Then, when the store is mobbed with sales customers, breeze in, pull out your list, and buy the patterns you want.

- *"Easy sew" patterns are a boon to the beginner and produce impressive, finished products.* Don't overlook them. For best results, follow the pattern's suggestions in selecting your fabric.

- *Many designers are developing their newest fashions in "designer" patterns.* Buy them only if you think the design isn't too trendy and can be worn next season, *and the next.* Conservative patterns not only can be worn longer but are easier to assemble.

- *Steer clear of the "designer" patterns from Paris and Italy.* They tend to be expensive and require inner dresses or jackets to achieve their style. They are only for the veteran home tailor.

- *When you find a pattern you like, stick with it!* Make it in different fabrics and lengths.

- *Paper sewing patterns will last longer if they're sprayed with a fabric protector (like Scotch Guard) before they're used.*

FABRICS

- *The best months to buy fabric are April, June, September, and November.*
- Some good sources for fabrics are the following:
  - *Sales at yardage stores.* There are usually three or four a year.
  - *The remnants table in any store's fabric section.*
  - *Mail order from abroad.* Everything from English woolens to Thai silks and Hong Kong brocades are available. Check ads in the classified sections of popular women's magazines.
  - *Old dresses and suits* can be disassembled and the fabric reused for new garments.
- *Learn to choose the right fabric.* A label should say how the fabric will behave and how much maintenance it will need, but you can tell more by examining the fabric yourself.
  - Bunch up a corner for a few seconds, let it go, and see if it wrinkles.
  - Drape a section to see how it hangs.
  - Hold it up to the light to see just how thick it is. Can you see through it?
- *When you buy fabric, make sure you get a permanent care label that can be sewn onto a seam or waistband so that the garment can be properly maintained.*

KNITTING

Knitting can be an enjoyable, satisfying money-saver, and it uses time that otherwise would be wasted. Knitting is perfect while you watch TV, talk on the phone, attend PTA, ride in the car, or have coffee with friends. With many stitches you don't even have to watch your hands.

How to Learn

- *Many shops that sell yarns and other supplies run classes for beginners.*
- *Barter one of your talents or services for knitting lessons.* With two or three lessons, you're launched. You can take it from there, and if you hit a snag, you've got an authority to call on.

Buying Yarn

- *Get it on sale!* Local yarn shops always offer specials; you just have to inquire when they are.
- *Mail order is an economical way to purchase yarn.* The Canadians and Irish supply excellent yarns, and even with the postage and handling, you save.
- *If you're going to the trouble to make a sweater, then purchase a good yarn,* even if you have to order it by mail. In certain parts of the country only synthetic yarns are available. Polyester yarns look bad, wear worse (they pill), and can't hold in body warmth like natural wools.

RECYCLING CLOTHING

Take the clothes you don't wear very much out of your closet and see if there are new ways to put them to use. It often takes very little to convert a garment that's become unfashionable into something new and versatile. It may be as simple as changing a hemline or converting flare-legged pants into straight leg trousers. A garment with a hole or a stain can often be saved by making it into something else. What can be taken in, let out, or restyled? A day of sewing—or $100.00 spent on alterations at the tailor—can often produce a whole new wardrobe. Be inventive about finding new uses for old things. Or maybe your friends can use them as they are.

Here are some suggestions for ways to recycle:

- Worn-out dresses can be saved. If the top wears out, make the bottom into a skirt, or vice versa. Or if a long skirt hem gets ragged, make the skirt into a shorter one.
- Cut an unserviceable baggy dress in half and make it into a separate skirt and top that you can wear either together or with different skirts and tops.

- The same can work for slips. When a full one wears out, cut the bottom half off, stitch in a hem, and you've got yourself a camisole top you can wear with slacks. If the bottom is still good, sew elastic around the waist and you've got a half-slip.
- Drapery material, especially the old flowered patterns, works well for skirts or jackets.
- Bedspreads, especially those soft chenilles, can be transformed into robes or caftans.
- Robes and lounging pajamas from the '30s are easily converted into sporty street clothes.
- Dyeing can make something new from something old. Those old 100 percent wool olive drab army overcoats, for instance, are excellently constructed and toasty warm in the winter cold. Dyeing can make them into handsome overcoats for daily use. And dye those sweaters that don't quite match anything.
- If you didn't save your narrow-lapelled coats and slim ties from the '60s, you're probably stuck with wide-lapelled coats and fat ties from the '70s. Now that fashion is putting you out-of-fashion again, have your existing clothes retailored. It's cheaper and smarter than buying new ones!
- Shirt and blouse collars always start to go first. When the collar of a shirt gets frayed—if the shirt itself is in decent shape—simply have the collar reversed. Any dry cleaner with a tailor can handle this job. If you sew, do it yourself. The job will be easier if you liberally coat the collar with spray starch first. You can also shorten long, droopy shirt collars yourself, or have them done by a professional. For the latter, look in the Yellow Pages under "Shirts—Repairing."
- Sweaters can be restyled—and should be if you've not been using them. Change collars, lengths, or styles (V-necks into cardigans, for example).
- Old nylon stockings can be used as sweater sleeve liners if wool is too itchy on your arms.
- One of the greatest household mysteries is the destination of all those missing socks. Resign yourself to the inevitable and save the singles. There are two things you can do:

  — If you hold onto them long enough, eventually you'll be able to match them to other widowed socks.
  — Make them all one color. Dye them a dark color, or place them in a pot with enough water to cover them and boil them gently for at least 15 minutes. Let them cool and then dry. They will all be the same color.

- When a garment is lengthened, the crease from the previous cuff or hem is often difficult to remove. Apply white vinegar to the wrong side of the fabric and steam press. The crease and any shine will disappear.
- Remove buttons, snaps, and zippers from garments about to be converted to rags or thrown into the trash. (If the clothing is bound for Goodwill or the Salvation Army, however, leave it intact.) These notions can be used later. Sometimes an article of clothing in a thrift shop or yard sale is worth buying for the notions.
- Instead of being hassled with buying new shoelaces when the ends start fraying, dip the ends in fingernail polish, clear or otherwise.
- The nonsewer can now mend or seam most washable fabrics without a needle and thread. A new clear adhesive costing under $2.00 is available in hardware and houseware stores. Manufactured by Advance Color Corp. (P.O. Box 54870, Los Angeles, CA 90054), this stuff can even be used for shortening trousers or skirts and mending torn pockets or hems.
- A new set of heels and soles costs a lot less than a new pair of shoes. Visit your cobbler.

MAINTENANCE

Taking care of your clothes can double their life, and your clothes will look better on you during that time. So will your clothes budget.

MINIMIZING WEAR AND TEAR

- *Always be aware of the condition of your clothes.* When you take them off, check for rips, tears, and smudges; when you are dressing, check snaps, zippers, and buttons. "A stitch in time saves nine" applies here. Mending a small rip prevents it from becoming a big one; spot-cleaning a stain prevents it from setting and doing permanent damage; tightening a button before it falls off can mean not having to replace several others to match a new one.
- *Hang up what you take off.* The garment lasts longer, and you'll spend less time at the laundry. Hang slacks upside down by their cuffs so that the weight of the trousers and the belt will help pull wrinkles out. Keep sweaters folded up.
- *Alternating clothes every day gives them a chance to revitalize.* Hanging allows a garment to breathe and return to its natural shape, but this process takes longer than overnight. Remember this the next time you say, "I'll hang it up tomorrow."
- *Save unnecessary wear and tear on expensive clothes* by changing into something more casual as soon as you return home.

- *Protect good clothes.* Apply makeup before dressing, don't cook without an apron, and roll up your sleeves before washing your hands.
- *In inclement weather there are two objectives: protecting yourself and protecting your clothing.* Use a raincoat, take an umbrella, and wear rainboots or galoshes. Roll your trouser legs up or tuck them into boots, if possible. Even a leather handbag or attaché case should be carried in a plastic shopping bag.
- *When slacks are damp, give them a good, strong finger crease to save having to press them.*
- *Launder or dry-clean soiled clothes as soon as possible.* Dirty clothes attract moths and insects, and once grime has "set" in a fabric, it's harder to remove.
- *Don't stuff your pockets.* Overstuffing can rip the pockets and stretch clothes out of shape. Avoid pens that might leak (or at least make sure they're capped), watch keys and sharp objects that can gouge holes, and don't force calculators and other large objects into your pockets.
- A common problem with woolen slacks is that they eventually get shiny bottoms. To avoid this, if you do a lot of sitting in one place (like in your office chair), *use a fabric-covered seat pad.* Leather and plastic are the bottom shiners.
- As shirts get old, little balls of fuzz appear, especially around the collars. *Shave them off with a safety razor.* You can also shave the knots or balls from sweaters or gently work them off with sandpaper.
- *Iron-on patches applied to the inside of the knees of jeans will make them last longer.* Also apply them to the insides of sleeves of shirts that get a lot of rough use.
- *When elastic sewn directly into a garment splits or wears thin, just patch the damaged spot with more elastic.* There's no need to replace the whole thing.
- *Forget buying expensive and ecologically harmful aerosols for static cling.* Starch your slip very slightly or draw out the static electricity by running a wire coat hanger between your dress and slip.

REMOVING STAINS

Removing stains from your garments makes them last longer and saves money on commercial cleaning. You should remove stains yourself and continue to wear a garment until it needs cleaning.

Some Basic Spot Removers

- *The average commercial spot remover is two parts water and one part rubbing alcohol.* Make yourself up a bottle.

- *Or buy dry-cleaning fluid at your local hardware store.* Ask for it by its generic name trichloroethylene and save. It should cost around $3.00 a quart.

- *A cheap spot remover is electric-dishwasher detergent.* Apply to wet fabric, scrub gently with an old toothbrush.

- *Many small spots can be quickly removed with a cotton swab dipped in cleaning fluid.*

- *Fine sandpaper or an emery board can often remove spots on white garments.* Rub gently.

    A handy USDA reference book entitled "Removing Stains from Fabrics" is available from the U.S. Government Printing Office, Washington, DC 20402.

    Also see the chart of stains and the household products that can remove them beginning on the next page. It's quite thorough and is applicable not only to clothing but also to carpets and other fabrics around the house.

General Rules for Removing Stains

The following are general rules governing the treatment of stains:

- *Never use hot water.* It only sets the stain.
- *Treat the stain as soon as you can.*
- *Treat from the opposite side of the fabric when possible.*
- *Test any chemicals on an inside seam before you put them on the stain.*
- *Always rinse in lukewarm water if you use a chemical.*
- *Use a dilute solution of cleanser a couple of times rather than blitzing the stain (and the fabric) with a strong solution.*
- *Always rinse or dab from the outside in, in a circle larger than the stain.* This keeps the stain from spreading as the cleaning agent dissolves it.
- *Never soak wool, silk, or flameproof or non-colorfast fabrics.* Wash first in lukewarm water and an enzyme presoak (such as Axion).
- *Don't use dry cleaning chemicals on plastic (polyester).* They melt it.
- *Never mix any of the following:*
    — Acetate and polish remover (acetone)
    — Permanent press cotton and chlorine bleach
    — Acrylic fabric and peroxide or acetone
    — Polyester and chlorine bleach or dry-cleaning fluid (trichlorethylene)
    — Silk or wool and chlorine bleach or dry-cleaning fluid.

Stains and the Household Products That Can Remove Them

TYPE OF STAIN	WHAT TO USE TO REMOVE IT	INSTRUCTIONS
Alcoholic beverages (See also *Wine*)	Liquid detergent Few drops of white vinegar in water	Dilute immediately with cold water, sponge with detergent, rinse in vinegar/water solution.
	3 tbsp. glycerin in cold water Few drops of white vinegar in water	Soak in glycerin/water solution; rinse with vinegar/water.
	Rubbing alcohol	Spot with straight alcohol; for acetate fabrics dilute with 2 parts water. Then wash normally.
Animal accidents (see also *Urine*)	1 tbsp. Borax in 2 cups water Seltzer	Sponge area with solution until stain disappears. Seltzer will help take up remaining smell, especially on rugs.
Antiperspirants	Detergent and warm water	Sponge with solution.
	Equal parts ammonia and water	*For wool and silk garments.*
	Straight ammonia	For other fabrics.

Ballpoint pen: See Ink

Berries: See Fruit

Stain	Treatment	Instructions
Beer	Cold water	Sponge down—the more the better.
Bird droppings	3/4 cup baking soda and 1 tbsp. soapless detergent in 1 gallon warm water	Scrub down; follow with a rinse and wash.
Blood	Meat tenderizer and cold water	Apply tenderizer; drip on enough water to make a paste; leave 15–30 minutes; rinse with cold water.
	Laundry starch and cold water	Apply starch, drip on enough cold water to make a paste. Let dry. Brush it and the stain away.
	Strong enzyme presoak solution 1 tbsp. ammonia in cold water	Apply presoak solution followed by a cold water wash and then the ammonia solution.
	Ice cube or cold water Carpet or upholstery shampoo Dry-cleaning fluid	Dampen carpet with ice or water; apply cleaner, then dry-cleaning fluid.
	1 tbsp. table salt in 1 cup cold water	Dampen and loosen blood stains with this solution.
	Ice cube	With washcloth under stain, rub with ice cube and blood will run into the cloth.

NOTE: Use only cold water; hot water sets the stain.

Stain	Agent	Treatment
Butter or *margarine*	Cornmeal	Absorbs greasy stains.
	Dry-cleaning fluid	Also absorbs greasy stains.
Candle wax or *crayon* (See also *Chewing Gum*)	Scouring powder (a brand containing bleach)	*For linen and white cotton.* Wet thoroughly; apply cleanser and scrub with brush; let set until stain disappears. Then wash.
	Paper towels, brown paper bags, or blotter	Scrape off excess with dull knife. Sandwich stain area between pieces of paper, and press with warm iron. Sponge off any remaining wax with solvent. Use grease solvent on candle wax; dry-cleaning solvent works better on crayon.
	Grease solvent or dry-cleaning solvent	
Candy (See also *Chocolate*)	Dishwashing liquid detergent	Sponge with cool water. Massage in detergent; then rinse. When dry, dab cleaning fluid onto stain with clean white fabric, cotton, or gauze. If yellow residue remains, dab with hydrogen peroxide.
	Dry-cleaning or other cleaning fluid	
	Hydrogen peroxide	
Carbon paper	Glycerin	Work into stain; rinse thoroughly. Repeat until stain disappears.
	Dry-cleaning fluid	Sponge area.
Catsup or *chili sauce*	Detergent	Sponge area with cool water, let sit for half hour. Apply detergent and rub into stain; then rinse.
Chewing gum	Ice cube	Either place garment in a plastic bag and freeze it, or rub gum with an ice cube in a plastic bag (so as not to wet the fabric). In both cases, gum will become brittle enough to be scraped off.
	Dry-cleaning fluid	Any remaining can be removed with dry-cleaning fluid.

	White vinegar	Soak garment.
	Egg white	Rub onto garment before washing.
Chocolate	Club soda	Soak before washing.
	Talcum powder	Will absorb stain. Rub in.
	Milk	Keeps stains from setting.
	Shortening	Rub into stain before laundering.
Coffee	Borax and warm water	As soon as possible, sponge stain.
	Vinegar and water	Soak overnight in solution; dry dripping wet in sunlight.
	Household bleach	If fabric is bleach-safe, use with water to remove stain.
Collar ring	Hair shampoo	Apply shampoo to collar with a small paint brush or toothbrush. Will dissolve body oils responsible for stain.
	Chalk	Apply a thick layer to collar ring. It will absorb stains. Leave overnight; then wash.
	Paste of white vinegar & baking soda	Apply; rub in; launder normally.
Cosmetics (See also *Lipstick*)	Sudsy detergent solution	Sponge; let dry. Repeat until stain disappears.
	Dry-cleaning fluid / Liquid detergent	If grease-base makeup, spot with dry-cleaning fluid; then sponge with cool water. Massage in liquid detergent; rinse with lukewarm water.
	Equal parts water and hydrogen peroxide	Use to bleach any residual stain. (This works well on stains from foundation or powder and on lipstick.)

Crayon: See Candle Wax

Curry: See Coffee

Stain	Treatment	Instructions
Egg	Cold water	Never use hot water; it will set the stain. Soak in cold water an hour or two. Wash.
	Detergent	If the egg is dry, scrape off as much as possible. Sponge with cold water. Apply detergent to spot and wash.
Felt-tip pen	Water	If water-soluble, soak immediately; then use soap and warm water.
	Hairspray	If not water-soluble, apply liberally; let sit a few minutes; rub vigorously with clean, dry cloth.
Fruit	Detergent and boiling water	Stretch stained area over bowl and pour boiling solution onto stain from a height of several feet.
	Glycerin, hydrogen peroxide, *or* lemon juice	If the above doesn't work, rub stain with any of these and repeat boiling water treatment.
	Glycerin *or* eucalyptus oil Vinegar and water	*For fabrics that cannot be washed in hot water*, soak in cold water and rub glycerin into stain. Wait a few hours, rinse in vinegar/water solution, and launder.
Glue	Nail polish remover	Apply to opposite side of fabric. Will loosen glue so that it can be peeled off. Make sure fabric can take it.

Stain	Treatment	Instructions
Grass	Molasses	Pour onto stain and let sit for several hours. Wash garment in soapy, warm water.
	Rubbing or denatured alcohol	*For stains remaining after a normal wash* with detergent (that was applied directly to stain) and bleach; let garment dry and then sponge stain with alcohol. Use diluted 50–50 alcohol/water solution on colored fabrics.
Gravy	Lard	Rub into stain before washing.
	Cold water	Soak; then launder.
Grease	Detergent *or* cake of dry soap	Rub into stain; rinse in hot water.
	Grease solvent, and talcum powder *or* cornstarch	Apply powder and solvent to stain, let dry, brush off.
	Salt dissolved in ammonia	Sponge onto stain.
	White flour White paper towel *or* napkin	After covering spot with flour, place paper on top and press with hot iron; paper and powder absorb grease.
	2 tbsp. washing soda with 1 cup warm water	*For noniron fabrics,* apply mixture, let sit for 5–10 minutes, and rinse.
	White vinegar *or* club soda	*For suede,* sponge on liquid. Use sueded brush to restore nap.
	Club soda	*For double knits,* sponge soda on fabric.

Stain	Treatment	Instructions
Ice cream	Shortening	Rub stain with small amount; then wash in hot water.
Ink, Ballpoint	Dry-cleaning solvent	Apply to stain to remove; then wash.
	Eraser	Ballpoint pen eraser may do the trick. If eraser doesn't work, it is a good idea to experiment. If possible, mark an inconspicuous part of the garment and try any of the following:
	Warm water	Some ballpoint inks are water soluble.
	Denatured alcohol *or* petroleum jelly	Apply to stain; soak in detergent solution; launder.
	Hairspray	Apply liberally; let sit a few minutes; rub vigorously with clean, dry cloth.
	Cuticle remover	*For leather*; removes stains.
Liquid ink	Cold water	For washable inks, run through fabric until water is clear.
	Paste of milk and cornmeal	Apply to stain for a few hours, brush off.
	Sour milk *or* buttermilk Salt	Soak overnight. Rub salt into stain beforehand to speed milk's efficiency.
	Lemon juice	Can dissolve stain. Apply directly.
	1 part alcohol 2 parts water	Soak garment in this solution.
	Thick paste of baking soda and water	Cover stain with paste and hold over pot of boiling water to steam-clean stain. Launder.

Iodine	Cold water	Soak garment; then wash.
Jam and Jelly	White ink *or* ammonia	Cover stain; then wash normally.
	1 oz. washing soda *or* Borax powder dissolved in 2 cups warm water	Soak in solution; wash normally.
Lipstick (See also *Cosmetics*)	Petroleum jelly, glycerin, salad oil, rubbing alcohol, hydrogen peroxide, *or* lemon juice	Rub into stain; wash in soapy, hot water. Use care with alcohol and peroxide. When using lemon juice, dilute if using on colored fabric; otherwise use full strength.
	Thick mixture of powdered soap and water	With white towel under spot, sponge thoroughly with mixture. Wash normally.
	White bread	Rub stain off with bread.
Mercurochrome	4 tbsp. ammonia in 1 qt water	Soak garment in solution.
	Rubbing alcohol	When safe for fabric, sponge on. If spot is obstinate, place pad saturated with alcohol over spot. Leave until stain is gone. Keep pad damp.
Mold and *Mildew*	Table salt and lemon juice	Rub mixture into stain; place garment in sun.
	Bleach	Use when washing.
	Sour milk *or* buttermilk	Soak garment overnight; rinse and dry in sun.
	Equal parts rubbing alcohol and water	*For leather;* sponge stain away.

Mud		Let mud dry first, and brush away as much as possible. To remove remaining stain, try any of the following:
	Raw potato	Rub stain; then launder.
	Cold water	Soak; then wash normally.
	Denatured alcohol	Sponge on.
	Glycerin *or* liquid detergent	For washable fabrics, rub into stain and then launder.
Mustard	Nail polish remover	Test to make sure it won't damage fabric; then apply to back of stain.
Nail polish		
Paint	Turpentine Bleach	*For oil-base paint,* sponge with turpentine; then wash with bleach.
	Liquid detergent	*For water-base paint,* sponge with detergent and wash.
	Detergent solution	In either case, if stains are still visible, soak overnight.
	Rubbing alcohol	Can sometimes remove dry water-base paint.
		Note: Treat before paint dries if possible; otherwise you're in trouble.
Pen: See *Felt-tip Pen, Ink*		
Pencil	Pencil eraser	Erase!

Perspiration	Ammonia	For newer stains. Apply with sponge; then rinse and wash normally.
	White vinegar	For older stains. Same procedure as for ammonia.
	Table salt in water	Soak washable fabrics in solution.
	Thick paste of baking soda and water	Apply; leave for 15 minutes; wash normally.
Rust	3/4 oz potassium persulfate in 1 pint water	Soak rust spot.
	Lemon juice Salt	Hold spot over boiling water and squeeze lemon juice onto it. Or apply salt, squeeze lemon juice over it, and place in sun.
	Cream of tartar	Cover stains, gathering up area so that powder will remain in contact with stain. Soak in hot water for 5 minutes; launder.
	Barkeeper's Friend commercial rust remover	Follow directions.
Salt water	Warm water Rubbing alcohol	Dissolve salt stain by sponging with warm water. If stain remains, sponge again with rubbing alcohol. Launder.
	2 tsp. rubbing alcohol 1 tbsp. milk	*For shoes.* Rub onto shoes; let dry; repolish.
Scorch marks	Washing soda and water	Rinse in cold water right away; then sponge with solution.
	Corn starch	Dampen mark and sprinkle corn starch over it. Let dry. Brush away.

Stain	Treatment	Instructions
Scorch marks	Raw onion *or* a dampened slice of stale bread	Rub over scorch; then soak in cold water and wash.
	Hydrogen peroxide	*On white or color-safe fabrics*, use straight. *For linen and cotton*, place dampened cloth over mark and apply warm iron.
Shoe polish	Rubbing alcohol	If fabric will take it, sponge with alcohol; or, if not, use 1 part alcohol to 2 parts water.
	Mineral oil *or* glycerin / Cleaning fluid	Work mineral oil or glycerin into stain; follow with cleaning fluid.
Soot	Borax powder	Add to wash. Removes minor marks.
	Art gum eraser	Erase spots.
	Salt	Rub salt on stain; remove it and soot with stiff brush.
Spaghetti	Lemon juice	Sponge stain; rinse.
Tar	Liquid bleach	If fabric is bleach-safe, apply directly to fabric after dampening it.
		Scrape off excess with dull knife, then try any of following:
	Shortening	Softens tar so that it can be scraped away completely. Leave on for 10 minutes.
	Turpentine *or* dry-cleaning fluid	Sponge area.
	Kerosene	Test colorfastness first. Sponge kerosene onto area; wash with detergent.

Stain	Treatment	Instructions
Tea	Washing soda and water *or* hydrogen peroxide	Sponge stained area.
	Boiling water	Pour over stain.
Tobacco	Rubbing alcohol	Sponge area.
	Molasses	If fabric won't take alcohol, cover stain with molasses and let sit for several hours. Wash in soapy, warm water.
Urine (*Animal and Human*)	Warm water Solution of 1 tbsp. white vinegar to 2 cups water	Sponge with water; then apply vinegar/water solution.
Vomit	Washing soda and water Vinegar and warm water	Sponge thoroughly with soda and water; rinse with vinegar and water.
Water marks	Silver spoon	Rub back of silver spoon on mark.
Wine (*red*)	Boiling water	Hold fabric over bowl, pour boiling water over stain until it disappears.
	Salt	Cover stain with thick layer of salt, rinse out in cold water, and wash.
	Paste of salt and lemon juice	Apply paste, rinse, and wash.
	Boiling milk	Dip stain in milk.
White wine		Can dilute red-wine stains. Follow with cold water rinse.

Yellowing

Solution of 1 gallon hot water, 1/2 cup electric dishwasher compound, 1/4 cup liquid bleach, 1/4 cup white vinegar

For 100 percent cotton, whiten by soaking overnight in solution. (Use *only* stainless steel, plastic, or enamel container.) Wash, adding vinegar to rinse water.

For nylons, let mixture cool (hot water sets wrinkles). Soak in room-temperature solution for 1/2 hour. Wash, adding vinegar to rinse water.

For dull white polyester, omit bleach from soaking solution and vinegar from rinse. Allow to soak overnight.

Mixing these will ruin the fabric, create a permanent stain, or release toxic gases that could make you very sick.

MACHINE WASHING

Economizing

- *Your highest cost is for the hot water used, whether hand or machine washing.* Cut down and save $60.00 a year in water heating. Cold-water washing has other advantages as well. It makes clothes last longer, reduces fabric shrinkage, prevents colors from bleeding, and keeps permanent pleats pleated and white nylon white. However, cold water detergents can leave a residue in fabrics in a hot water wash, and flame-resistant garments can lose their resistance.

- *Washing machines take energy to operate, so make every load count.* Unless you have a water-level setting for the size of the load, operate the washer only when you can fill it to capacity. The same goes for the dryer and the iron. Crank them up only when there's enough work to make it worthwhile.

- *Use a measuring cup so you don't waste laundry detergent.* And use just enough detergent to create the lightest suds level. Soap manufacturers will often recommend that you use too much so you'll buy their product again sooner.

- *If your washing machine is not operating up to par, try cleaning it before calling a repairman.* Add a gallon of white vinegar to a warm-water wash cycle. The vinegar will wash away accumulated scale, soap, and detergent residue. A common ailment is a clogged filter screen that impedes the flow of water into the machine. You can clean this yourself, although it may take a wrench to uncouple the water hose. Check your instruction manual or phone a repairman.

Bleaching

- *Clothes will last longer without bleach, which weakens fibers.* Using a lot of extra bleach gets clothes no whiter, it only damages them more.

- *Plain lemon juice makes the cheapest, safest, and simplest bleach.*

- *If you must use bleach, keep it to a minimum and use it in less concentrated doses.* Punch a hole in the bottle an inch or so below the spout and add the bleach to the wash a few drops at a time. Use more bleach only occasionally if needed to whiten yellowed cottons and nylons (see below).

Avoiding Fabric Softeners

- Consumer Reports *claims that fabric softeners actually make clothes look yellow and dingy*, and CR is rarely wrong.

- *Plain white vinegar works better and is cheaper than commercial fabric soft-ener.* All you need is a quarter cup per load. There's no vinegar odor and the added advantage is that vinegar neutralizes soap and detergent residue.

Other Machine Washing Tips

- *A teaspoon of epsom salts per gallon of rinse water keeps the colors of garments from running or fading.*

- *Wrinkles in wash-and-wear fabrics can be minimized by rinsing those fabrics in cold water.*

- *Whiteness can be restored to cotton and nylon by using the hottest possible water and doubling the normal amount of soap or detergent.* For added effect, stop the washer after five minutes and add a cup of chlorine bleach diluted in a quart of water (or the same proportion of vinegar and water). Run the machine another five minutes, stop it for ten minutes of soaking, and complete the wash cycle. (For presoak com-pounds, see *Yellowing* in the chart on page 180.)

HAND WASHING

Almost everything except clothing with unwashable linings can be hand washed instead of dry-cleaned. Even silks and woolens can be washed in cold water in the sink or bathtub. In fact, hand washing is *better* for lambs-wool, cashmere, and the like because dry cleaning is a harsher process that depletes the natural oils in these fibers.

Tips for Hand Washing

- *Woolite isn't everything it's cracked up to be.* For delicates, a mild solution of Ivory Flakes is more gentle and effective. Another efficient soap is liquid dishwashing detergent. It's as mild as special soap products, and cheaper.

- *Vinegar works exceptionally well in hand washing.* Added to rinse water, it cuts down on soap residue so efficiently that at the most, only a couple of rinses are necessary. This saves water and time.

- *Both glycerin and hair rinses are good for final rinses of sweaters.* They condition and soften.

- *Nylon pantyhose last longer if washed in very cold water.* When they're new, wet them with cold water, put them in a plastic bag, and freeze. When they're thawed and dried you'll have longer-lasting pantyhose.

Gloves

- *Wash leather gloves in either shampoo or soap containing lanolin.* This re-stores the natural oils in the leather. Put the gloves on and wash as if you were washing your hands. Don't wring them dry; press them flat and into shape on a towel, then roll it up. Dry them away from heat. And don't worry if the leather stiffens or changes color. Simply knead it back to its original softness and color. If you're washing doeskin, pigskin, or chamois gloves, however, add a few drops of olive oil to keep them soft and pliant.

- *To clean white kid gloves, put them on and dunk them in a bowl of rubbing alcohol.* Wash them as you'd wash your hands. Remove them carefully: roll them off instead of pulling. When they're dry, rub them with egg white. It works—and they'll never look better.

- *You can also dry-clean white kid gloves.* Slip them on and rub white corn meal or moist bread crumbs all over. Again, remove them by rolling down. Then buff with a flannel cloth.

- *Eventually white kid gloves become too dirty to clean. A good way to extend their life indefinitely is to dye them.* Soak them in strong black coffee for excellent results.

OTHER CLEANING HINTS

- *Be advised that some manufacturers don't test the care instructions for their fabrics;* they go by what the textile maker tells them. So mistakes can happen. If your clothes are damaged after you've followed the manufacturer's instructions, return them to the retail outlet and request a refund.

- *Pay special attention to the care labels on stretch fabrics (ski pants, etc.); they are very fragile.*

- *Use the commercial dry-cleaning machines at the laundromat.* A full load (8 pounds) can be dry-cleaned for between $3.00 and $4.00. That's at least two-thirds cheaper than having each piece done individually. These machines are perfect for bulky articles such as overcoats with unwashable linings, sweaters, blankets, etc. They also work for articles such as slacks and shirts that require special pressing or steaming, but everything must be put on hangers hot out of the machine to prevent wrinkling. Another advantage is that clothes can be cleaned and ready to go within an hour.

- *Dry-clean your own ties.* Fill a small jar with dry-cleaning fluid. Roll up a tie, put it in the jar, screw on the lid, and shake vigorously. Remove the tie and let it dry. Presto! You've saved yourself at least $1.50.

- *It's the sweatbands of men's hats that collect oil and dirt. Excessive buildups can damage and shorten the life of a hat.* Wipe sweatbands periodically with a damp cloth that has been rinsed in soapy water. You can also keep sweatband deposits to a minimum by coating the band of a new hat with paraffin.

- *Socks that won't come clean can be boiled in water with a slice of lemon.*
- *You can clean velvet by holding it pile side up over steaming water to which a little ammonia has been added.* Finish by brushing well and ironing lightly on the wrong side. This raises the nap and removes wrinkles.

DRYING

Line Drying

Line drying can cut your energy bill, and there are several advantages in addition:

- *Clothes last longer;* all that lint you remove from the dryer filter is the fabric slowly wearing down.
- *Clothes smell fresher*, even in the city.
- *Elastic lasts longer;* electric drying wears it out.
- *The sun bleaches whites*, making them appear cleaner. Brightly colored and dark clothes can fade on the line, however, so always hang them inside out or in a shaded area.
- *Clothes, bed sheets, and especially wet bath towels can be freshened without being washed.*
- *In winter, drying the family wash in the basement or elsewhere indoors can contribute up to 26 pounds of moisture to the dry indoor heat.*
- *Outdoor winter drying can be slow, and clothes can freeze, but when you bring them inside and hang them up you'll notice that a fresh smell permeates the house.* In a short time, the clothes will be thawed, dried, and ready for folding.
- *When the temperature is hovering around freezing, wipe the line with vinegar so clothes won't stick to it.*

Electric Drying

- *Don't overdry clothes.* It's not good for them, and it wastes energy.
- *Drying permanent press clothing at too high a temperature or leaving in the dryer after the cycle is complete causes permanently dried-in wrinkles.*
- *Don't overload a dryer, and don't underload it either.* The proper load makes best use of the heat generated.
- *Especially during summer, the dryer should be vented outside to get rid of moisture-laden air and to speed up drying time. In the winter, venting the dryer inside can add both heat and moisture to the house.*

- *Keeping the lint filter clean reduces drying time and your energy bill.* At least once a year, you should also clean the lint buildup on the outside of the dryer drum, the motor, and the exhaust pipes. Use a vacuum cleaner and a brush.

- *Instead of using tear-off fabric softener sheets in the dryer, pour a few capfuls of liquid fabric softener into a washcloth.* Wring the excess back into the container, then toss the saturated cloth into the dryer (as you would a tear-off sheet). Or better yet, try vinegar instead.

IRONING

- *Aluminum foil spread between the padding and cover on an ironing board reflects heat back up through the cover while you're ironing, making for more efficient ironing and energy savings.*

- *Starching the ironing board cover also makes for more speedy ironing, and the cover stays cleaner longer.*

- *Whenever there's some showering (or bathing) going on, hang clothes that need pressing (including ties) in the bathroom.* Steam penetrates material, thus eliminating wrinkles—and ironing! This is a good technique to use while traveling.

- *"Iron" handkerchiefs, fabric napkins, scarfs, doilies, or other fine fabrics by plastering them when wet to any smooth surface (a tabletop or counter top, a wall, or the tile and glass around the bathtub or shower).* Tape the top corners if it's a vertical surface. They'll dry almost as wrinkle-free as if they'd been ironed.

- *If you insist on ironing handkerchiefs, then at least iron in twos and threes.* The material is thin enough for the heat to penetrate.

- *Are you using a hotter setting than is necessary? If so, you are wasting energy and ruining the garment.* Always read labels; a "cool setting" means just that.

- *When ironing different types of fabrics, begin with those that require a lower setting and work up.*

CARING FOR SHOES

- *Studies have found that if you wear different shoes each day, three pairs will last as long as four that are not alternated.* Shoes, like clothes, need time to take a breather—to dry out and resume their natural shape. A full day will do it; overnight won't.

- *Keep a pair of shoe trees for every pair of leather shoes you own.* When your feet aren't in the shoes, the trees should be. They will make your shoes last longer. Wooden shoe trees are best because they absorb moisture. (Shoe trees can often be found in thrift shops. Just be sure you buy the right size.)

- *Improper care of rain-soaked shoes can shorten their life span.* When you remove them, apply a light film of mineral oil to keep them from becoming stiff. Stuff them with newspaper so that they will keep their shape, and dry them well away from any direct heat source. A good drying idea is to hook the heels of your shoes over a chair rung so that air will be able to circulate freely around them. This keeps the drying shoes pretty much out of the way as well. When the shoes are thoroughly dry, give them a shine.
- *Stretch your own shoes instead of taking them to the shoe repair shop.* Slip plastic bags into them, fill with water, and place in freezer overnight. Water expanding as it freezes will stretch shoes evenly and safely. You can repeat the process several times until shoes fit.
- *When colored shoes get scuffed and scratched, camouflage the damage with crayons.*
- *Suede shoes and other outerware can be steam-cleaned at home.* Remove any excess dirt with a suede brush or dry sponge. Then hold the shoes over a pan of boiling water until the nap is raised by the steam. Stroke the shoes to cleanliness with a soft brush and let them dry.
- *For a temporary solution to scuffed shoes (when you don't have time to shine them), use hand cream.* Rub on and buff.

STORAGE

Basic Hints

- *The ideal clothing closet should be cool and dry.* Consider installing a dehumidifier if you live in a humid locale. A low-wattage light bulb (turned on, of course) can also be used as a "damp chaser."
- *Keep seldom-worn garments covered to prevent their getting dusty.*
- *Let damp clothes dry before storing them; otherwise both they and neighboring garments may become mildewed.*

Moth Prevention

Clothes that might have lasted for years on end are often destroyed by moths. It's upsetting to take out an old, reliable sweater and find it riddled with moth holes. But there are preventive measures.

- *Store your clothes in cedar,* which can be an expensive process.
- *Store your clothes in camphor moth balls,* which can be an odiferous process.
- *Make pomander balls and hang them in the closet.* These old-fashioned closet sachets are cheap and easy to make, and their fragrance should keep for years.

  Completely cover the peel of an orange by sticking whole cloves into it. Mix ground cinnamon and orrisroot powder in a paper bag (a teaspoon of cinnamon and a tablespoon of orrisroot powder for a small orange; double for a larger orange). Put the orange in the bag and shake until it is covered with this fixative powder. Store in a dry place for about two weeks; it will shrink and emit a spicy fragrance. Remove it from the bag and hang it in the closet.

These make nice gifts as well. Store them in plastic so they'll keep. For variation you can also use apples, lemons, or limes.

- *Make herbal moth-repellant potpourris.* Potpourris are mixtures of spices and dried flower petals made into sweet-smelling sachets.

Mix any of the following herbs together: bay leaves, cedar leaves, pennyroyal, rosemary, sassafras, southernwood, wormwood. Add some orrisroot or calamus for preservation, and some cloves if you're so inclined. Sew the mixture into small bags and place among your woolens.

All of the herbs for pomander balls and potpourris are available at stores that sell herbs. Check the yellow pages under "Herbs."

SOURCES

Readers' Digest Complete Guide to Sewing. If you can get only one book to help you with home sewing, get this one. Well worth the price whether you're a novice or a master. W. W. Norton & Co., 500 Fifth Ave., New York, NY 10036. $18.95.

Complete Guide to Clothes Repair by Maureen Goldsworth. A thorough guide to making your clothes last longer. Good value, especially for those without a sewing background. Stein & Day Publishing Co., Scarborough House, Braircliff Manor, NY 10510. $5.95.

Finally It Fits—The No-Scare Home Patternmaking System for Everyone, Every Size by Ruth Amiel and Happy Gerhard. Provides complete instructions for making your own patterns—opens up new horizons in clothes designing. Times Books, Keystone Industrial Park, Scranton, PA 18512. $6.95.

Factory Outlet Shopping Guide by Jean Bird. This is available in six regional editions covering the Atlantic seaboard. Available from F.O.S.G. Publications, Box 239AF, Oradell, NJ 07649. $3.95.

"Tender Loving Care for Wool," a low-cost pamphlet from people who should know: The Wool Education Center, 200 Clayton Street, Denver CO 80206. 15¢.

Two pamphlets available from the U.S. Department of Agriculture, Washington, DC, 20250, for 95¢ each are:
"Buying Women's Coats and Suits" (Home and Garden Bulletin, No. 31);
"Men's Suits—How to Judge Quality" (Home and Garden Bulletin, No. 54).

⑥

TRAVEL

6

TRAVEL

These days, more and more dollars take you fewer and fewer miles. But traveling well for less requires not so much lowering your sights or standards as planning ahead, educating yourself about travel economy, and rethinking your approach to travel. Simple maneuvers like booking in advance, traveling in October rather than in August, staying in an old hotel rather than a new one, or finding a package deal that incorporates the things that are most important to you will enable you to save money without markedly cramping your style.

GENERAL TIPS

- *While you're away for a long weekend or a vacation, your house will cost you less if you take a few simple steps:*
  — Empty the refrigerator and turn it off.
  — Unplug electric clocks and instant-on TV sets.
  — Turn off the hot water heater.
  — If you have a gas stove, turn off the pilot lights. (Don't blow them out; that doesn't stop the flow of gas. Be sure to seal them.)
  — Lower the thermostat.
- *Before you take a trip, it's essential to plan it well enough to know what you're getting into.* Otherwise you can blow your budget and savings plan to smithereens when you have to pay credit card charges and other bills that arrive after you return. If you obtain the prices for all your accommodations, fares, fees, and so forth *before* you leave, you'll know just how much you'll be spending. Also, if you go ahead and make a booking, that price will be guaranteed, and you won't be affected by price hikes that go into effect between the time you make your reservations and the time you go. Besides, planning a trip is part of the fun.

- *Different modes of transportation provide different kinds of discounts.* For instance, Amtrak lets kids under the age of 5 ride free, while the airlines charge half fare for children from 2 through 12. So a family with youngsters under five can save substantially by taking the train. Alternatively, if the kids are students, try to capitalize on any special student fares, or on family fares, military standbys or whatever you can possibly qualify for.

- *If you have a student in the family, he or she can obtain discounts all over the world with an international student card.* It costs only $8.00; proof of student status is required. Write to the Council on International Educational Exchange, 205 East 42nd St., New York, NY 10017; telephone (212) 661-1414.

- *You can save hundreds of dollars by traveling to a place when others aren't there, and you can have more fun because they aren't.* Peak season rates can be three times as high as off-season rates. Ask when off-season rates go into effect and when they end: traveling during these "shoulder" seasons enables you to cut costs and still enjoy the weather, or whatever it is that has people flocking there during peak season. The time to stay away from the Caribbean is mid-December through mid-March; for Europe, it's June through September.

- *If you can't travel off-season, put on your thinking cap and try to come up with places that will be pleasant to visit and not jam-packed with tourists.* In other words, avoid Yellowstone. Try Saskatchewan, upper Michigan, or the open spaces of the Midwest.

- *There are still countries where the dollar has power—seek them out.* It was a favorable exchange rate that enabled expatriates like Hemingway and the Fitzgeralds to live like royalty abroad. When you're considering going to a particular country, ask people who've been there recently just how far their dollars went. And always remember, if you stay on the beaten path, it always costs more.

- *Some European countries offer special air fares and discounts on lodgings and sightseeing to induce you to visit.* Check with the national tourist office or an airline that serves the country. Most nations maintain a tourist office in New York City. You can also write to their embassies in Washington for the address of the tourist office.

- *If one family member has to go on a business trip or to a convention, he or she can take the rest of the family along.* This gives the family a vacation while saving money, since the company may pay for a large portion of the trip.

- *Instead of taking the family car on a vacation, look into combination packages that include a rented car (along with a hotel) on the other side.* They come in all shapes and sizes—fly/drive, rail/drive, bus/drive, etc. These can make a trip much easier and more pleasant.

- *An average of 200 parks are located within a 100-mile radius of most cities.* They can all be reached by bus, so save the gas and use public transportation to get there.

- *Travel with a purpose!* Visit a new place where you can shape up, learn a craft, or participate in a house-building program. Or if you're over 60, visit an Elderhostel (see page 208), where you can live on a college campus and take courses in whatever subject interests you.

- *Eating on vacations can deplete funds fast.* Have breakfast in your room or on the campground—cereal, milk, sweet rolls, or fruit. Carry along an immersion heater so that you can boil a cup of water for your morning tea or coffee. Have a picnic for lunch. Roadside lunches in a field beat the plastic plants, fake brick, and styrofoam beams of restaurants along the road. If you're abroad, hit the local marketplaces and feast there.

- *If you're squeamish about heading off for faraway places because you'll be leaving your family doctor behind, you can obtain a list of English-speaking doctors who practice where you're going.* Write to Medical Assistance for Travelers, 350 Fifth Ave., Suite 5620, New York, NY 10001. Be sure to tell them where, exactly, you'll be.

GETTING INFORMATION

Informed travelers get the best travel deals and are best able to fend for themselves in a crisis. But there are other reasons for doing your homework before a trip. Face it—you'll be on strange turf, and the more you know about local history, cuisine, or whatever, the more rewarding your trip will be.

- *For domestic travel, contact chambers of commerce, tourist information bureaus (write to the state capitol), visitors' and convention bureaus, and the U.S. National Park Service* (Department of the Interior, 18th and C Streets, Washington, DC 20240).

- *Airlines provide information on the places they serve.* (You can often dial airlines, travel agencies, and other companies toll-free.)

- *Your local library can be a treasure trove of information.* While you're there, don't forget back issues of travel magazines. These often contain advertisements (usually in the back) for inexpensive flights, hotels, etc. Take a bundle of postcards along so you can address them and send them off with inquiries.

- *Borrow a recent guidebook if you can.* Most guidebooks are adequate. Check with friends to see which they recommend (and can loan you). Also try reading a guide's account of a place you've visited and see if it's up to snuff. The Fodor volumes on East Asia and the Caribbean, for example, are inaccurate and generally inadequate. They're especially not recommended for the do-it-yourselfer. (See pages 216–220 for specific listings.)

- *Because positive word of mouth is the best recommendation, bar none, try to get information from friends or friends of friends.* If you can find no one to compare notes with, ask your travel agent (if you're using one) for the name of someone who did take the trip you're planning and call them up. They'll probably be delighted to rehash their experience. Make a list of questions to ask; this is one way to make an objective decision about any tour or package plan.

- *For those who do a lot of traveling, there's a newsletter that can keep you informed on bargains, virgin paradises, and, in general, the latest happenings in the field.* Write to Travel Smart, Communications House, 40 Beechdale Road, Dobbs Ferry, NY 10522.

- *Work with a travel agent.* If you're planning a trip, a savvy travel agent can be invaluable. Air fares are especially confusing, since they have been deregulated; besides, there are also special—and constantly changing—package deals that include accommodations, meals, transportation to and from the airport, and even theater tickets. (See Package Plans, next section.) Travel agents are experienced in all of this; it's their job to keep up with the latest that's available. And you don't pay their commissions. The airlines they book you on, the hotels you stay in, etc., pick up that tab. You just have to know enough to insure that you get a good deal.

- *Two organizations have specialized in travel for the handicapped for over a decade:* Flying Wheels Travel, Box 382, 143 West Bridge St., Owatonna, MN 55060, telephone toll free (800) 533-0363; and Wings on Wheels, 19505L 44th Ave. West, Lynnwood, WA 98036, telephone (206) 776-1184. A new arrival on the scene is Whole Person Tours, 137 W. 32nd St., Bayonne, NJ 07002, telephone (201) 858-3400. You might also write to the Society for the Advancement of Travel for the Handicapped, 26 Court St., Brooklyn, NY 11242, telephone (212) 858-5483, for the names and addresses of travel and tour operators in the United States and Europe that can accommodate the handicapped.

PACKAGE PLANS

A package can be either a good deal or a bad one.

- *The more that's included in a package, the more you save (and pay).* Weigh the components and take note of anything that doesn't quite suit you. Wouldn't you rather eat out than take all your meals in the hotel? Do you really want to go on a night club tour? And what about those tennis court privileges that you'll never use because you don't play? Similarly, packages can offer false economies. A reduced rate in a posh hotel will still cost you a lot more than a comfortable, less expensive establishment; and besides, if you're doing a lot of sight-seeing, you need the room only to sleep in.

- *Look into off-season package plans—they're your best buy.*

- *Many of the big hotel and motel chains offer package deals.* Some are tied in with air fares; others aren't. Big-city hotels offer weekend packages; resorts offer midweek packages. Contact these places yourself and get the lowdown. Call toll-free if you can.

- *There are also unescorted standard itinerary tours that can save you money.* Instead of being booked on a tour with a group, you do the tour yourself. There can be some pitfalls here, and there will be no tour director to complain to, so you'd better trust whoever sells you the tour.

- *Try to verify that you've booked through a reputable packager.* The Better Business Bureau can tell you (see page 460); better still is the word of someone you know who's taken a trip offered by the packager.

- *Making inquiries is essential.* Cover yourself so there will be few unpleasant surprises along the way.

  — Are any deposits required? Are they refundable? When?

  — What happens if the tour is canceled?

  — What type of hotel will you be staying in? If they say grade A, ask what rating system is used. Tops could be AAAA. And what are the facilities at the hotel and in your room?

  — What will you pay extra for, and what is included in the price? Baggage handling? Sight-seeing? Museum admissions? Tipping? Meals?

- *So away you fly, and that "oceanfront" hotel you're booked into actually faces a swamp or the airstrip you landed on. Protest immediately; otherwise it will be too late.* Complain to the tour director, show him or her a copy of the tour brochure (you should carry it with you), shoot a cable off to the tour company office (be sure to show a copy to the director beforehand—you might save the price of the cable). And recruit other members of the tour; group complaints are more effective.

- *If you can't get satisfaction right away and realize you'll have to complain after the fact, document your problem as best you can—even take pictures.* Write to the Civil Aeronautics Board, OCCCA, 1825 Connecticut Ave. NW, Washington, DC 20428, or to the American Society of Travel Agents, 4400 McArthur Blvd., Washington, DC 20007. And remember, there's always small claims court, in which you can seek settlement.

TRANSPORTATION

BY AIR

Air Fares: How to Get More for Less

The deregulation of air fares, which began a few years ago, has created prices at all altitudes.

- *Booking in advance almost always saves you money.* And that extra bit of planning enables you to save by flying at midweek or at night when rates are lower.

- *Both domestic and international carriers sporadically offer, at a flat rate, unlimited-use fares on the routes served by the carrier.* If your vacation can be properly timed—because there is almost always a time limitation— to take advantage of one of these, you're in luck. They're one of the best bargains around. One such fare, sponsored by Eastern, offered a 21-day unlimited mileage deal for a cost of $499.00 per person (if you traveled with someone) or $649.00 (if you went alone). Since Eastern flies everywhere from Mexico to Maine, this was quite a bargain.

- *If you're flying internationally, always inquire about APEX (Advance Purchase Excursion Fares).* You have to buy your ticket seven to 21 days before departure, and you have to stick more or less to your schedule, but it can be economical to do so.

- *Almost all airlines offer special fares.* When booking, always inquire about budget fares. There are usually others besides those for flying off-season, at night, or midweek.

- *Bear in mind that, because of the restrictions, the lowest fare isn't always the best if you want some flexibility.*

- *Investigate flying standby.* If you've got the time to gamble, you can save up to 50 percent over regular economy fares on international flights. Most planes don't take off completely full anyway, so there's a good chance you can fly with those who paid full fares.

- *There are "no frills" carriers, many of which were at one time charter carriers and now provide scheduled, low-priced service.* Examples are People, World, Capitol, and Trans International.

- *A free stopover en route to your destination can be a real bonus; these are often offered free of charge.* It's strictly up to you to inquire here. No one's going to offer you a free stopover.

- *Stopovers can often be obtained without extra charge if you get a tour-basing (IT) fare.* The tour-basing deal requires that you prepurchase a portion of your land arrangements—perhaps three nights in a hotel, or accommodations and tours worth $200.00; it varies. Besides a possible free stopover, tour-basing arrangements usually offer you hotel accommodations at reduced rates.

- *When booking, always make sure you get a direct flight.* Non-direct flights can sometimes cost 10 to 15 percent more. And remember, there's a difference between nonstop and direct. A direct flight can make umpteen stops.

- *When you're making travel arrangements and are informed that you'll have to stop over and change airlines to get where you're going, ask if the fare you're being quoted is a published joint fare.* If it's not, you're entitled to a $25.00 deduction per airline change-over. By way of explanation, say you're flying from New York to Oklahoma City, Okla., and the only way to get there is to fly Delta to Atlanta and change over to Eastern to continue on to Oklahoma City. There are two ways your fare could be calculated:

  — A joint fare—a special New York to Oklahoma City rate that is substantially less. You're better off with this one.

  — The straight charge: Delta's New York to Atlanta fare plus Eastern's Atlanta to Oklahoma City fare. In this case you're entitled to the $25.00 reduction. But it's up to you to ask for it. They won't offer it.

- *All airlines have "Promotional Fare Guide" booklets.* It's never a bad idea to study them before making airline reservations.

- *When dealing with travel agents or airline representatives, it's up to you to ferret out the cheapest fares.* If you don't ask whether a fare is a published joint fare you won't be offered a $25.00 reduction (see above); if you don't ask for a night flight you won't be offered a chance to save 20 percent; and so on. *Always emphasize your flexibility for the sake of getting a cheaper fare.* Remember that commissions on budget fares are low, so travel agents might not knock themselves out to get you a bargain.

But you can do it yourself. And you can probably do your homework toll-free.

- *Air fares are in such a muddle that even the airlines' employees can be totally confused about pricing.* So call as many carriers as you can. Employees have been known to give fares cheaper than the published rates. If and when they do, confirm it and have them mail you the tickets.

Other Tips on Air Travel

- *Some folks make getting bumped pay off.* They always fly during peak travel hours on heavily-trafficked routes and check in as late as possible (no less than 15 minutes before flight time) in the hope that they'll hit the jackpot, which is a free flight later, topped with a hefty cash settlement or, next best, a flight in first class for coach fare. When you're bumped, if the airline can get you to your destination within two hours (for domestic flights) or four hours (for international flights), they have to reimburse you only the cost of your ticket (up to $200.00 and fly you for free. If they cannot comply with the two- and four-hour time limits, they pay double the money (up to $400.00). Being bounced—if you're not in a big rush—can be like winning a game of roulette.

- *You have certain rights if your flight is delayed more than four hours or if you miss a connecting flight because of a delayed arrival.*

  — Most airlines will foot the bill for a telephone call or cable to family or friends on the other end.

  — You're entitled to a free hotel room if you're stranded overnight, along with taxi fare to and from the hotel.

  — You're usually provided with meal vouchers you can use in the airport restaurant.

- *If you request either a vegetarian or kosher meal when you book your flight, you might find that it's slightly better than standard airplane fare.* It's always worth a try.

- *If you have a young child or long legs, you can get more leg room as well as room to crawl in by sitting in the first row in the coach section (bulkhead seats, facing the dividing wall) or by sitting in seats next to the emergency exits.* Request these seats as far in advance as possible.

- *Flight insurance is the worst of deals.* Don't bother—you're twice as safe in a plane as you are riding a bicycle. If you've got a life insurance policy, that's plenty.

- *Airlines and almost all other travel companies give high priority to billing (same day) and low priority to crediting (up to two months).* If you pay for travel arrangements with a credit card and then have to cancel and rebook, have the airline apply the original charge to your new tickets; otherwise you'll very likely be charged interest on both the original and new charges.

● *Many people trying to save a buck with a charter flight have lost it.* But no longer. The Civil Aeronautics Board has enacted passenger-protection legislation governing charter flights. You can cancel a ticket within seven days if the charter organization doesn't live up to its side of the bargain and changes departure dates, hotel accommodations, price, or destinations. And new public charters that require no advance purchase or minimum group size and provide open-ended stays and discount prices have appeared recently. They're worth looking into.

Complaining to the Airlines

Most travel complaints are directed at airlines. Here are some hints about complaining.

● *You'll probably have to write a letter.* In it you should state:
— Your complaint in full
— The settlement you want
— The carrier, flight number, date, and the name(s) of airline employee(s) involved.
● *If you can't get satisfaction from the airline, you have a couple of alternatives.*
— Write to the Civil Aeronautics Board, OCCCA, 1825 Connecticut Ave. NW, Washington, DC 20428. They handle 20,000 to 30,000 complaints annually.
— Contact the Aviation Consumer Action Project, a non-profit organization that handles airline passengers' gripes. They also publish a booklet entitled "Facts and Advice for Airline Passengers" that has an informative "Constructive Complaining" chapter. Here's the address: P.O. Box 19029, Washington, DC 20036. Enclose one dollar for postage and handling.

DRIVING

Taking Your Own Car
● *The best way to vacation in the family car is to stay in one place, using your car only to get around once you've driven there.*
● *Make sure your car is running well before you take it on a trip.* An improperly maintained vehicle can leave you stranded, or, at the least, cost you more for the gas and oil it wastes.

- *When you get lost, ask for directions instead of driving all over the countryside unnecessarily wasting gas and driving yourself crazy.*

- *If you're traveling during a gas shortage, remember that most states have toll-free numbers you can call to get information about gas availability.* The American Automobile Association keeps tabs on gas supplies as well.

- *AAA members are eligible for travel counseling and can obtain information on everything from roads under construction and speed traps to motels, restaurants, and tourist attractions along the way.*

- *If you're motoring to Canada or to Mexico, check with your insurance agent to see whether you're covered while you're there.* For Canada you can get a Non-Resident Inter-Province Motor Vehicle Liability Insurance Card; in Mexico you may be limited to only a 48-hour stay if you make no provisions for insurance before leaving home.

- *Don't forget that you can get free road maps by writing to Exxon, Mobil, or Texaco.*

Note: The Auto-Train between Lorton, Va., and Sanford, Fla., used to be a viable alternative for traveling south. The car came along as a passenger on the train with you and the family. It declared bankruptcy, however, in 1981. It's been replaced with a company called Auto-Truck that provides service between the New York metropolitan area and California or Florida (and all points in between). To ship your car to Miami will cost you $429. The toll free number is (800) 223-4050; New York state residents call (212)354-7777.

Rentals and Drive-aways

- *The latest bargain in rental cars is "Rent-A-Wreck."* These agencies provide inexpensive relief from Hertz and Avis: the cars are dependable, though older, and the price is right. Look for one in your area. They're springing up everywhere.

- *Many of the established rental agencies offer package deals, unlimited mileage rates, and special offers.* They have toll-free numbers as well. The catch is the insurance, which they require you to get, unless your own insurance covers you behind the wheel of any car. Coverage usually extends to other cars only if your own car is in a repair shop; then your insurance may cover you in another, "substitute" vehicle.

  The insurance that rental agencies provide is costly. A prime example is found in the Miami–Fort Lauderdale area. Compact cars are advertised at, say, $69.00 a week, with unlimited mileage. You reserve your car (toll-free) and congratulate yourself. But when you arrive you realize that $69.00 does not include the requisite $6.00 per day for insurance (that's another $42.00), or, of course, the cost of gas.

- *When inquiring about cars, here's a checklist of things to ask about:*
  - — How much is the rental fee per day or week?
  - — How much is charged per mile?
  - — Is insurance required? If so, is a cheaper rate available for deductible coverage? (Also call your insurance agent to see how you might be covered. An inexpensive binder attached to your present policy could save you money.)

- *Car rental agencies at airports usually charge more than those located elsewhere.* If you've made no reservations for a car, don't panic. Upon arrival, get the Yellow Pages and start calling. You'll almost surely find something at a reasonable price, and the more economical rental agency will probably even send a van to the airport to collect you.

- *There are auto-transport and drive-away agencies in larger cities.* They'll give you someone else's car to deliver to your vacation destination. You're usually given an inadequate gas allowance and a time limit. You can save wear and tear on your own car and the money for gas and parking you might otherwise pay. Look in the Yellow Pages under "Automobile drive-away."

THE BUS: LEAVING THE DRIVING TO THEM

- *The bus is the cheapest way to travel, especially on unlimited travel passes offered by Greyhound and Trailways.* Prices change, but as this book goes to press, you can pick up a seven-day pass for $186.55, a 15-day pass for $239.85, and a 30-day pass for $346.45. Children under 12 travel half-fare and those under 5 ride free.

- *The bus companies also offer promotional fares to various cities.* Check them out as well.

- *Food in many bus stations is costly and unsatisfactory.* We recommend bringing your own: make trips to local supermarkets; have picnics on the bus, if the carrier allows it.

- *There are special motor coach tours in Canada and the United States that can provide a relaxing vacation while you cover a lot of ground.* Travel agents usually have information on these, or you can contact Greyhound and Trailways in care of the New York Port Authority Bus Terminal, Eighth Ave. and 41st St., New York, NY 10014. Also Grace J. Talmage Associates publishes a quarterly *Domestic Tour Manual* that gives the complete motor coach story. The cost is $5 an issue; wrtie to P.O. Box 39, Abington, PA 19001.

- *There's a cheap bus network in Europe called Magic Bus, which provides discount bus and train service among many European cities.* The clientele is said to include a nice mix of nationalities and ages, and the price is right. For ticket information, contact Magic Bus, 15600 Roscoe Blvd., Van Nuys, CA 91406.

THE TRAIN

- *Phone Amtrak toll-free at (800) 523-5720 to find out what special rates are available.* Their family plan enables one adult (usually head of household) to pay full fare and the rest of the family to get the following discounts: spouse and children between the ages of 12 and 21, 50 percent; children between 2 and 11, 75 percent; children under two ride free. There are no restrictions on these tickets. Amtrak also offers an assortment of package tours in the United States and Canada—everything from white-water rafting to a trip to the San Diego Zoo. (In Canada, write to Via Rail Canada, P.O. Box 8116, 1801 McGill College, Montreal, Quebec, Canada H3C 3N3.)

- *Before you leave for Europe, pick up a Eurailpass.* You can't buy them abroad. These passes cost anywhere from $210.00 to $530.00, they're good for anywhere from 15 to 90 days in 16 countries, and they entitle you to unlimited first-class rail travel. Europe, unlike the United States, has an extremely efficient, well-maintained, and comfortable rail system. For more information, write Trains, Box M, Staten Island, NY 10305.

- *If you travel by rail in Europe, one way to save on hotels is to travel at night and sleep on the train.* The trains are comfortable, so you'll sleep well.

BY SEA

This is not the cheapest way to go, but it is certainly one of the most pleasant and exciting. It's really a pity that the days of leisurely, inexpensive sea travel are almost over.

- *There are air/sea packages available—you fly one way, go by ship the other.* Cunard/BA offer one of these, if you're heading to England and would like to sail on the QE2. There are others; check with your travel agent.

- *Freighters are an especially delightful way to travel.* They can cost half of what a cruise ship might. You also get more of shipboard life, eating your meals in the officers' mess and having the run of the ship. Freighters carry fewer than a dozen passengers (because a ship's doctor is required if there are more than a dozen).

  There are several travel agencies that specialize in freighter travel.

Air and Marine Travel Service
501 Madison Ave.
New York, NY 10022
(For $2.00 they'll send you their semiannual four-page "Trip Log Quick Reference Freighter Guide.")

Freighter Cruise Service
5925 Monkland Ave., Suite 103
Montreal, Quebec H4A 1G7, Canada

Freighter World Cruises
180 South Lake, #335F
Pasadena, CA 91101

McLean-Kennedy
410 St. Nicholas St.
Montreal, Quebec, Canada

Maggie Horn
601 California St.
San Francisco, CA 94108

Pearl's Freighter Tips
175 Great Neck Road, Suite 306F
Great Neck, NY 11021

Taylor Travel Service
3959 Main St.
Buffalo, NY 14226

TravLtips Freighter Travel
163-07 Depot Road
Flushing, NY 11358
(For a membership fee of $15.00 you can subscribe to their newsletter and use their reservation department.)

BICYCLING

Bicycling vacations, while not always recommended for the entire family, can be rewarding, healthful, relaxed, and inexpensive experiences. And by the end of this decade, the Bureau of Outdoor Recreation (U.S. Department of Interior) has estimated, there will be over 200,000 miles of bike routes in the United States.

- *Domestic airlines charge only $20.00 to check your bicycle as a piece of baggage. And the bike can be checked in lieu of one bag on trains and buses and on international flights.* Get the facts straight with the carrier before you travel. They will usually furnish you with a packing container.

- *Bikecentennial is a nonprofit, membership-supported organization for American and Canadian tourists.* It furnishes books, trip planning, maps, group tours, and other services to members. For information, write Bikecentennial, P.O. Box 8308, Missoula, MT 59807. (Also see page 218.)

- *More information can be obtained from:* American Wheelmen, Box 988, Baltimore, MD 21203; International Bicycle Touring Society, 2115 Paseo Dorado, La Jolla, CA 92037; and Highroad to Adventure, American Youth Hostels, Delaplane, VA 22025.

ACCOMMODATIONS

In the United States you can travel from coast to coast and seem to stay in the same hotel room every night. And the costs can be exorbitant. There are money-saving, comfortable, and fascinating alternatives to the Holiday Inns and Ramada Inns spread across the country.

SOME PRACTICAL SUGGESTIONS

- *Older hotels have much more character than new ones, and they're usually cheaper.* And always remember that a room in a hotel across the street from the beach is going to cost you less than one with a view of the beach. The same goes for hotels at ski resorts and lakes, and for any centrally located accommodations. A slight inconvenience can save you lots of money.

- *Always keep an eye out for "children free" signs at hotels and motels.* Hotels that let children stay in a room with the parents at no extra charge, often providing roll-away beds, can save you a lot. Pack sleeping bags in case the kids have to bed down on the floor.

- *If you're staying in a motel or hotel in an urban area, make sure they—not you—will pay for parking your car.* This is an expense you shouldn't have to shoulder.

- *You risk being charged if you're not out by check-out time.* If you want to stay later, ask at the desk for permission to do so. It's usually granted if the hotel is not heavily booked.

- *Some hotels (usually the more expensive ones) will let you make a special reservation that will guarantee your reservation for a late arrival.* If the room is not available when you arrive, the participating hotel must provide you with free transportation to a comparable hotel and free lodging for the night. You can also avoid being billed for a guaranteed room you can't use if you call the hotel to cancel before 6:00 p.m. their time, 4:00 p.m. in resort areas. Make a note of the cancellation number you are given.

MOTELS

Small, privately-owned "mom and pop" motels can be a real treat. Good food usually accompanies clean accommodations. Otherwise, if you're stuck on the highway and need reasonably priced accommodations, motel chains such as Family Inn, Econo-Travel Lodge, Days Inn, Budget Host, Motel 6, Red Roof Inn, Knight's Inn, and Regal 8 offer rooms for substantially less and furnish more or less the same amenities as the bigger chains.

GUEST HOUSES

Guest houses, or tourist homes, are usually large older houses whose owners rent out rooms. They are often centrally located, and they can be lovely old residences that are a treat to stay in. These places offer a personal touch: often the proprietors will find you a babysitter, give you reliable information about the area you're visiting, and so on. Many guest houses will accept visitors only through bed-and-breakfast referral agencies. Although these are only a couple of years old in the United States, they've been around a lot longer in Europe (see page 210). They will send you brochures about lodgings, confirm your reservations, and make attempts to insure that your needs are met (you can specify if you want air conditioning, privacy, etc.).

Here's a listing of bed-and-breakfast booking agencies:

Bed & Breakfast Atlanta
1221 Fairview Road NE
Atlanta, GA 30306
(404) 378-6026
Lodgings in and around Atlanta.

Bed & Breakfast International
151 Ardmore Road
Kensington, CA 94707
(415) 525-4569
Lodgings in California and Washington.

Bed & Breakfast League
2855 29th St. NW
Washington, DC 20008
(202) 232-8718
Lodgings in 19 large cities in the United States. Annual membership fee: $45 single, $55 family.

Digs West
8191 Crowley Circle
Buena Park, Ca 90621
(714) 739-1669
Lodgings near Disneyland.

Florida Suncoast Bed & Breakfast
P.O. Box 12
Palm Harbor, FL 33563
(813) 784-5118
Lodgings in and around St. Petersburg.

Guest Houses Reservation Service
P.O. Box 5737
Charlottesville, VA 22903
(804) 979-7264
Lodgings in and around Charlottesville.

International Spareroom
Box 518
Solana Beach, CA 92075
(714) 755-3194
Lodgings in 32 states.

Northwest Bed & Breakfast
7707 SW Locust St.
Tigard, OR 97223
(503) 246-8366
Lodgings in locations from Los Angeles to British Columbia. Annual membership fee: $15 single, $20 family.

Pineapple Hospitality
384 Rodney French Blvd.
New Bedford, MA
(617) 997-9952
Lodgings in Southeastern Massachusetts.

Rent a Room
1032 Sea Lane
Corona del Mar, CA 92625
(714) 640-2330
Lodgings in Southern California.

Urban Ventures
322 Central Park West
New York, NY 10025
(212) 662-1234
Lodgings in Brooklyn, Manhattan, and Queens.

An interesting cooperative guest house system that has sprung up on the American scene is offered in *The Traveler's Directory*. For $15.00 you get a listing that can land you up to 700 prospective house guests, who can also put you up in their homes when and if you ever pass their way. There are also members abroad.

For more information write to The Traveler's Directory, 6224 Baynton St., Philadelphia, PA 19144.

HOUSE SWAPPING

Swapping homes is a super, economical way to get to know another place well. You can vacation in new and exciting accommodations—from rustic to elegant—here or abroad. There are even farm–city exchanges (for instance, 120 families so far are participating in the Illinois Farm Bureau Exchange). The rural hosts get a taste of city life, and the city folk take care of the farm—feed the livestock, ride horses, and get a taste of the country. It's an excellent opportunity for the kids.

Some Advantages of House Swapping

- There's no hotel tab. Your listing in a house-swapping directory will run from $15.00 to $50.00.
- You can get valuable, money-saving information about what to do, where to go, where to shop, etc., from the people with whom you're swapping and their friends and neighbors.
- You can save money by cooking in or eating out at reasonably priced, recommended restaurants.
- Often a car is included in the exchange.
- There are no worries about your vacant house being burglarized or your pets and plants not being tended while you're out of town.

Disadvantages? Well, a swap may take upwards of four months to arrange, so plan early.

House Swapping Services

The *International Home Exchange Journal* is published four times a year and contains some 400 listings. For $25.00 a year you receive the *Journal* and get your home registered. Write to International Home Exchange Service, P.O. Box 3975, San Francisco, CA 94119.

Other organizations include the following:

Adventures-in-Living
Box 278
Winnetka, IL 60093

Holiday Exchanges
Box 878
Belen, NM 87002

Inquiline, Inc.
35 Adams St.
Bedford Hills, NY 10507
Registration is $50.00 and includes a photo of your home. For another $100.00, Inquiline will make all the arrangements for you.

Interchange Home Exchange
888 Seventh Ave.
New York, NY 10019
Registration is $12.00, photo included. They'll make arrangements for you for $110.00.

Vacation Exchange Club
350 Broadway
New York, NY 10013
For $18.00 you get registered; a photo of your home will cost another $6.00. An unlisted subscription costs $12.00.

ACCOMMODATIONS ON COLLEGE CAMPUSES

Many universities open their dormitories to paying guests during the summer. The cost is a reasonable $5.00 to $9.00 a night, and you can usually use the recreational and dining facilities on the campus. For more information, contact the following organizations:

For colleges in the United States:
CMG Publishing Co.
P.O. Box 630
Princeton, NJ 08540

For colleges in Canada:
Canadian Bureau for International Education
141 Laurier West
Ottawa, Ontario, Canada K1P 5J3

For colleges in England:
University Holidays
AAD Associates
Box 3927
Amity Station
New Haven, CN 06525

HOSTELS

Hostels may be a bit Spartan, but the money you save in these cheap, clean accommodations can be spent seeing the sights and enjoying yourself. There are hostels for all age groups in many parts of the world. Membership in the American Youth Hostels organization, for example, lets you stay in more than 200 hostels in this country, and in a formidable 5,000 more in 50 countries around the world. (YM/YWCA's, church groups, and other organizations also sponsor hostels.) Accommodations vary from place to place, naturally; but for the most part, they are usually sex-segregated with communal bathrooms, kitchens, and other public rooms.

Hostels can come in quite handy. You can check into one and then use it as a base while you get to know the city and scout around for an inexpensive hotel. If your trip is not a long one, hostels work well because they simply give you a place to lay your head at night—all you need when you're doing a lot of exploring.

For more information:

American Youth Hostels, Inc.
National Administrative Offices
1332 Eye St. NW, Eighth Floor
Washington, DC 20005

Canadian Hostelling Association
333 River Road
Vanier City, Ottawa, Ontario, Canada K1L 8B9

ELDERHOSTELS

A new arrival on the hostel scene is the Elderhostel movement, a national program for those over 60. It combines education and hosteling. Over 200 colleges in 30 states offer low-cost residential academic programs during the summer, typically lasting a week. Hostelers don't have to have any previous formal education, just an interest. The courses they take are usually not for credit, but curricula vary from campus to campus. One thing is certain— this is an excellent way to take a vacation. And there is always a good selection of courses, often supplemented by field trips and required reading as well.

For more information, write to Elderhostel, 55 Chapel St., Newton, MA 02160, or to AARP (American Association of Retired Persons, see page 90).

TENTING TONIGHT

You can buy a tent at any price and sleep cheaply under the stars. About the cheapest campgrounds are our national parks. Campers pay from $.50 per person to $3.00 a carload. If you're going to be visiting a lot of these parks, you can even lower that cost by buying a $10.00 Golden Eagle Passport. The "Passport" is good for a full year and entitles you, your family, and your car to enter recreation areas, monuments, and parks run by the Federal Government without the normal admission charge. For information, write to:

National Park Service Headquarters
U.S. Department of the Interior
Room 1013
18th and C Streets NW
Washington, D.C. 20240

You can also order informative brochures from the U.S. Superintendent of Documents, Washington, DC 20402. Titles include *Camping in the National Park System*, *Fishing in the National Park System*, and *Boating in the National Park System*.
Other sources of information on camping include the following:

- *The Sierra Club sponsors outings, many of them family-oriented.* They publish an annual booklet describing their trips. Write to 530 Bush Street, San Francisco, CA 94108. You might also request a listing of some of their other publications, which make excellent gifts and would be of interest to any one interested in the outdoors.

- *Another wildlife conservation society is the Wilderness Society.* It operates trips of all sorts. Get information by writing to the Wilderness Society, Western Regional Office, 4260 Evans Ave., Denver, CO 80222.

- *The American Automobile Association publishes* AAA Camping, RV *(Recreational Vehicle)* and Tent Sites, *in 11 volumes covering the United States and Canada.* It is free to AAA members.

- *An organization that adds convenience to any camping vacation is Camper 800,* a reservation agency that charts trips and makes reservations for you in some 2,000 privately owned campgrounds in the 50 states. Tourist packages, including tickets to tourist attractions or to special exhibitions, are available. Phone toll-free, (800) 828-9280; in New York State, (800) 462-9220 between noon and 10:00 p.m. seven days a week.

If you don't feel like buying a tent, you can rent one at over 200 campgrounds in the United States and Canada. Kampgrounds of America (Box 30558, Billings, MT 59114) is the biggest tent renter. Also, some states, such as Arkansas and Ohio, rent campsites complete with tents. Check with the National Park Service about their facilities.

ACCOMMODATIONS IN EUROPE

One way to get real insight into a country is to stay in small local hotels or guest houses. Most Hilton and Intercontinental hotels look rather alike; quaint, charming, and regionally authentic they're not. Expensive they are!

- *The British have had the bed-and-breakfast setup for decades, and you can pay from $12.00 to $15.00 a night.* The British Tourist Authority has a Family Holidays plan that can place you in an English country house for less than $100.00 a week. Make inquiries about bed-and-breakfast and family holidays plans through the British Tourist Authority, 40 W. 57th St., New York, NY 10019. The British Automobile Association (AA Britain) publishes *Guide to Guesthouses, Farm Houses, and Inns*, which is available in many bookstores for $6.95.

- *France is another country with lots of tourist homes.* You can be a house guest for $35.00 to $40.00 a night for two, with breakfast. Write Chez des Amis, 139 West 87th St., New York, NY 10024. They've also got information on vacation stays with French and British families.

- *Most national tourist offices have complete hotel listings and prices; if you've not reserved a room, check in at the local tourist office upon arrival and they'll help you find accommodations.* There's always an office at the airport or the train station. For other listings, check the *Official Hotel and Resort Guide* as well as hotel and travel indexes in your local library, or try the AAA European Accommodation Directory, available from the American Automobile Association.

- *If you arrive early enough in the day, it's not disastrous to be without accommodations.* In fact, it can be the opposite. Check your luggage at the train station and, assuming you've studied up on the city itself, take local transportation to the area you'd like to stay in. Take a leisurely walk around and check out various hotels. Proprietors will always show you rooms, so try to get one that's just right, one with a nice view, comfortable beds, a reasonable price, etc. This shopping around can kill part of a day, but it is informative and enjoyable, and will land you accommodations that will enhance your stay.

MONEY

LOCAL CURRENCY

Here's how most Americans spend money abroad. Let's say a tourist is visiting Egypt, where there are 100 piasters per Egyptian pound. A piaster is worth 1.8 cents; a pound is $1.80. So when the tourist wants his photo taken atop a camel in front of a pyramid and an Egyptian camel driver asks for anywhere from seven to 10 pounds, the tourist forks over what's requested. The prime factor here, often not considered, is that the average daily wage of an Egyptian worker is 25 piasters, or $.45 American. So the seven to 10 pounds the camel driver wants is 20 to 40 times the average Egyptian's daily earnings. The camel driver knows a sucker when he sees one. He is making more in a day than his brother earned last month.

When you arrive in any other country, don't spend dollars; spend the local currency. You can do a mental conversion to dollars, but think local: How much would the local people be paying for the same service, and why should you pay 20 times as much?

And always bargain, although nowadays you have to work harder because so many tourists before you have spoiled so many places. Often when you try to bargain, local vendors won't even bother because they know they can get the price they want from somebody else. Another bargaining problem is this: a vendor asks eight pounds for a basket. You bargain, get it for five, and walk off congratulating yourself. The vendor is self-congratulatory as well: the basket cost him only five piasters; you paid many times too much for it. *When you bargain, don't halve the price—slash it, and start there.*

You can tell from the moment you arrive in a foreign country just how much of a rush you're going to get; it's almost directly proportional to the onslaught you get when you walk out of the air terminal and start looking for transportation into town. If you're traveling alone, the foolproof way to get from airport to hotel without getting fleeced is to drop by the tourist desk and ask how much a taxi should charge to go to your hotel and how much you should tip. Then convert a few dollars at an exchange booth, breeze out of the terminal, get a taxi, and establish *that* price before you pull away. If the driver won't come around, there's always another taxi.

Whether it is a Caribbean island or China, most tourists are totally insensitive to the local economy. They quickly do rough conversions to U.S. dollars, comparing prices to what they would pay back home, and reach for their wallets. And then they wonder why the general opinion of American tourists is low. Those people living in poor countries resent your bucks; no swindler respects the person he's swindling. Tourists also wonder why trips cost them so much. There are actually places in the world where tourists can spend less per day than they do at home, but very few bother to manage it.

TRAVELER'S CHECKS

Traveler's checks are the safe way to play. Their most important advantage is that if you lose them they're replaceable. But even though American Express claims it replaces tens of millions of dollars in checks for tourists every year, the traveler's check business has been a boon to the companies that distribute them for three reasons:

1) They invest your money to make more money.

2) For letting them use your money, they charge you one percent of the face value of the checks.

3) When you cash them in, you may be charged again, either with a service fee or with a lower-than-normal exchange rate.

The traveler's check business is worth $35 billion annually, and is growing by 12 to 15 percent annually. That's a lot of "float" for generating large profits.

- *There are, however, some companies that will provide you with free traveler's checks.* Barclays Bank (in conjunction with Visa) is one, and since it is worldwide, Barclay/Visa checks are every bit as convenient as American Express. And Thomas Cook checks are usually provided free to members of clubs affiliated with the American Automobile Association. Some banks in this country provide free traveler's checks as a personal service to their clients, so that's an alternative you should also investigate.

- *Before you go abroad, it can be a good idea to buy traveler's checks in the currency of the country you're visiting.* You'll be protecting yourself if the dollar's value drops between the time you purchase the checks and the time you spend them. On the other hand, if the dollar's value increases after you buy the checks, you're locked into a less favorable exchange when you're ready to spend. Another drawback is that you might not be getting the best exchange rate when you buy in this country (although if you live in a large city and can buy checks from a branch of the country's national bank, you can obtain checks at the worldwide rate of exchange). Check the trends, then decide whether to exchange your dollars now or later.

- *It's always a good idea to find out which banks have branches where you're going and what kinds of deals they can give.* Companies like Thomas Cook and American Express have offices only in the larger cities, but a national bank has branches everywhere, and its checks are recognized everywhere as well.

- *Take along some cash as well.* By keeping a limited supply of small bills, you'll be able to leave a country without taking any of its currency with you. If you want to buy a souvenir or a beer at the last minute, exchange a couple of dollars instead of cashing a $20.00 traveler's check. Remember, if you leave a country and take its currency with you, you will take a beating when you try to cash it in at home.

- *About losing your checks:* American Express launched a multi-million-dollar advertising campaign based on their efficiency in replacing lost traveler's checks; they are, in fact, pretty reliable, even though they've been ripped off for millions by those who have claimed to have lost their checks and been reimbursed, thereby doubling their money. Still, no matter how easy a traveler's check company makes it for you to replace stolen or lost checks, remember that if they don't have an office for you to dash to, you're probably going to have to spend money on expensive cables or telegrams to get new checks. Do this only if you've been cleaned out. Otherwise, go personally to the company's offices when you get to a city where one is located. The lesson here? *Keep traveler's checks in different places and keep a record of the numbers separate.* Another reason to keep close track of the numbers of your traveler's checks is that today many savvy burglars snitch only a few checks instead of an entire booklet, banking on your poor bookkeeping to enable them to get away with the theft.

BAGGAGE

- *Soft luggage saves you energy, since it's easy to carry, and money, since it's cheaper than traditional luggage and less likely to tip the baggage scales into the overweight category.* Another advantage is that there's almost always room to stuff in an extra item.

- *You're in for a hard time if your luggage gets lost.* To be on the safe side, here are a few precautions:
  - Put name tags and labels both outside and in, complete with your address and phone number.
  - As you pack, make a list of everything that's going with you. This can come in handy two ways: (1) If your luggage is lost, it can help you in filling an insurance claim (so you should carry the list with you, not in the suitcase); and (2) it can be used as a reference when you're packing up for your next vacation. Make adjustments if you took too much or too little. It makes packing a breeze.

- *A note about filing for lost luggage: Airlines require proof of value of all items inside the lost suitcase.* Some cautious travelers go so far as to take a picture of their packed, open suitcase before they depart. If you want to go one safe step farther, simply buy excess-baggage insurance at the airline counter when you check in. You can purchase it for as little as $.10 per $100.00 of coverage. Actually, this is like taking an umbrella with you in the morning to make sure it won't rain. Losing your baggage happens when you least expect it, and rarely when you're insured. So maybe coverage *is* worth it.

- *Some facts about what you can expect from the airlines if they misplace your luggage:*
  - The airline's liability is $750.00 tops. Reimbursement can take months, and it's at a depreciated rather than a replacement rate.
  - Airlines are obligated to pay any emergency expenses (for medications, etc.), necessary rentals (sports equipment rentals included—save your receipts), and the cost of replacing toiletries.
  - They'll usually foot the bill for half the cost of replacing clothing. If you demand more, they may pay, but if they find your baggage they often insist that the clothing be turned over to them.
  - It's up to the airline to pay the cost of delivering lost luggage to your hotel or home.
  - Abroad, the amount of your reimbursement can be negotiable. Always tell the flight representatives that the amount they offer isn't enough and see if they'll improve the offer. If they tell you that the amount they're offering you is the airline's maximum offer, it very well might be. But if you feel you didn't get enough, write to the airline when you get home. It's anxious to keep you as a customer and might come through with more.
  - The recovery rate of lost baggage is 98 percent.

CUSTOMS

Getting caught cheating is no fun. Here are some of the rules:

- No duty is assessed on merchandise worth up to $300.00.
- For merchandise worth over $300.00, you pay a 12 to 22 percent tax—which may still make your purchases worthwhile.
- Those 21 or older are allowed a quart of liquor and a carton of cigarettes duty free.
- The penalty for not declaring goods can be up to six times the normal duty.
- You can ship an unlimited number of gift packages worth no more than $10.00 in value, but the same person cannot receive more than one a day.
- There is no duty at all on stamps, coins, books, oil paintings, or antiques that are more than 100 years old.

- Cars are charged 3 percent of their dutiable value.
- You can't bring in food of any kind.

Customs agents usually slap heavy fines on those they feel are intentionally trying to cheat them. So even though ignorance is no excuse for wrongdoing, plead it. And if you do get caught and the inspector asks, "Is there more?" 'fess up. They'll undoubtedly press on with their search if you say no, and then you're really in for it.

For more information on customs rules and regulations, there are four pamphlets published by the U.S. Customs Service (P.O. Box 7118, Washington, D.C. 20044) that can keep you out of trouble and enable you to bring in as much as is legally possible: *U.S. Customs Trademark Information, Know Before You Go, Customs Hints for Returning U.S. Residents,* and *Importing a Car.*

THINGS TO WATCH OUT FOR

- *Be cautious if you're offered special coupons or vacations certificates for air fares, hotels, car rentals, etc.* They can actually cost you three to four times their actual value, because the distributors are not authorized representatives.

- *Major airlines—including Pan Am and TWA—have been taken to court by the Civil Aeronautics Board for the following shenanigans:*
  — They have sold prospective passengers special fares, only to switch them to full coach fare at the airport and put them aboard a half-empty plane.
  — To compete with charter and "no frills" airlines, major carriers have advertised low fares. The only catch is that these fares have so many loopholes and restrictions that it's almost impossible to fly as cheaply as the advertisement would have you believe. You'll have to fly night coach, book months in advance, not change your flight or pay a penalty fee if you do, and so on.

- *Remember, "All that glitters is not gold."* For that free pool you can use, there's a charge for towels and a chair; or the free meals are served between 2:00 a.m. and 5:00 a.m. (as in some Las Vegas hotel packages); or you are given lowest priority in using the "free" golf course and tennis courts.

- *When you give money to a fly-by-night "go-between" agency or representative, you risk having them take a vacation on your hard-earned money.* If you're not sure you're dealing with a reputable agency, call the hotel they're booking you into to see whether you have a reservation, and do the same with the airline you're scheduled to fly. A phone call to the Better Business Bureau, the Office of Consumer Affairs, or the attorney general's office in the state you plan to visit can tell you if there have been any complaints against the outfit you're dealing with. Also ask if it's licensed or bonded.

• *Fine print can be a bore and an eyestrain, but reading it beats what can happen to you if you don't read it.* Charter flights and package tours provide shysters with a multitude of opportunities not to deliver what is promised, and the fine print they don't expect you to read helps them do it.

• *Special clubs or travel associations can also be shams, even when they claim that major hotel and motel chains are participating.* For starters, most major hotel and motel chains never make deals with travel clubs or associations. Check it out!

• *Never, never buy a cut-rate plane ticket abroad from anyone but a reputable agent.*

• *Carry credit cards and traveler's checks, and watch it when people offer you higher-than-normal exchange rates.* There are thriving black markets where you get a higher exchange rate, but many an unsuspecting tourist is also given counterfeit money. (Also, many are not; but always remember that you're violating the law every time you get a higher black-market exchange rate, even though money will go farther.)

• *Advertising pays off—but not for you.* If you flash large amounts of cash, dress to the nines, or wear expensive jewelry, you're asking for it. Thieves, pickpockets, purse snatchers, and swindlers—and they come in all shapes and sizes—support themselves royally on the booty they steal from innocents abroad.

• *If you can, keep your hotel room key with you.* When you leave it at the desk, it signifies that you're not there, and it could be picked up by someone other than you. Nicer hotels have safe deposit or security boxes. Leave your valuables in them. Also, after your room has been made up, put the "Do Not Disturb" sign on the door outside.

• *Limit your shopping at airports.* Here the markups are always higher, except on liquor and tobacco. Do your gift and souvenir shopping in town where you can bargain.

SOURCES

GUIDEBOOKS

Arthur Frommer publishes a wide range of guidebooks: the "Dollar-a-Day" guides (Europe is now $15.00 a day; the original best seller was $5.00), the

Dollarwise Guides (which cover accommodations and facilities from budget to deluxe, with emphasis on the medium-priced), and the more compact, pocket-size *Arthur Frommer Guides*. Be careful if you're using these guides: so many people buy them that sometimes when an establishment gets a recommendation from Frommer, its proprietors raise prices and clean up. It's also more fun to hit out-of-the-way places instead of those where the clientele are all Americans with a Frommer guide sitting on the table beside them. However, there are exceptions. If all Frommer guides were as well-written and as comprehensive as Nancy McGrath's *Dollarwise Guide to Egypt*, we'd recommend no other series. Because each Frommer guide is individually authored, some are better than others. All are available for anywhere from $1.95 to $4.50 from the Frommer/Pasmantier Publishing Corp., 380 Madison Ave., New York, NY 10017.

Temple Fielding's travel guides make for entertaining reading, whether you're going or not. They're not recommended for the shoestring traveler, but are quite informative nonetheless. If you buy *Fielding's Favorite* travel book, you get an extra service: a toll-free number you can call seven days a week for up-to-date information on such matters as exchange rates, recent changes in prices, weather predictions, political warnings, availability of gasoline, and more. *Fielding's Europe* is $11.95; *Fielding's Low-Cost Europe*, $5.95. All are available from Fielding Publications/William Morrow & Co., 105 Madison Ave., New York, NY 10016.

BOOKS ABOUT TRAVEL

The Art and Adventure of Traveling Cheaply by Rick Berg. While enjoyable to read, it may not be just right for family travel. But it is a must for the shoestring traveler abroad. This books goes into the nitty gritty—how to deal with border troubles and black markets; how single women should handle the unwelcome attentions of foreign men; how to earn quick money, get information from local hustlers, and much more. And/Or Press, P.O. Box 2246, Berkeley, CA 94710. $4.95 postpaid.

The Travel Catalog by Karen Cure. A compendium of hundreds of things to do and see while you're traveling. Addresses and travel information are included as well. It's entertaining just to read about all the vacation attractions that are available to you—everything from the greatest roller coasters and toy collections to the most beautiful scenic drives and nude beaches. Holt, Rinehart and Winston, 383 Madison Ave., New York, NY 10017. $6.95 postpaid.

Your Trip Abroad. Provides information about obtaining passports and visas and protecting yourself while you travel abroad. Request item #167H. The Consumer Information Center, Dept. 44, Pueblo, CO 81009. $1.75.

TRANSPORTATION

Flying

How to Fly for Less: Consumer's Guide to Low Cost Air Charters and Other Travel Bargains, edited by Jens Jurgen. Because it's updated annually, it stays relatively current, and at $5, it can easily pay for itself. Travel Information Bureau, 44 County Line Road, Farmingdale, NY 11735. $5.00

   Superflier: The Air Traveler's Handbook by Laura Torbet and Kalia Lulow is an exceptional and complete consumer's guide to air travel, including your rights as a consumer. Available from Playboy Press, 747 Third Ave., New York, NY 10017. $2.50.

By Train

How to Camp Europe by Train by Lenore Baken. Using a Eurailpass to travel from campground to campground can make a family vacation in Europe a reality. This books tells you how to plan it from scratch and then how to eat cheaply and well and get around efficiently and economically once you're there. Ariel Publications, P.O. Box 255, Mercer Island, WA 98040. $6.95.

By Sea

Tramp Steamers: A Budget Guide to Ocean Travel by Meme Black. For the *complete* story on the joys of freighter travel and how to go about it, this is the source. Addison-Wesley Publishing Company, Reading, MA 01867. $6.95.

By Bike

AYH North American Bike Atlas describes the countless trips you can take in this continent, including the Caribbean. American Youth Hostels, Inc., AYH National Campus, Delaplane, VA 22025. $2.45.

The Bicycle Touring Book: The Complete Guide to Bicycle Recreation by Tim Wilhelm and Glenda Wilhelm. Rodale Books, 33 East Minor, Emmaus, PA 18049. $9.95 postpaid.

Bike Touring: The Sierra Club Guide to Outings on Wheels by Raymond Bridge. Sierra Club Books, Box 3886, Rincon Annex, San Francisco, CA 94119. $6.95 postpaid.

The Cyclist's Yellow Pages: A Complete Resource Guide to Maps, Books, Routes, Organizations and Group Tours. Bikecentennial, P.O. Box 8308, Missoula, MT 59807. Membership is $15.00 a year, and you get the Yellow Pages and a publication list free along with it.

ACCOMMODATIONS

Motels

America on $8 to $16 a Night: 4,000 Dining and Lodging Discoveries. Travel Discoveries, 10 Fenway North, Milford, CT 16460. $5.95 postpaid.

National Directory of Budget Motels: A Nation-Wide Guide to Low-Cost Chain Motel Accommodations, edited by Raymond Carlson. An annually revised directory of chain motels in the United States that cost $12.00 to $17.00 a night for a single. Pilot Books, 347 Fifth Ave., New York, NY 10016. $3.50 postpaid.

Where to Stay, USA. The Council on International Educational Exchange, Books Dept., 205 East 42nd St., New York, NY 10017. $4.95, plus $.50 handling.

Guest Houses

Guide to Guest Homes and Tourist Homes USA. Tourist House Associates of America, RD 2, Box 355A, Greentown, PA 18426. $4.95.

National Guide to Guest Homes compiled by Maxine R. Coplin. Covers 16 states. Home on Arrange, 220 Redwood Highway No. 113, Mill Valley, CA 94941. $4.95, plus $.84 handling.

The New England Guest House Book by Corinne Madden Ross. East Woods Press, 820 East Blvd., Charlotte, NC 28203. $6.95, plus $1.30 handling.

The Southern Guest House Book by Corinne Madden Ross. East Woods Press, 820 East Blvd., Charlotte, NC 28203. $6.95, plus $1.30 handling.

College Campuses

Lovejoy's College Guide. Lists U.S. colleges and universities. Simon and Schuster, 1230 Avenue of the Americas, New York, NY 10020. $6.95.

Low-Cost Vacations on Campuses. CMG Publishing Co., P.O. Box 630, Princeton, NJ 18540. $5.00.

Mort's Guide to Low-Cost Vacations and Lodgings on College Campuses. CMG Publishing Co., Box 630, Princeton, NJ 18540. $6.00.

Hostels

Hosteling USA by Michael Frome. The official handbook of American Youth Hostels, in a recently published revised edition. East Woods Press, 820 East Blvd., Charlotte, NC 28203. $6.95, plus $1.30 handling.

Youth Hosteler's Guide to Europe by the Youth Hostels Association Service. Written for the shoestring traveler. Includes maps, charts, and walking and cycling tours, with complete listings of youth hostels and much other pertinent information about travel and accommodations in 22 countries. Collier

Books Order Dept., Front and Brown Streets, Riverside, NJ 08075. $4.95 postpaid.

Campgrounds

Campground and Trailer Park Guide. Lists hundreds of thousands of sites. Regional editions available. Rand McNally and Co., Box 7600, Chicago, IL 60680. $8.95.

RV Campground and Services Directory. Trailer Life Publishing Co., 29901 Agoura Rd., Agoura, CA 91302. $8.95, plus $1.50 handling. Canadian edition $9.95.

Woodall's Campground Directory, North American Edition. Lists and rates over 17,000 campgrounds. Regional editions are also available. Woodall Publishing Co., 500 Hyacinth Place, Highland Pk., IL 60035. Distributed by Simon & Schuster, 1230 Avenue of the Americas, New York, NY 10020.

IMPORTING

How to be an Importer and Pay for your World Travel by Mary Green and Stanley Gillmar. One way to pay for your trip abroad is to be your own importer, especially if a country that produces interesting handiwork or antiques is on your itinerary. Celestial Arts, 231 Adrian Rd., Millbrae, CA 94030. $6.95 postpaid.

SOURCES OF FURTHER INFORMATION

GENERAL INFORMATION
  FOUR SPECIAL BOOKS
  U.S. GOVERNMENT PRINTING OFFICE
  CONSUMER INFORMATION CENTER
  CORNELL UNIVERSITY
CONSUMER PROTECTION
  CONSUMERS UNION
  BETTER BUSINESS BUREAU
  FIGHT BACK
RECYCLING
COMMUNITY ENVIRONMENTAL COUNCIL
  REYNOLDS ALUMINUM
BARTER
  THE BARTER PROJECT
  THE NATIONAL COMMERCE EXCHANGE
  BOOKS
COOPERATIVE BUYING
ALTERNATIVE LIVING
  RODALE PRESS
  GARDEN WAY

SOURCES OF FURTHER INFORMATION

GENERAL INFORMATION

FOUR SPECIAL BOOKS

There are four sources of information that reflect the spirit of *Helpful Hints for Better Living* and deserve special mention here.

The Ecotopian Encyclopedia for the 80's: A Survival Guide for the Age of Inflation by Ernest Callenbach. A fine reference guide with A to Z listings, providing pertinent information for better, more efficient living. The original title in 1972 was *Living Poor with Style*, and that remains the central theme. And/Or Press, Box 2246, Berkeley, CA 94702. $9.95.

Living More With Less by Doris Janzen Longacre offers a spiritual approach to economizing. The Library of Congress marks it for inclusion in the "Conduct of Life" category, and that's what this sensible and touching book is all about. It was commissioned by the Mennonite Central Committee, one of the most effective helping organizations in the country. For information about this book, contact Herald Press, 616 Walnut Ave., Scottdale, PA 15683. $6.95.

The Next Whole Earth Catalog. Quite simply, an inexhaustible guide to everything dealing with better, less wasteful living. Point/Random House, 201 East 50th St., New York, NY 10022. $12.50.

Sylvia Porter's New Money Book for the 80's contains 1,300 pages of advice on personal money management from the pro. In paperback from Avon Books, 1790 Broadway, New York, NY 10019. $9.95.

U.S. GOVERNMENT PRINTING OFFICE

The Government Printing Office is one of the best sources of low-cost information, and it provides a great opportunity to get some return from the assorted departments, research projects, and consultant studies your taxes

223

have funded. The GPO has over 25,000 publications and periodicals for sale. To keep it all manageable, the material is broken down by subject. The 250 subjects range from Accident Prevention to Zoology with stops for Camping, Food Storage, Insurance, Retirement, and so on. Each subject has its own bibliography, with titles as varied as "Starting and Managing a Small Retail Music Store," "Living on a Few Acres," and "Sex and the Spinal-Column-Injured." Just like going through your attic on a rainy day, but more informative.

A good start is *A Comsumer's Guide to Federal Publications*, the free subject index. It contains a form for ordering the free indexes for the subjects you want to explore. At that point, you'll have paid only postage. The publications themselves start at about $1.00 and go up from there.

This takes time. If you're lucky, things will go faster at your local GPO bookstore. It stocks many titles and has access to all the rest. Boston, Cleveland, Columbus, Dallas, Denver, Detroit, Jacksonville, Los Angeles, New York, Philadelphia, Pueblo, San Francisco, and Seattle all have GPO stores.

Besides the free catalog of government periodicals mentioned above, there's also another for posters, charts, and pictures (No. SB-057). There is also a free monthly catalog, *Selected U.S. Government Publications*, which contains only the new and consistently popular items.

All of the catalogs are available from the Superintendent of Documents, U.S. Government Printing Office, Washington, DC 20402.

CONSUMER INFORMATION CENTER

A free catalog that lists over 200 publications, over half of which are also free, is available from the Consumer Information Center. You can order money-saving booklets on every subject, from health care to real estate. Write to Consumer Information Catalog, Pueblo, CO 81009.

CORNELL UNIVERSITY

Hundreds of booklets covering a wide range of topics in the areas of home energy, maintenance, and ecology are available for 60¢ and up from Cornell University. Write to Cornell University Distribution Center, 7 Research Park, Ithaca, NY 14850, for their free "Know How" catalog listing available titles & costs.

CONSUMER PROTECTION

CONSUMERS UNION

Consumers Union is a nonprofit group that tests and reports on products and services. It's worked since 1936 to inform consumers about what they'll get for their money, and to create and maintain decent living standards for consumers. It maintains law offices in Washington, DC, San Francisco, and Austin, and initiates law suits and petitions to government agencies on behalf of consumers.

Consumers Union supports itself mostly through subscriptions to *Consumer Reports* (2.9 million readers), although there is some income from noncommercial grants and fees. It doesn't accept advertising or samples from anyone. The Union has recently also started a consumer magazine for kids 8 to 12, *Penny Power*, to offset some of the influence of commercials and to help develop good consumer attitudes and buying habits.

A publishing arm of Consumers Union, Consumer Reports Books, produces paperback books on a wide variety of topics, including: *The Heart Attack Handbook, How to Buy a Used Car,* and *You and Your Aging Parent.* In addition, the *Buying Guide* summarizes CU findings on dozens of products by scores of manufacturers.

For more information about the Consumers Union and its publications, write the Office of Public Information, The Consumers Union, Mt. Vernon, NY 10553.

BETTER BUSINESS BUREAU

If you're wondering about the reputation of a businessman, try your local Better Business Bureau. They won't give you recommendations, but they will tell you if a firm has a long record of complaints and angry customers. They also publish the *Better Business Bureau Guide to Wise Buying* ($7.95). It gives basic advice on buying common goods and services, as well as warnings about common scams and swindles. For the book, or for a listing of free pamphlets that cover about the same ground, write to the Council of Better Business Bureaus, Inc., 1515 Wilson Blvd., Suite 300, Arlington, VA 22209.

FIGHT BACK

Another excellent reference for ways to avoid being victimized by consumer cheats and frauds is *Fight Back (And Don't Get Ripped Off).* Author David Horowitz, a man you may recognize from Johnny Carson's "The Tonight Show," is NBC's consumer specialist, and his book is worthwhile for its information, encouragement, and resources. Available from Harper and Row, 10 East 53rd St., New York, NY 10022. $2.95, and very much worth it.

RECYCLING

COMMUNITY ENVIRONMENTAL COUNCIL

For information and details about recycling centers, municipal composting and proven recycling programs, contact Community Environmental Council, 924 Anacapa St., Suite B4, Santa Barbara, CA 93101. If you wish, they will send you a copy of *Recycling: The State of the Art,* for $10.

REYNOLDS ALUMINUM

If you live in a "no-deposit no-return" state, call Reynolds toll-free at (800) 228-2525, to see if there's an aluminum recycling center near you.

For information on recycling, contact Public Relations Manager, Reynolds Aluminum Recycling Co., 6603 West Broad Street, Richmond, VA 23261. Reynolds will also advise you on setting up your own recycling center for aluminum cans and scrap. It's a good way for kids to make extra money, and aluminum cans can be recycled at only 5% of the cost of making new cans. That's high-yield ecology!

BARTER

THE BARTER PROJECT

Dedicated to the return of the barter system, the Barter Project provides listings and publications that can get you started. Write to The Barter Project, The National Center for Citizens Involvement, 1214 16th St. NW, Washington, DC 20036.

THE NATIONAL COMMERCE EXCHANGE

At the National Commerce Exchange you'll pay a fee for a listing of your business or your barterable skills. Goods are bartered on a 10 percent commission, payable in bartered services. For more information, write National Commerce Exchange, 6501 Loisdale Road, Springfield, VA 22150.

BOOKS

Three books on the subject of barter are:

Barter: How to Get Anything from Automobiles to Vacations Without Money by Constance Stapleton and Phyllis Richman. Scribner's, 597 Fifth Ave., New York, NY 10017. $4.95.

Let's Try Barter by Charles Morrow Wilson. Devin-Adair Co., 143 Sound Beach Ave., Old Greenwich, CT 06870. $4.95.

How to Barter and Trade by Jack Trapp. Cornerstone Library, Scribner's (see above). $4.95.

COOPERATIVE BUYING

Information on cooperative buying, coop funding, and starting a coop is available from The National Consumer Cooperative Bank, 1630 Connecticut Ave. NW, Washington, DC 20009. Or try The Cooperative League of the U.S.A., 1828 L Street NW, Suite 1100, Washington, DC 20036.

ALTERNATIVE LIVING

RODALE PRESS

Rodale Press is one of the oldest, biggest, and best sources of information about organic gardening, alternative foods and energy, and alternative life-styles. Rodale has a big experimental farm, an outreach program that will put you in touch with learning centers and apprenticeship programs, and a broad list of publications. For information and a list of books and magazines not specifically listed in *Helpful Hints for Better Living*, write to Rodale Press, 33 East Minor St., Emmaus, PA 18049.

GARDEN WAY

These folks started out selling a rotary tiller and a garden cart, but their publications are now among the best. The topics covered include gardening and preserving, alternative energy sources, building, cooking, and country living skills. For a publications list write to Garden Way Publishing, Rt. 1, Box 105, Pownal, VT 05261.

INDEX